Roosevelt & His Rough Riders

Roosevelt & His Rough Riders
The 1st U.S Volunteer Cavalry in Cuba, 1898

ILLUSTRATED

The Story of the Rough Riders
Edward Marshall

With an Account of the Rough Riders at Santiago
by Theodore Roosevelt

Roosevelt & His Rough Riders
The 1st U.S Volunteer Cavalry in Cuba, 1898
The Story of the Rough Riders
by Edward Marshall
With an Account of the Rough Riders at Santiago
by Theodore Roosevelt

ILLUSTRATED

FIRST EDITION IN THIS FORM

First published under the titles
The Story of the Rough Riders
and
The Rough Riders (extract)

Leonaur is an imprint of Oakpast Ltd
Copyright in this form © 2023 Oakpast Ltd

ISBN: 978-1-916535-54-1 (hardcover)
ISBN: 978-1-916535-55-8 (softcover)

http://www.leonaur.com

Publisher's Notes

The views expressed in this book are not necessarily those of the publisher.

Contents

Preface	9
The Building of the Regiment	11
The Regiment at San Antonio	21
At Tampa, and the Trip to Cuba	31
In Cuba, Before the Fighting	42
The First Shot	55
The First Battle	65
Death and Suffering	78
After Las Guasimas	87
The Beginning of San Juan	106
The Charge of San Juan	115
The Men Who Died	128
After the Fighting was Over	133
Last Days in Cuba	142
Home Again	150
In New York	164
Roster	166
The Rough Riders at Santiago *By Theodore Roosevelt*	227

Executive Mansion Washington
February 21, 1899

All of our soldiers in Cuba did well. It was an honour to the First United States Volunteer Cavalry to be with them, and it was an honour to the army to have this splendid regiment at the front.

William McKinley

A Tribute from the Secretary of War

The First United States Volunteer Cavalry was an admirable regiment, and did good service during the war. Officers and men alike acquitted themselves most creditably. They were promptly organised, were equipped with smokeless-powder carbines, and took part in every military engagement in Cuba, except the light at El Caney. Wherever they were they did well.

R. A. Alger

Major-General Leonard Wood's Opinion of the Regiment.

Notwithstanding the fact that my connection with the regiment, as commanding officer, ceased on June 30th, the day before the San Juan charge, my interest in it has never lessened for a moment. I was naturally proud of my connection with it at the beginning. I am proud now of the fact that I went into the war as its colonel, and I am proud of its record. When I began to do what I could at San Antonio, to organise the regiment into a creditable military body, I said to the men of it:

> Make yourselves as much like regular soldiers as you can in the shortest possible time. If you think only of that you will be thinking exactly of the right thing and you

will have enough to think about to keep you very busy. If you devote your time and attention to that, the regiment will be a success.

The men did make themselves so much like regulars that it was hard to tell the difference, and the regiment was a success.

It would be utterly useless for me to recapitulate now the history of the good work the Rough Riders did. They were not the only good soldiers in the army, but they were among the best, and they did not do any bad work.

Leonard Wood
Maj Genl
USV

From Lieutenant-Colonel (Formerly Major) Brodie.

Never in the history of the world had such a regiment been organised. It was made up of men of the frontier, who were joined by volunteers from nearly every State and Territory in the Union. The former were accustomed to adventure, and the latter joined the regiment because they were looking for it, so there was no man in the whole organisation who was not anxious to face hardship and brave death. We had all either seen or wanted to see hard work. We got it. The regiment contained no shirkers. I was wounded at Las Guasimas. It is one of the regrets of my life that I could not have been with the men at San Juan. I rejoined the regiment at Montauk.

We were as lucky in our two commanding officers as we were lucky in our men. Wood and Roosevelt were of the very few worthy to command a regiment like the Rough Riders. They were strong of mind and body, knew the military business, were self-forgetting, patient and brave. Both have since won high honours, and both have absolutely deserved them. To neither of them, in all his life, can any honour come which is too high.

Alexander O. Brodie.

Preface

The author makes no apologies for devoting an entire book to the story of one regiment in the Spanish-American War. The history of the Rough Riders is really the history of the war, for from its beginning to its and these men were at the forefront of the fighting, and did work on a par with our very best regulars. The American people has already formed its estimate of them. Captain Lee, who was the English military *attaché* during the entire campaign, told me that they were the best regiment of volunteer soldiers ever organised, and this English estimate quite agrees with that made by George Lynch, an experienced correspondent from London. He said:

> No European, who has had an opportunity to study the Rough Riders, fails for a second to appreciate the American soldier. It would be madness to back the English, German, or French fighting machines against men like those in the First Volunteer Cavalry.

The Rough Riders were the first volunteer regiment organised, armed, and equipped. They were the first volunteer soldiers to land in Cuba. They raised the first flag flown by the military forces of the United States on foreign soil since the Mexican War. They were the first regiment of the army to fire a shot at the Spaniards, and the first man killed was one of them. Indeed, they bore the brunt of the first battle, and they bore it with unexampled bravery. In the second battle, their colonel and his men led the van and headed one of the most desperate charges in the history of warfare. From first to last they were always in the lead, and always a credit to themselves and to their country.

If these men do not deserve a history book devoted entirely to them, then I am ignorant of any men who do.

My own connection with the regiment began the day after they landed in Cuba (where I had gone as war correspondent for the *New*

York Journal*)*, and lasted just twenty-four hours. It was then quickly put a stop to by a Mauser bullet. Not more than six weeks ago Colonel, now Governor, Theodore Roosevelt sent me the medal of the regiment, and was good enough to say that he was glad to consider me a member of it. Like medals and like letters were sent to Richard Harding Davis, the able correspondent of the *New York Herald* and *Scribner's Magazine*, and to Captain McCormack of the regular army. Both of these gentlemen were with the Rough Riders in the Battle of Las Guasimas, and, I think, afterwards at the Battle of San Juan.

The fact that I was shot while on the battlefield with this regiment, naturally made me feel a deep sympathy with it, a hearty pride in all its achievements, and constant interest in everything it did in Cuba and, after its return, in America. When Mr. John H. Cook, the President of the G. W. Dillingham Company, asked me to write a history of the regiment I was, therefore, greatly pleased. Of course, it was impossible that I should not have at hand some of the required material. My long illness, however, had not permitted me to gather it in a systematic or sufficient way, and so I have had to call to my assistance several members of the regiment, as well as others.

I am deeply indebted to Colonel Leonard S. Wood (now Major-General and Military Governor of Santiago Province), Captain James H. McClintock, Major Alexander Brodie, Lieutenant F. P. Hayes, and Privates George W. Burgess, Sam. W. Noyes, and "Judge" Murphy. I have borrowed anecdote and fact freely from the newspaper press, and only regret that the almost universal anonymity of American journalism makes it impossible for me to thank and credit the writers by name. Richard F. Outcault, who has made the drawings for the book, has caught the spirit of the regiment and the scenes in which its work was done, admirably. I am further indebted to Mr. W. R. Hearst, the proprietor of the *New York Journal*, whose constant kindness has permitted me to take time to write this book while still a member of the *Journal* staff.

CHAPTER 1

The Building of the Regiment

Rough, tough, we're the stuff,
We want to fight, and we can't get enough,
Whoo-pee.

This was the cry of the Rough Riders. It is just as well to put it at the head of the chapter on organisation as it would be to put it anywhere else, for it unquestionably expressed the sentiments of the men who joined the regiment, from the very beginning.

The moment that the newspapers sent broadcast the tale that such a regiment was contemplated, excitement began in nearly every State in the Union, and did not end until the announcement was made that the regiment was complete.

As it stood finished, the troops which made it up, theoretically, came from the following sections, although men from the East and from other States and Territories were scattered through each troop.

Troops A, B, and C, from Arizona.

Troop D, from Oklahoma.

Troops E, F, G, H, and I, from New Mexico.

Troop K, from Eastern colleges and cities.

Troops L and M, from Indian Territory.

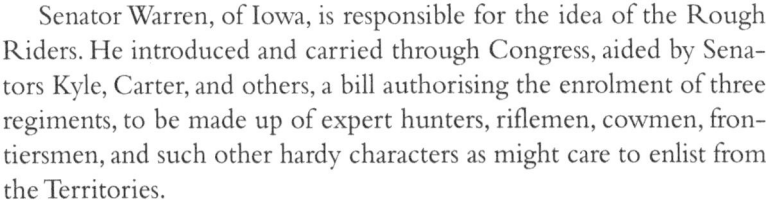

Senator Warren, of Iowa, is responsible for the idea of the Rough Riders. He introduced and carried through Congress, aided by Senators Kyle, Carter, and others, a bill authorising the enrolment of three regiments, to be made up of expert hunters, riflemen, cowmen, frontiersmen, and such other hardy characters as might care to enlist from the Territories.

Captain Leonard Wood, of the Medical Corps, was the President's chief medical adviser, and had had much experience in Indian fighting in the West.

Theodore Roosevelt was Assistant Secretary of the Navy, and had had some knowledge of men and things on the frontier, through his life on his own and other ranches.

It was the President's intention to offer to Wood the colonelcy of one regiment, to Roosevelt the colonelcy of a second, and to Griggsby, of Montana, the colonelcy of the third. Wood and Roosevelt received their offers at about the same moment. Roosevelt promptly declined his, on the theory that he had not had sufficient military experience to warrant him in taking command of a regiment. He asked that he might be given the second place in the regiment commanded by Wood, which was done. Thus, the Rough Riders began. Alexander Brodie, who afterwards became major of the regiment, was probably the first man to systematically start towards the organisation of this particular regiment. He was shot at Las Guasimas, and after the war he ran for Congress from his section, with disastrous results. No more gallant soldier ever wore Uncle Sam's uniform.

Major Brodie started about the organisation of the regiment with characteristic impetuosity. Before he telegraphed to the President that he engaged himself upon the enterprise at all, he telegraphed to each county in Arizona, saying that he wanted men; that he wanted good men, and that he wanted them quick. Brodie's first fear was that he would not receive sufficient replies, so that he could tender the services of a respectable number. He made the conditions of enlistment very rigid. He demanded, first, that the men should be good horsemen; second, that they should be good marksmen; and, third, that they should be of good moral character.

He asked for as many references as you would ask for if you were investigating the antecedents of a prospective servant girl. He had an idea that this request would bar from service in the regiment many men otherwise desirable, and it undoubtedly did. But his amazement was writ in large characters on his face and in his language, when he found that Arizona contained enough men, exactly to his liking and ardently anxious for enlistment, to form a full regiment. This information he telegraphed to the President with great glee. But the President wired back to Brodie, that Arizona's quota of troops previously decided upon by Congress assembled, was insufficient to enable him to accept the services of a whole regiment from that Territory. He added to the message, and this well-nigh broke Brodie's heart, that not more than two hundred men could be taken.

Brodie started on a process of sifting, and presently gathered at Prescott the best three hundred and fifty out of the lot. From these he selected two hundred, after having examined them first as to their qualifications for killing Spaniards and, second, as to their qualifications for entering into the heavenly choir, in case they should by chance be killed themselves.

James H. McClintock, afterwards captain of B Troop, probably gave Brodie more assistance than any other one man. McClintock would have been a bad man himself had he not been prevented by the restraining influence of the profession of journalism, which he followed. He had been the editor of half a dozen papers in the Territory, some of which are as dead as he came near to being at Las Guasimas; some of which now survive on half-total disability, as he does; and some of which are as active and as sturdy as he was when he helped Brodie to organise the Arizona troops.

I shall not attempt to tell a chronological history of the organisation of this regiment, because I do not believe that anyone could prepare such a chapter. The regiment was organised, as most of its members had previously lived, and as it fought at Guasimas and San Juan—helter-skelter.

Arizona furnished the regimental colours and the regimental mascot. The universal sympathy which existed between the people of the Territory and the object of the organisation, could not be more plainly shown than it was by these two episodes. The ladies of the Women's Relief Corps at Phoenix gave the flag, which was presented by the governor. As Captain McClintock received the colours, a chorus of female voices from the Territorial Normal, School sang "God be with you till we meet again." The regimental mascot was given to the regiment by Robert Brow, a prominent and jovial gentleman of Prescott, and if the band played at all during the ceremony, the tune was probably either "We won't go home till morning," or "The Streets of Cairo." Thus, extremes met.

The flag was a beautiful silk standard, sewed together by devoted women who did not mind sitting up all night in order to get it ready in time, and it is said that there was much difficulty in finding the material of which to make it. The same rumour tells of a blue silk ball-gown, which may or may not have been used as the field for the flag's white stars. It was understood and hoped that President McKinley would, when the regiment was in Washington, formally present the colours to it in behalf of the ladies of Phoenix, but for some reason this plan fell through.

The regimental mascot was a mountain lion cub, who had been named Florence by Mr. Robert Brow's patron, who brought her in to him, and possibly turned her over to him in payment for a stack of blue chips. She was an extremely handsome animal, with soft, deep, tawny fur, and eyes which were deceptively mild in their appearance. Nothing could possibly be more satisfactory and comforting than the gentle purr of this pleasant cat, and nothing could certainly have been sharper or more lacerating than the points of the claws which, for a certain portion of the time, she kept amiably concealed in the velvet pads of her muscular paws.

Florence was fond of soldiers, and never attacked them. She hated civilians, and the man who did not wear a uniform was reasonably certain to carry her signature away with him if he went near enough for her to reach him. This is literally true.

The flag was the first to be raised by the army during the war, and the day we landed floated proudly on the summit of Mount Losiltires. It was gallantly borne through every engagement in Cuba, and has now been returned to the Women's Relief Corps of Phoenix, who point with pardonable pride to the many bullet holes which are in it.

The mountain lion was very wisely left at Tampa when the regiment sailed. Some of the troopers advocated her transportation to Cuba on the theory that the colonel could sick her on the Spaniards just before each battle, with disastrous results to the enemy, but still, she was left at Tampa. She has now gone back to Arizona. Probably Mr. Robert Brow has her again. She did her duty nobly, and deserves a pension.

One more word about Arizona, which does not entirely concern the Rough Riders. This Territory, both on the first and second calls for troops, had her full quota organised, armed, and equipped before any other State or Territory in the Union.

At Whipple Barracks, when the two hundred selected men marched away to take the train for San Antonio, they left behind them fifteen hundred to two thousand sorrowing ones, who would have gone with them at the drop of the hat, and who mourned because the hat fell not.

It was on the 3rd of May that the Arizona men started for San Antonio.

It was on the 8th of May that the very last men of all—those of K Troop—left Washington for San Antonio. These were the "dude warriors," the "dandy troopers," the "gilded gang." When their train pulled into San Antonio, and they started stragglingly to march to camp, they encountered a contingent of three hundred and forty cowboys from New Mexico. Oil and water are not farther removed than were the everyday natures of these two groups of men. Yet, instantly they fraternised, and from that moment—through the hardships of it all, through the blood and death and fever of it all—these men were brothers.

Concerning the voyage of the Washington swells, I will quote an item from a newspaper. It indicates some interesting things about the regiment:

> A well-known New York clubman had enlisted. When departing for San Antonio he engaged a sleeper, and was shown to his place by the porter. Just as he deposited his baggage, Sergeant Thaddeus Higgins, an old cavalryman of the regular service, who had charge of the party, tapped him on the shoulder.
> 'Take these things back there,' he said, jerking his thumb in the direction of the ordinary day coaches provided by the government for the troopers.
> The clubman looked surprised. It was his first experience in military discipline.
> 'That's where you belong,' added Sergeant Higgins, with the thumb still pointed to the rear.
> The clubman was made of good stuff. He saluted, picked up his things, and went back to the day coaches. He did not sleep at full length until the train arrived at San Antonio.

Definitely, the Arizona contingent started for San Antonio May 3rd; the troop from Guthrie, Oklahoma, started May 4th, and the four troops from New Mexico started May 6th.

And it may be as well now to go back to some of the experiences which Colonel Roosevelt, then Assistant Secretary of the Navy, was having in Washington.

From the very start, as I have said, Colonel Roosevelt was considered the head of the regiment. The fact that he had declined to accept the colonelcy on the ground that he did not have enough experience, and that the post of commanding officer had been given to Captain Leonard Wood of the Medical Staff, had no effect on the belief of the people, that Roosevelt was the colonel; that Roosevelt was the organiser; and that Roosevelt would carry the regiment through to victory, although this belief was not wholly accurate. All kinds of applications for places in the regiment were made to him.

For instance, on April 27th, Representative Catchings, of Mississippi, called upon him to offer the services of a company from Vicksburg, under the guidance of Jack Conley, known to be one of the most daring characters in that State. Roosevelt had to decline. At that very moment letters and telegrams lay on his desk, which told of over fifteen thousand men who wanted to join the regiment. Probably no military organisation has ever been made up of men selected from so large a number of applicants, or of men so carefully selected. I could fill a chapter easily by telling of the men who wanted to be Rough Riders, but couldn't.

The Rocky Mountain sharpshooters, alone, comprised more than two hundred men, and among them were many who had seen service during some of the regular army's most desperate Indian campaigns, and men who are known as being among the best hunters of big game in all the West. A large delegation of men from Harvard College called upon Roosevelt one day in Washington and offered their services in a body. Indeed, delegations of that kind from most of the Eastern colleges went to him, but went to him in vain. His secretary answered more than five thousand individual applications for places in the regiment, and answered ninety-nine *per cent.* of them with declinations. Finally, Roosevelt decided, after a consultation with the Secretary of War and General Miles, the commanding general of the army, to organise a troop in Washington.

It may not be amiss to speak rapidly of the personalities of some of the men whom he accepted for this troop. There were among them some of the best football players in the country; a noted steeplechaser; a crack polo player; famous clubmen; honor men in almost all the Eastern colleges; and many famous amateur athletes. Two others—J. C. Clagett, of Frederick, Maryland, and L. *M.* Montgomery, of Bradley,

Maryland—rich farmers, were so anxious to join that they offered to pay their own transportation and furnish their own horses and equipments. An idea of K Troop is given below.

Woodbury Kane was a polo player of note, and a hard rider on the hunting field. He came of a fighting family; played football at Harvard.

Craig Wadsworth was one of the "fighting Genesee Wadsworths," whose name had always been among the foremost in the annals of the country in war. He had led the Genesee Valley hunts for some years, and at other times had led many a german in New York ballrooms.

William Tiffany was a nephew of the late Mrs. August Belmont, and grandnephew of Commodore Perry. He spent several years on the plains of Montana.

Reginald or "Reggie" Ronalds was the son of Mrs. Pierre Lorillard Ronalds, who is the best known American in London, is a great friend of the Prince and Princess of Wales, and has a voice that has held Europe and America under its spell for two generations. Ronalds once played tackle on a famous Yale football team.

Dudley S. Dean, captain of the Harvard football team of '91, was in charge of the business of the Mexican Central R. R. at Las Vegas, Mexico, up to the time when he resigned and came North to enlist.

Guy Murchie was the well-known Harvard coach.

Waller was the champion high-jumper of Yale. Stephens was a great polo player from Colorado.

Henry W. Bull, of California, was one of the leading members of the Harvard crew.

Hollister was Harvard's champion half-mile runner. Horace Devereaux, from Colorado Springs, was the leader in one of Princeton's most famous football teams.

Basil Ricketts was the son of the late General Ricketts, and was born just across the street from the place at which he entered service that day.

Sterne was a well-known polo player.

Percival Gassett, of Boston, was a grandson of Commodore "Mad Jack" Percival, who commanded the frigate *Constitution*. Gassett had served for three years in Troop A in Boston, and in Light Battery A. He bore a medal for marksmanship.

There were three New York policemen in the troop; Henry Haywood, Edwin Eberman, and William Breen. Eberman also served in the Sixth Cavalry at Pine Ridge, and wears a medal for gallant conduct there. Two other ex-cavalrymen were in the troop, First Sergeant

Higgins, of New York, and Private Price. It is interesting to note that the policemen who joined the regiment were given indefinite leave of absence with full pay by the city. Poor Haywood was killed July 1st.

I devote considerable space to these men, not because their work was any better than that of the men of whom I do not speak by name, but in order to illustrate the extraordinary materials of which the regiment was made. That such chaps should have joined at all was, perhaps, more to their credit than it was to the credit of the Westerners who joined, for they had more to lose in going, and the hardships of a soldier's life meant more to them than they did to the me who had known hardships all their lives. There were those among this dude contingent, however, who had done service on the plains, and who could ride as well, or throw a rope as well, or shoot as well, or do any of the things which are associated with life on the frontier, as well as the men who were properly known as cowboys.

It was on the 6th of May that Theodore Roosevelt was sworn in as Lieutenant-Colonel of Volunteers. The ceremony took place in the office which he had occupied as Assistant Secretary of the Navy, and there were a good many prominent men there to see the famous civilian fighter change to a military fighter. There were senators and representatives there and many army officers. General Corbin administered the oath.

That same day most of the members of Troop K were mustered in. They were in the Army Dispensary building in Washington when Roosevelt made his first speech to them. It was the first speech he had made as an army officer, and he evidently enjoyed the situation. During the Santiago campaign he made almost as many speeches to his soldiers as he did to the voters of New York State during his political campaign, and the soldiers always enjoyed them. He said to the men who had gathered there:

> Gentlemen: You have now reached the last point. If any one of you doesn't mean business, let him say so now. An hour from now it will be too late to back out. Once in, you've got to see it through. You've got to perform without flinching whatever duty is assigned to you; regardless of the difficulty or danger attending it. You must know how to ride, you must know how to shoot, you must know how to live in the open. Absolute obedience to every command is your first lesson. No matter what comes you mustn't squeal. Think it over—all of you. If

Sgt. Philip A. Smeed. Harry S. Van Bland. Jules M. Coville. Sherman Bell.
Carlos Aud.
Henry Fincher.
A Group of K Troop Men.
From a photograph by William Dinwiddie.

any man wants to withdraw, he will be gladly excused, for there are thousands who are anxious to have places in this regiment.

Of course, no one withdrew. The comic paragraphers had a deal of fun over the enlistment of these men these petted ones of fortune who were going to war—but the comic paragraphers stopped saying funny things when the petted ones of fortune, later, stood up like the real men they were and took, without whimpering, their doses of steel medicine on the battlefields of Cuba.

They gave their lieutenant-colonel a rousing cheer, and three times three times more rousing cheers. Afterwards they cheered him in the staid and quiet precincts of the Navy Department until all the clerks, who had never heard such a disturbance within its sacred walls before, swarmed into the hallways and wished that they were going to war too.

In the meantime, Colonel Wood was busy at San Antonio. The men began to pour in there from the Territories in which they had been enlisted. By May 10th the regiment was all there, and was being licked into shape with a rapidity that was probably never equalled before.

Chapter 2

The Regiment at San Antonio

The life of the regiment at San Antonio was almost as interesting as the life of the regiment, afterwards, in Cuba. Probably there never was banded together such an incongruous mass of men as this one which gathered in the Texan city for the purpose of being put into shape as a cavalry regiment.

The men were at first put into the old Exposition building, because there were no tents for them. All the officers expected clashes between the Eastern contingent and the Western men; but the clashes did not come. The men mixed fraternally, and officers ceased to be surprised when they found that an Arizona bronco-buster had chosen as his bunkie some Eastern college man.

Colonel Roosevelt quickly won the love and confidence of the men who were under him, by refusing to accept for himself any conveniences which he could not offer to his men. He slept as they slept, and ate what they ate. Another thing which pleased them was the early announcement that it had been arranged in Washington, through his personal efforts, to arm the regiment with Krag-Jorgenson carbines. The Rough Riders thus became the only volunteer regiment of the army properly equipped with modern guns.

After the tents came, the men left the Exposition building and made a regular military camp on the Exposition grounds. A very large majority of them had never seen a shelter-tent before, and knew much less about how to make a military camp than some of them knew about differential calculus, and others about stopping stampeding cattle. Many of the officers quartered themselves in the buildings thereabouts, but Roosevelt slept in his shelter-tent with his poncho and his blanket. The regiment, by the way, had no regimental or officers' tents assigned to it until it arrived at Montauk, after the war was over.

There were men admitted to the regiment after the mobilisation at

Five Bronco-Busters.

San Antonio, and there were men who left it after that. Some of these were finally rejected on their physical examination, and some were dropped or dropped themselves for other reasons.

One of the latter class was a German, who must certainly have been accepted by mistake. While the Rough Riders were not all educated men, they were mostly chaps with breech-loading, rapid-fire-high-speed-projectile minds. The German's head lacked these characteristics. He was undeniably stupid. He suffered. He went.

It came about in this way. The men in his troop had decided that they did not care to accompany him to Cuba, but they took him aside, and with many words explained to him their high regard. They told him that he was a man whose reputation for bravery had gone before him, and that as the Spaniards had crossed the Mexican border into Texas, and were momentarily expected to attack that camp at San Antonio, he had been selected as the one man of all men to protect it from their devilish wiles. Night was approaching, and the last snow of the tardy spring was falling. They gave him three candles and they posted him in a remote place by a tree.

"If one regiment of Spaniards attacks you," said they, "light one candle; if the attack is made by two regiments, then light two; if three regiments come upon you in the night, light all of them, and may God have mercy on your soul. We are sorry that we cannot give you a gun."

The German accepted the responsibility, and his leave-taking was impressive. Solemnly the men of his troop filed up, and sadly and affectionately they shook his hand. They assured him that it was a great thing to be the first man in the war to die for his country, and he wept in dialect as he thanked them for the chance.

Strict military regulations had not been put in force at San Antonio, else it would have been impossible for the twenty men to leave the camp who stole away at midnight toward that watchful German. But they left it, and when they came upon the German, his regret was that he had not more than three candles, for he was convinced that the entire Spanish Army of not three, but three thousand regiments had begun a night attack. Also, he became impressed with the idea that there are other things nicer than dying for one's country.

His disappearance might have been recorded as desertion. But it was not.

Another episode—B Troop had no cook. That is, its cook had expressed his opinion of his assignment to that duty by remarking:

"What the hell do I know about cooking? All I do is to throw the stuff together, boil it and then yell 'dinner!'"

This, unfortunately, was too true, and great was the grief of Captain McClintock and Lieutenant Alexander there at. Desperate, they dined at a restaurant. That meal was a taste of Paradise. McClintock said: "I'm going to get that cook!"

He disappeared into the kitchen, and great was the woe and loud the protests of the proprietor of the restaurant while McClintock was explaining to the cook the beauties of service in the uniform of Uncle Sam. No recruiting officer in the service of the queen ever worked harder to earn his fee than McClintock did to get that cook. His eloquence won the day, and the cook enlisted. Then did B Troop begin to feast like lords. But suddenly the cook was missing. No search availed the grief-struck officers. Days passed. Frank W. Schenck had gone.

When he reappeared, McClintock's joy at his return was too acute to permit much scolding. He, however, demanded an explanation of his five days' absence, and Frank W. Schenck replied with honeyed sweetness, that he had gone to San Antonio (a mile away) and started to return on time but had missed his car.

At Montauk, the same cook obtained a furlough, and went away. When he returned, he brought a Mrs. Frank W. Schenck with him. He had gone all the way to San Antonio to be married, and that first puzzling absence was at last made clear. For courtship must precede marriage.

The Easterners were scarcely less at home on the Western broncos, than the Westerners were on the McClellan saddles. They missed the great Mexican pommels which had been theirs since childhood, and one of them announced that riding a McClellan was like clinging to a chip at sea. One night the men had to handle thirty half-broken terrors. They rejected their saddles altogether, and worked the animals with ropes alone.

    Nothing could have been more inspiring to the onlooker or more interesting to the participant than the first regimental evolutions on these wild Western ponies. There would be five or six horses in every troop whose refusal to stay in line was firm and permanent. It was frequently necessary to stop the entire manoeuvre while some cowboy paused to throw his unwilling little brute. Bridles were scarce at first, and some of the men got on with the simple hitch of a lariat around their animal's lower jaw. For a horse to bolt was common, for one or two to rear so enthusiastically that they eventually fell backward, excited no comment. Nothing less than the stampede of an entire troop amid the howling of the men was considered really exciting.

    The second mounted regimental drill occurred May 24th, and with it came one of these stampedes. Dozens of the troopers were thrown, and among the victims were as many Western cowboys as members of the gilded Eastern gang. They had attempted to charge, with Roosevelt in the lead. That some of the men were not killed in the ensuing mix-up was wonderful. Hallett Allsop Borrowe was thrown beneath two strapping cowboys and had his new uniform blouse literally torn off his back. The Government provides not for such contingencies, and Borrowe had to buy his own new blouse. Afterwards the charge was tried again with some success.

    The next day Joseph Jenkins Lee, of Baltimore, and Roscoe Channing, who was Yale's great half-back in '96, were assigned their mustangs. They took what they themselves called a trial canter. That there were more trials than cantering about it was shown by their condition when they returned. Inasmuch as they took solemn oath that they had not been thrown, the regiment concluded that they must have paused by the wayside to mix mud pies.

    The first man sent to hospital was Private Greenway. He tried to stop his mustang with his kneecap.

    Just before the regiment departed for the concentration camp at Tampa, the gathering and shipping of the livestock afforded much pleasure and instruction to the men. That any of the men who entered the corrals lived to go afterwards to Cuba was not the fault of the merry mustangs who plunged therein. "Judge" Murphy was the sergeant of the guard. His heart had been broken by the work of getting the horses out. He had been at it for twenty hours, and war seemed cruel to him. That was when he learned to love Captain Capron. He was between two plunging brutes in the middle of the corral, finding it difficult to keep awake, even in such distressing circumstances. Captain Capron, long and big, climbed over the surrounding fence and said:

"Go up and go to sleep on one of those boxes. I'll do your work for you. I don't want to kill my men—yet."

Afterwards at Las Guasimas, they were glad to die for him and he was glad to die with them.

The second wounded man was Marshall Bird, whose subsequent wonderful escape at Guasimas is mentioned in the story of that battle. Bird was thrown while he was a member of a detail going after horses, and it was thought for a time that his skull was badly fractured, but he turned up for duty and went on with the others. It may be well now to devote a few brief words to the startling experiences of the Eastern men who went west. When they arrived in San Antonio, May 10th, they gathered by pre-arrangement at the best hotel in the city. They made elaborate toilets and they ordered as fine a breakfast as San Antonio provided.

"It's all off after this," they said to themselves, and they enjoyed that breakfast with great joy. There were in this little party, G. Ronald Fortescue, Henry W. Sharp, J.B. Tailor, Henry W. Bull, Kenneth Robinson, William Tudor, Jr., R.H. M. Ferguson, William Quaid, Jr., H.K. Devereaux, E. C. Waller, Jr., George Kemp, Maxwell Norman, J. A. Massie, Woodbury Kane, William Tiffany, "Ham" Fish, Craig Wadsworth, and Reginald Ronalds. After the breakfast was over, it was, as they had said, "all off." They donned their flannel shirts, their duck trousers, and their blouses, put on their campaign hats and went to work.

They were assigned sleeping quarters in a somewhat remote part of the Exposition building, evidently on the theory that they and the Westerners might disagree, but this was wrong. For instance, Woodbury Kane met Henry Remming and formed a friendship that day which lasted all through Cuba. He was set to work digging a trench in front of the officers' quarters, and finished his job with cheerfulness, despite his blistered hands and stiffened back. Craig Wadsworth was ordered to devote two hours to chopping wood. Goodrich and Kane afterwards took lessons in handling lassoes, and got badly tangled up.

A couple of days later, a rift in the lute appeared when Tiffany complained that he had no clean shirt. He finally got a pass, so that he could hunt his washerwoman up, and was unmercifully guyed. Poor Tiffany—he is dead now. The only charge of favoritism ever made among the Rough Riders came less than a week after Roosevelt landed in San Antonio. Woodbury Kane was given charge of the rapid-fire

Captain Woodbury Kane,
Promoted for Gallantry in the Fight of July 1st.

William Pollock,
Pawnee Indian.

guns, and Hamilton Fish, Craig Wadsworth, and Maxwell Norman were made non-commissioned officers in Troop K. The Westerners thought for a while that too many promotions were being given to the Eastern men, but this unpleasantness soon blew over.

Much excitement was created at one time by the announcement that Borrowe was keeping his valet at a hotel, and that he daily made a pilgrimage to the place to shave and take a bath. The valet was sent East. The same day a New Mexican cowboy refused point blank to obey an order given by Sergeant Tiffany. He said, "Wait till you get to be a brigadier-general before you give out orders in such a high and mighty fashion," and Tiffany made threats about the guardhouse. It was all forgotten in a day or two. This same day two members of the New York Stock Exchange joined the regiment. They were J. Lorimer Worden and C. E. Knoblauch. Worden is an athlete, and Knoblauch a giant who boxes, wrestles, swims, and rides expertly.

A few days later, Woodbury Kane had trouble. He sawed up an ammunition box to make a desk, and the ordnance officer called him picturesquely down. Kane was extremely sorry.

Perhaps the most impressive day in San Antonio was Sunday, May 22nd. The whole regiment, fully uniformed, was arrayed in squadron formation before Colonel Wood's tent early in the morning. The object was the reading of the articles of war, and the ceremony lasted nearly an hour and a half. The stately passages were pronounced in solemn sentences by the captains of the troops, and the men were much impressed.

After breakfast, religious services were held in the great Fair building, and twenty Western terrors melodiously acted as the choir. The only instrumental music was furnished by a silver bugle at the expert lips of Trumpeter Cassi. Loud as he blew, the sound of his cornet was lost in the fine harmonies of the cowboy choir, when they started in with "*How firm a foundation*," and when the rest of the regiment joined in the chorus, the sturdy Ringing was plainly heard in San Antonio, a mile away. From the Arizona plains came the soloist. He was A. R. Perry, and famous in the regiment as the best bronco buster of them all, but his untrained voice was clear and high and melodious, and when he sang "*Onward, Christian Soldiers*," many of his comrades cried.

San Antonio was hot, dusty, and disagreeable. The men, Easterners and Westerners alike, found camp life hard, beyond their dreams. The officers of the regiment worked themselves and their commands night and day, in order to make soldiers out of them, and no regiment

From a photograph by Field.

The Dock at Port Tampa, Florida, on the Day of Sailing.

was ever put into fighting shape so quickly. No detail was neglected which could quickly place the men on a par with the regular troops, with whom they would be brought into competition when the first expedition to Cuba started, and the men took it all cheerfully, and did their work with gladness. This was because among them there was but one thought—the desire to go on that expedition.

Officered as they were, with the President's own Medical Adviser in command, and the ex-Assistant Secretary of the Navy as their Lieutenant-Colonel, they knew that they would be considered kindly when the opportunity came, and they were anxious to see to it that that consideration found no flaws in them.

When Colonel Wood announced to the men that marching orders had at last arrived, the news was received with cheers which lasted for many minutes. Indeed, nothing except the sound of taps coming from the bugles with the night, could still the exuberant spirits which infected the regiment. No wilder hurrah was heard in Cuba when we learned our victories than that which went up in San Antonio when marching orders were received. Lieutenant-Colonel Roosevelt read the message, and then he and Colonel Wood embraced like schoolboys.

CHAPTER 3

At Tampa, and the Trip to Cuba

It was on May 29th that the Rough Riders went away from San Antonio with high hopes in their hearts that they would not pause long again until they paused in Cuba. Indeed they had better luck than any other regiment in the army, for between the embarkation at San Antonio and the moment when they actually faced the Spanish bullets, less than thirty days intervened.

Every captain had orders to send his troops to bed early that Saturday night, for Wood and Roosevelt already had inklings of the imperfect transportation which the Government could furnish to the regiment. They knew the trip before them would be long and wearisome, and they wanted their men to be well prepared for it.

The work of breaking camp took all of Saturday. Colonel Wood ordered all superfluous baggage left behind, telling the men that they could take with them only such necessaries as they could find room for in their blanket rolls. Hundreds of boxes were sent by express that day to Western ranches and Eastern mansions. Kane, Tiffany, and Ronalda sheepishly admitted that their rejections included the swallowed-tailed coats and low-cut vests of full-dress suits. Just why these gentlemen took dress suits to war with them I do not know.

The last packing was done after supper. Then most of the cooking utensils were stowed away, leaving the men only their blanket rolls to pack, and their shelter-tents to "strike" (or take down), before they started on their journey.

At three o'clock the sweet notes of reveille rang out, and Camp Wood woke up. The dawn was cool and lovely, and the men were as full of energy as they afterwards proved themselves to be full of fight. Breakfast was a hasty meal, prepared under great difficulties, because so many of the cooking utensils had been packed up; Drilled as they had been in the preparation of the blanket rolls, there were those among the men who packed theirs so badly that many of their little treasures were shaken out before they reached the railway. They were shaken out to stay, for when the ride once started, Colonel Wood permitted no stoppage.

The cars into which the men were huddled were infinitely less comfortable than the cars making up the trains on which most of the regular troops went South. I travelled from Chickamauga to Tampa with the Ninth Cavalry, and the negro troopers were furnished with emigrant sleeping cars. The men of the Rough Riders had no such luxury. They slept in their seats, if they slept at all.

The experiences which the men had had with their Western horses at drill and regimental manoeuvres, were as nothing to the time they had in loading them on the stock cars for final shipment. It is well here to call attention to the fact that these horses were practically neglected during the five days' trip which followed. This was no fault of the regiment, but can only be laid at the door of the railway companies.

Roosevelt left on the last section. Wood remained to see that everything got off all right, and followed on a regular passenger train. It was fully half-past ten at night before that third section pulled out, and when it went, the sleeping car berth which had been reserved for Lieutenant-Colonel Roosevelt was occupied by a private soldier. Roosevelt found him suffering from an illness, and had him taken in and put to bed. From then on, until the regiment reached Tampa, Roosevelt took pot-luck with his men in the dingy day coaches which Uncle Sam had furnished to them.

There was a good deal of trouble in getting food for the men during that long day's wait in the San Antonio railway yard. Their dinner finally consisted of a thin slice of canned beef between two hardtacks. This was the first day the regiment went hungry. Many others followed after they reached Cuba.

The first man to be taken sick on the trip was Private Nicholson, of Troop K. His home was Baltimore, and he had the measles. It is believed that he may have carried this disease into the regiment, for many men afterwards came down with it.

All along the line the men were received with the utmost enthusiasm by great crowds waiting at the stations. Even as early as four o'clock in the morning, in some instances, pretty girls were dressed in white, and waiting to give them posies as they passed. The most enthusiastic reception of all occurred at New Orleans, where tremendous crowds were at the Southern Pacific and Louisville and Nashville

Troop H, shortly after Arrival at Tampa.

stations to bid them Godspeed as they passed through.

There were unaccountable delays, and for hours the men, who were kept closely in the cars by guards stationed at all entrances, sweltered and sweated in the heat of a New Orleans day. They bore the hardship of this kind of travelling with a certain rough philosophy, but the remarks they made about the railway companies are not printable in this volume. They were dirty, hot, and hungry, and while it cannot be said that language ever suffers from dirt or hunger, that used by the Rough Riders on this occasion was certainly hot.

It was early in the cool dawn that the regiment reached Tampa. It was dumped without consideration by the railway company at Ybor City, although it could easily have been taken half a dozen miles nearer to its camping place. The baggage cars were run off into some remote district, thoroughly out of sight, and the regiment's mess kits were hidden in them. They had been assigned three days' rations. Their journey had taken five days, and they were hungry.

Probably a trooper's remark on this occasion, "that war is hell," was spoken with more feeling than marked the expression of any sentiment afterwards during the entire campaign. Roosevelt and Wood were both wildly indignant over the way the regiment had been treated by the railways. Roosevelt made the acquaintance of at least a dozen officials of the road before the day was over, and those officials can be classed with the Spaniards whom he met afterwards and who never wanted to renew their communication with Colonel Roosevelt. So crowded was the train that grain, hay, and other forage for the animals had to be packed in the aisles of the passenger coaches, and the tops of the freight cars carried tons of supplies of all kinds.

The animals were unloaded in the stock pens, and plainly showed the effects of the starvation and neglect which they had suffered on the way. But like the men, they were glad enough to get there, no matter how.

The ride from the point of disembarkation to the camping grounds was not less than eight miles long. It was made with some pretense of troop formation, but not much. The men rode through Tampa, with its filthy shanties and deserts of sand, to a point back of the Tampa Bay Hotel. Their destination had previously been used as the Sixth Cavalry's drill ground.

Not much effort was made to form an elaborate camp here, for the men were tired and it was the belief of everyone that they were only pausing for a day or two before they were to be sent to the transports and on to Cuba. They simply formed in lines—a row of tents and a row of horses at their picket lines. It was not a good camping ground. Rains were frequent, and the formation of the soil was such that the water would not soak in. Those who had the money were comforted by the proximity of the Tampa Bay Hotel, but those who had not, were less pleasantly situated than they had been in San Antonio.

The arrangement of the tents close to the picket lines brought a plague of flies about the men, and Tampa contributed its pleasant little share of tarantulas and centipedes. It is scarcely worthwhile to go into great detail about the stay of the men at Tampa. It was an unpleasant period, but it was only preliminary to the embarkation. It was simply one of the necessary evils which led up to the glorious Cuban campaign, and the men have forgotten as much of it as they can forget.

It is only fair here to make some slightly detailed mention of Troops C, M, I, and H. These included the unfortunates whose memory of Tampa is their memory of the war. Probably no grief stands out as more acute and painful in the minds of the men who formed these troops than that which came to them when they found that they were to be left behind. Nearly every regiment of the army was forced to desert some of its men in this way, and the men who stayed behind deserve quite as ample credit as the men whose privilege it was to hurry to the front. Theirs were the long and aggravating days of inactive discomfort; of weary, weary waiting. Major Hersey was left in command of those who stayed in Tampa.

After Major Brodie was wounded and promoted to the lieutenant-colonelcy, Captain Jenkins was made the junior major, and through a special dispensation from General Coppinger, Hersey became the ranking major, and joined the regiment in the field. Afterwards, Major Dunn took command at Tampa. The troops at Tampa suffered terribly from sickness. For instance, there were eighty-three men in C Troop. When the war was over, and they finally started North, only forty-five men were left who could travel, or who had not already been sent North. It has been shown that the men in Tampa really suffered more from sickness than the men who went to Cuba.

The hospitals were so overcrowded that it was almost impossible to find room for ailing Rough Riders there, and many sufferers from typhoid and typhus-malaria were, perforce, neglected. Scarcely a hospital train went North which did not carry with it some of these unfortunate Rough Riders, and the lot of the men in Tampa was generally unhappy. They had eleven hundred horses and mules to look after.

Reveille was habitually sounded at 4.30. Drill came on at 5.30 and lasted until 8.30 or 9, and after that the men performed such dreary camp work as came in their daily routine. Then they could only lie in their shelter-tents out of the sun, and spend the horrid days in fighting mosquitoes, flies, and heat.

Their only hope was that they might be ordered to the front. Three times the glad news came. They were instructed to prepare their goods and strike their tents. The last time they were even told that transportation was all ready for them, and that the ship which was to carry them on to Cuban battlefields lay anchored, ready, in Savannah harbor. But each time when they were prepared to start, their orders were countermanded, and the dreary, dreary hopeless days at Tampa began again. I should have said before that the camp of this waiting contingent was transferred from Tampa to Port Tampa, after their more fortunate companions had sailed away, and that the sanitary conditions were as good as any.

An episode of the days at Tampa was the football game. There were a good many football players in the regiment, and some of them had college records not excelled. The game was progressing merrily, when Hamilton, the strong man, from Indian Territory, who had been to town as Major Hersey's orderly, came along. He could not keep out of the game and forgot that he still had his spurs on. He jumped for Ricketts and McFarrin, who had played on the University of Pennsylvania team. There was scarcely a man in the scrimmage that ensued who left it without wounds from Hamilton's spurs.

The newspapers have already told the story of how the troops were loaded on the transports; how the transports sailed out into Tampa Bay, and how the spectre of a mythical Spanish fleet drove them ingloriously back to their docks.

Finally, they started. The troops on board the *Yucatan* were A and B, from Arizona; D, from Oklahoma; E, F, and G, from New Mexico; K from the East, and L from Indian Territory. There was also a part of the Second Infantry on board, with its regimental band.

There had been the wildest excitement and heartburning among the men when it was found that some troops were to be left behind and some were to be chosen to go to Cuba. There was not a man in the whole regiment who did not voice in his heart that cry which he shouted from his lips:

Rough, tough, we're the stuff,

We want to fight, and we can't get enough.

But there were those of them who were to see no fighting and they took their disappointment then as bravely as their comrades afterwards took their danger, although the danger was much more welcome than the disappointment. Knowledge of the troops which had been selected was spread throughout the regiment the night before, and there were those among the Rough Riders who worked for transfer to the troops which were to sail under the favoured letters. More demonstrative than the others, because they were of the elect, were Woodbury Kane and Lieutenant Tiffany, who had been among the most ardent workers from the start. These two men had done more, perhaps, than any others to persuade the Westerners that because a man came from the East, and because he was college bred, he did not necessarily shirk his tasks nor fall off his horse.

The day of embarkation was a great day. Sergeant Higgins expressed it well when he remarked:

"Hell won't be worse crowded on the last day than this dock is now."

I have inserted a photograph of the embarkation in the book, and its wild mix-up only slightly pictures the insane confusion of the scene. On the transport, the quarters were anything but pleasant. Most of the bunks were in the vessel's hold—and she was a rattletrap old hulk that had been used in the freight-carrying trade—and they were badly built of rough and unplaned lumber. The work of the contractors who had put the berths up, proved to be so inefficient that many of them fell down when the men piled into them the first night. After that those particular Rough Riders were without beds. At the best, the bunks were so close together that the men could move about between them only with the very greatest difficulty, and when they crawled into them at night, they found them so narrow that turning over ordinarily meant splinters in their skins.

The transport's capacity was 750 men. At first 1,060 men were on board. One hundred were afterwards removed to another ship. Early in the voyage a waggish trooper hung the sign, "Standing Room Only," over the side of the ship.

Another came along, and with the same marking pot added: "And damn little of that."

In the meantime, of course, such luxuries as artificial ventilation had been utterly neglected, and the room on deck was greatly circumscribed by the building of a rough board superstructure. A little space was left clear, fore and aft of this, and if the men wanted air they had to seek these spaces, trust themselves to the somewhat shaky roof of the superstructure, or cling to the swaying shrouds.

It was on the first day out that the third man wounded met his injury. Thomas H. Young, who was the son of a Kentucky colonel, and whose father had applied for enlistment at the same time the son had, had a good place to sleep, where the fresh air came in through the cargo hatch. He had been a student in a New York law school and had shown himself to be an excellent soldier. He had especially won the favour of McClintock, who was the captain of his troop, and was slated for a non-commissioned officership, but that unlucky day a heavy cargo stanchion fell down on him and crushed his arm and head.

Young was one of half a dozen men who were taken to the hospital ship *Olivette* from the *Yucatan*, during the voyage to Cuba. I sailed down, as well as home, on the *Olivette*, and, with other correspondents, crowded eagerly to the rail at first whenever we heard that Rough Riders were to be brought aboard. After the first two or three had arrived, however, we held with equal firmness to the opposite side of the hospital ship, when such news came, for Young was the only Rough Rider who voyaged with us who did not suffer from some contagious or infectious disease. There were cases of measles, there were cases of typhoid, and there was one case of scarlet fever brought to us from the regiment.

Aside from these slight episodes, the trip to Cuba was uneventful to the Rough Riders. In the history of warfare, no such imposing array of troopships had ever been gathered together to carry an invading army. Thirty-four transports, arranged in three great lines, steaming so slowly that the alignment could be very well kept up, convoyed by one of the greatest battleships afloat, and by cruisers and gunboats, made a spectacle which every man who watched, realised was great, and in thinking of it, each man made the first letter of his thought a capital letter. Great in his mind, during that voyage, began with a tremendous G.

We went down on the inside of the Florida coast, and the first sign we had that there really was any Cuba on the map, was the flashing of great searchlights thrown from Morro Castle in Havana against the midnight sky. The *Segurança* was the flagship. She was not a pretty boat, but she steamed at nine knots while we steamed at less than five, and thus made her way about among us with some facility. In the mean-

From a photograph by William Dinwiddie.
Col. Leonard Wood in consultation with Lieut.-Col. Roosevelt at Daiquiri.

time, signal men were always wigwagging to the other boats from her dingy bridge, and smutty little torpedo boats were ever dodging about among the fleet, giving orders from her as to formation–as to who should come forward and who should fall back.

There were things which happened, before we passed Cape Maisí, of which we had no knowledge. The Spanish papers have, since the war, told of a trip which one of their torpedo-boat destroyers made through the middle of our fleet on a foggy midnight, when she did not know whether she was among friends or foes; when she did not know whether to fire or hold her ammunition, and when she was suddenly enlightened by a sturdy hail from the bridge of one of our warships, asking her if she were the *Porter*, one of our torpedo boats. The Spaniards promptly answered, "Yes," and when the warship threw her searchlight round, showing six or eight American ships in sight, she skipped for the Cuban coast and safety with all the rapidity there was within her boilers.

The *Yankee*, an American gunboat, converted from a millionaire's steam yacht, also nearly opened fire upon us when our flagship failed to give the proper night signal. But of these perils our men, Rough Riders and other troops alike, were wholly ignorant.

As our troopships passed Santiago, a shot was fired at only one of them, and that ship, strangely enough, was named the *Santiago*. The thing with the Rough Riders was still a picnic and not war. Indeed, there were dead among them before they learned that war is grim and war is awful and war is real.

So far as the trip on the transports was concerned, much more excitement was occasioned by pat hands at poker than was ever caused by dread of Spaniards.

Here is a story told by Col. Henry Wigham, an officer on the staff of the Governor of Arizona, and one of the men who helped to organise the Rough Riders:

> Among the troopers was a cowboy named Frank Briggs. He was a dead shot, a reckless frontiersman, and a good, game sport. Briggs wrote a letter to me after he had gone on board the transport, which I received at Tampa, and which said in part:
> 'I won $200 last night and $400 the night before. There is money to burn on this boat. If Charlie will only send me the dice he promised, I will be well stamped.'

A letter from an officer afterwards, to Colonel Wigham, spoke of the splendid work by Briggs, at Las Guasimas. He was as cool and accurate as though he had been in a turkey shoot back home, instead of in a battle on an enemy's hillside.

"Officers' school" was held every day in the morning, and in the afternoon the men were trained in handling Krag-Jorgenson carbines. Colonel Wood feared that the men would suffer from their inactivity during the trip, and made them exercise, as do the sailors on board a man-o'-war. It was a great lark for them to put their hands on one another's shoulders and rush about in a kind of trotting lock-step for an hour and a half each day.

The first Cuban land that came in sight was the blue point of Cape Maisí. The men cheered it with great enthusiasm, as they slowly ploughed through the southeastern passage. For a full half day before they landed, they again had sight of the hazy shores of Cuba and their cheering wearied.

Their first hurrahs at sight of Cuba were not so hearty as the cheers they gave when they parted from it, less than fifty days later.

This reminds me of a story told of Mr. W. R. Hearst. It is said that when he first landed in Cuba and looked about—at the umbrageous growth, at the fertile soil, at the towering palms, at the flitting birds, at the fragrant flowers—he remarked to George Pancoast, who was with him:

"My God! how could this paradise have been abandoned to mere savages?"

A month later, as he sailed away upon the *Silvia*, a special ship which he had chartered to take him North, he stood calmly at the rail and gazed with satisfaction at his last blue glimpse of Cuba. When he had found that Paradise, he had been well and strong, his muscles and his mind had overflowed with energy, his enthusiasm had been great. That day, as he leaned against the rail, the high temperature of Cuban fever burned his skin, his pulse beat 140 to the minute, and his eyes, erstwhile so bright, were yellow and bloodshot.

He shook his fist at Cuba on this occasion, and said:

"My God! how can even savages live there?"

On the 22nd of June, the Rough Riders made their landing at Daiquiri.

CHAPTER 4

In Cuba, Before the Fighting

It was at Daiquiri that I first saw the Rough Riders. I had happened to go away from Tampa on the very day they reached there, and had returned only in time to embark long after the *Yucatan* and its cargo of First Volunteer Cavalry men was out of sight.

I was among the first to land, because there was a *Journal* tugboat there to help me get ashore. While I was watching the soldiers of the regular troops disembark at the dock, the first boatload of Rough Riders came along. This dock was a mere skeleton. The Spaniards had ripped the planking off it before they retired, and, although there were thousands of feet of loose boards stacked up on shore, our men were in too great a hurry to nail them on the bare timbers which had been left. The engineers, who might have done this work, had been sent down the coast to build pontoon bridges for the Cubans, and so the United States army picked a precarious way ashore over slippery wooden girders.

This gave the Rough Riders their first opportunity to distinguish themselves in Cuba. Our soldiers, laden down with blanket rolls, ammunition belts, arms, and other heavy equipment, climbed up to the dock from the tossing surf boats with the utmost difficulty. The sea dashed quite over the dock at times, and the wet timbers afforded slight hold for either hands or feet. The men were thoroughly occupied in keeping their own balance, and frequently could not avoid letting some of their impedimenta slip from their hands into the boiling waters below the dock. There lay bugles, guns, revolvers, canteens, and other pieces of equipment galore.

In the boat-load of Rough Riders, which I have mentioned, were C. E. Knoblauch, whom I have already spoken of as a member of the New York Stock Exchange, and several other expert swimmers. They quickly volunteered to rescue the lost articles, and stripped for the work. All day long they plied at this thankless task.

Along toward night, while the Tenth Cavalry was struggling ashore, two of its coloured troopers slipped off the dock and went down into the boiling sea among the crunching boats and jagged rocks. Knoblauch; Buckie O'Neil, and their companions worked as never men worked before to save these two poor chaps from drowning, but the task was too great for human strength, and they had to make their way to shore as best they could—crestfallen and unsuccessful. The men who were drowned were the first victims of the same lack of foresight, which afterwards cost so many lives at Bloody Angle, and the men who tried to save them were the first men who had an opportunity to develop heroism during the land operations of the Spanish-American War.

So, the Rough Riders were "in it" at the start.

Over at the right of Daiquiri a sugar-loaf mountain rose sheer a thousand feet. It was called Mount Losiltires. On the very summit of this strangely shaped hill was a blockhouse. All the morning, during the bombardment, we had watched this tiny fortification with the greatest interest. It offered a shining mark for the gunners of the attacking ships, and probably a hundred shells were aimed at it. Many struck near it, and as we watched the clouds of smoke and dust resulting from their explosions slowly clear away, we expected to find that the blockhouse had been annihilated. But when the bombardment ended, it still stood there, outlined sharply and saucily against the Cuban noonday sky. At its side there rose a flagstaff.

I tried to borrow a flag of a number of transport captains, but with that charming indifference to any patriotic idea which they exhibited from beginning to end of the war, they unanimously refused to let me have one. I had in my possession a small flag belonging to the *New York Journal*; I decided to raise that flag as the first to be set flying over Cuba by anyone connected with the United States Army. There never was a harder climb than the one by which I reached the summit of Mount Losiltires.

There had been a path up the side of the mountain, zigzagging and rough at best no doubt, but now almost entirely obliterated in places by the terrific explosions of our shells. In one place a hole not less than ten feet deep and three times as far across had literally scooped out the side of the mountain—path and all. I never did harder work than I did in getting around this hole, clinging with hands and feet to tiny projections and little shrubs. William Bengough, a *Journal* art-

View of San Juan Hill and Block-house, showing the Camp of the United States Forces.

ist, had started with me, but the heat and the climb proved too much for him, and he stopped to rest before we reached the hole. Finally, I scrambled up to the summit.

The sun was blistering hot and the climb· had exhausted me. I sat down to get my wind. While I was sitting there, Surgeon La Motte, Colour-Sergeant Wright, and Trumpeter Platt, of the Rough Riders, came up by another and easier trail.

They had with them the flag which had been presented to Captain McClintock's troop by the ladies of Phoenix, Arizona. It was a beautiful silk flag and it is now a flag with a history. This history will be found elsewhere in this volume.

We consulted as to the best means of raising it. There were no lanyards on the weather-beaten old pole which the Spaniards had left behind them. We tried to devise a scheme of putting a flag up on that, but it was too small and slippery to climb, and we gave the notion up. Just at this moment the only patriotic civilian sailor that I saw during the whole war, came climbing slowly over the edge of the hill. I have forgotten his name; I wish I had it. The Rough Riders had investigated the blockhouse and found a little ladder inside, long enough to reach up to the tiny cupola with its loopholes. Wright and Platt had found this ladder, and presently Platt appeared on his knees on the hot, slippery tin roof. He remained on his knees not more than five consecutive seconds. The roof was too steep and Platt came to grief with great rapidity.

Then we paused for consultation. We had the flag, we were at the top of the hill, the blockhouse and the flagpole were there to our hands, but we could see no way of carrying out our brilliant design. Around the edge of the hill the Spaniards had dug trenches and built outside of them a low stone wall. Colour-Sergeant Wright took the flag on its own flagstaff, and waved it from this wall. Bengough came up and made a sketch of him as he stood there. I have it in my possession.

Then the patriotic sailor whom I have mentioned, and who had been quietly and with some amusement watching our efforts, volunteered his services. Wright and Platt lost themselves in speechless admiration as he crept like a cat out on the slippery roof. Wright had difficulty in finding words to express his amazement, a moment later, when the sailor rose to his feet, and lashed the flag of the Rough Riders, staff and all, to the little timber which stuck from the peak of the blockhouse.

The little bay in which the transports were anchored lay like a sheet of silver in front of us. Between it and the foot of our hill the coast of Cuba stretched like a map. The ships looked like toy ships from our point of vantage, and our soldiers looked like toy soldiers. The flag had been waving in the breeze perhaps a minute before these toy soldiers and the men on those toy ships got sight of it. And when they did, bedlam broke loose. Every steam whistle on the warships screamed its loudest, every soldier in the invading thousands yelled his hoarsest, and the Cubans, proud of the new Lee rifles which had been distributed among them by the navy, fired them off in greeting volleys to the bit of red, white, and blue which fluttered brightly at the top of Mount Losiltires.

Thus, the Rough Riders won their second glory. They had developed the first army heroes in the war, and now they had flown the first flag raised by the United States army on Cuban soil.

I remember with considerable interest an episode which occurred before we left the top of the hill. The three Rough Riders who were present proved themselves to be fine soldiers before the war was over, but on the afternoon of that 22nd of June we came near losing two of them.

It was evident that the Spaniards had left their trenches up there with considerable haste, for behind them remained many abandoned trappings. The commanding officer, for instance, had left the orders which had been sent to him from headquarters and copies of his own replies to them. One of his letters was amusing, found as it was in the midst of an abandoned post, which had fired not one answering shot to our bombardment. It was addressed to General Toral, and announced that he, the officer on Mount Losiltires, would take great pleasure in getting along without reinforcements, and that, should the American Army appear, backed by the entire navy of the United States, he could whip them and drive them back to Florida, single handed and without difficulty.

But as I have said, when the army did come, he fired not one single shot in opposition to its landing.

Being a Spaniard, he adopted other means to accomplish our undoing. There were many bottles of wine among the rubbish which the Spaniards had left behind them in the blockhouse, and there were other bottles of wine lying outside the blockhouse and on the stone wall and in the trenches. They lay there very ostentatiously. No one could possibly fail to see them. It was a hot day. The exertion of getting up the hill and raising the flag had been tremendous. That wine looked most inviting. Wright and Platt had opened a bottle and were about to drink of it, when Surgeon La Motte took it from them and smelled it. He threw the bottle on a rock, where it was dashed to fragments. Then he took the copper binding of an exploded six-inch shell, and with it broke every other bottle of that wine which the Spanish commanding officer had kindly left for the comfort and entertainment of the American Army.

Wright and Platt had had a narrow escape.

The wine was poisoned.

We made our way down the hill and left the flag behind us, to float there proudly until sunset.

The Rough Riders were encamped in a beautiful valley between the two low ranges of pretty hills which border the Daiquiri River. They had with them only "dog tents," and the grass in the valley was higher than the tents. This grass was full of land crabs and tarantulas. Nice little lizards, too, scuttled about here and there, and there were some extremely suspicious-looking snakes.

Colonel Wood and Colonel Roosevelt did not maintain such military discipline in the construction of their camp as did some of the other commanding officers, and the dog tents went up in a somewhat haphazard fashion. As soon as they were up and the men discovered their discomfort, they set about constructing for themselves more pleasant shelters. Neighbouring shrubbery was drawn upon for uprights and leafy boughs, and some good-natured Cubans instructed our gallant fighters in the mysteries of palm thatches. Before night fell, fully a quarter of the men were comfortably housed under these impromptu roofs. Regimental headquarters were positively embowered through the efforts of solicitous troopers. Probably no officers ever looked more carefully after the comfort of their men, and certainly no men ever looked more carefully after the comfort of their officers.

As the quick-setting sun went down red and fiery behind the hills, this Cuban solitude which had suddenly been transformed into the abiding place of six hundred men, with its myriad camp fires twinkling gayly, its cheery bugle calls and active bustle, presented as beautiful a picture as the brush of a painter could desire.

Travelling with the regiment was Burr McIntosh, also of the *Journal*, and a well-known actor. McIntosh was affected with that prying curiosity which leads a journalist to news, and sometimes into trouble. The first evidence of it came when he decided to test the speed of two tarantulas. At Tampa the boys had organised exciting races in which land turtles were the participants; McIntosh decided to try tarantulas. He did. They didn't speed to any appreciable extent, but they bit him with amazing rapidity. We wondered if journalism and the stage were about to lose a shining light. Surgeon La Motte did his best.

McIntosh, Major Brodie, Sergeant Hamilton Fish, and one or two others planned to tour the place in search of that celebrated medicine which is given so freely in New Jersey as a cure for snake bite. There was no whiskey in the camp. They searched elsewhere with commendable persistence. There was no whiskey in any other camp. They walked eagerly up the straggling little street, which has its beginning near the now celebrated skeleton dock.

At last, they found a storehouse full of Jamaica rum and great demijohns of sweet Spanish wine. They tried the rum and found it raw, even beyond the endurance of a Rough Rider. They carried a great demijohn of the wine back to camp with them.

That Sweet Spanish Wine.

McIntosh did not die of the tarantula bites, but when he woke the next morning to a realisation of the kind of head which sweet Spanish wine is capable of putting on a journalist and actor, he was sorry that he had not. He did not drink all of the wine, and there were others. I will not mention names, because these men are now looked up to as heroes by a grateful American public, and it would be cruel to take from them their laurels, but there were those among the Rough Riders who, however bravely they endured their wounds in days that followed, groaned miserably and were willing to go away from Cuba on the morning of the 23rd of June.

Most of the troops had disembarked before morning, and the landscape when the sun rose was dotted for a mile up the valley with the white tents of the United States Army. Down on the beach among half a dozen surf boats which had been crushed on the rocks, and amidst the many-colored, shining-sea-shells of the Caribbean, lay the two troopers who had been drowned the day before, and whom the Rough Riders had tried to save. A detail from the regiment was present at their unimposing funeral early in the morning. General Shafter was still on his flagship, the *Segurança*. Major-General Joseph Wheeler was in command on shore.

Most of the newspaper men were not allowed to land until late on

From a photograph by William Dinwiddie. *The First Camp of the Rough Riders, at Daiquiri.*

the 23rd. Those of us who had landed before had a hard time. The Cubans, who were naturally grateful to the New York *Journal*, had turned over to me as headquarters a big bungalow on a hill, and this kept the night dew off us. There were in our party Stephen Crane, John Hans of the *London Daily Mail*, Frank Nuttall of the *London Daily Telegraph*, and others. But saved as we were from sleeping out of doors, we were entirely without food. What little we got we begged from soldiers, although all of us bore credentials from the Secretary of War, directing all commanding officers to furnish forage and rations for us at the cost price. I may be pardoned for remarking here that I ate only one meal while I was in Cuba during the Spanish-American war.

The morning and early afternoon of the 23rd of June were devoted by the Rough Riders to perfecting the comfort and beauty of their camp at Daiquiri. They apparently expected to remain there a long time. But at one o'clock General Wheeler sent orders to Colonel Wood to be ready to move at a moment's notice. In the meantime, several regiments of regular troops had marched off towards Siboney. At half-past one orders came for the Rough Riders to move at once.

Their beautiful camp was transformed into a scene of desolation within an hour. The little shelters and palm thatches were ruthlessly destroyed. Dog tents came down and went into the blanket rolls of these dismounted cavalrymen with a rapidity which would have done credit to any regiment of regulars. The only trouble concerned the mule-trains. The scarcity of animals which handicapped the conduct of the Cuban campaign from the very start was severely felt by the Rough Riders. Much of the luggage of the officers was abandoned where it lay in camp. It seemed almost impossible to pack the mess truck alone on the few animals at hand, and the rapid-fire and dynamite guns presented great problems.

The captain of the *Yucatan* had gone out to sea with a good deal of the Rough Riders' plunder. There were not saddles enough for the officers to ride in. Colonel Wood had an extra horse—a beautiful little thoroughbred Kentucky mare. It was almost with tears in his eyes that he ordered a packsaddle put on her and told the men to load her with the regimental headquarters mess kit, and the pretty little beast turned pathetic eyes of protest on her master while this was being done. Wood felt so badly about it that he went away. He never saw the little thoroughbred again, I am told. She was among the first animals shot at Guasimas.

Colonel Roosevelt was without a saddle. The man who led his

troops so coolly at Guasimas and San Juan reached a state of excitement in the face of this early emergency which reminded me of the old days in New York when he was a Police Commissioner. His wrath was boiling, and his grief was heartbreaking. General Shafter had promised me before we left Tampa that I should be given plenteous transportation for *Journal* horses. I had consulted him before purchasing them, as I didn't want to buy animals that I could not take with me.

At the last moment, however, he had refused to allow any *Journal* horse a place on any transport, and the *Journal* staff was entirely without animals. This, however, left us with a large surplus of saddles. I had one myself, old and worn and perfectly comfortable, which I was especially fond of. In Colonel Roosevelt's distress I came to his rescue and loaned him that saddle. He rode it into the battle the next day and into oblivion, for it has never been heard of since.

I shall never forget the terrible march to Siboney. Colonel Wood kindly permitted me to march with him at the head of the column, in company with Captain McCormack and the regimental adjutant. Captain Capron was the senior captain of the regiment, and his command (L Troop) was at the head of the column. Just ahead of Colonel Wood a little Cuban boy, who could talk English, rode on a tiny native stallion, which succeeded in keeping Colonel Wood and his big charger at a very respectable distance. Colour-Sergeant Wright, bearing the heavy regimental standard—the same which we had raised the day before on Mount Losiltires—was just behind me, and was unquestionably the happiest man in Cuba. The heat was absolutely terrific, and before we had marched two miles every uniform was so soaked with perspiration that the men looked as if they had been ducked.

Tyree Rivers was the second regular army officer attached to the Rough Riders. He was an *aide* on Young's staff and an officer in the Third Cavalry, as Captain McCormack was the representative of General Wheeler. It is not fair to fail to mention his valorous work. He went from Siboney to Las Guasimas on a particularly sturdy mule, which he let me ride at intervals. After we had stopped at the end of the trail, and Colonel Wood had received word from Capron that signs of Spaniards had been seen, he sent Rivers off into the jungle at the right. Rivers came back, after he had started, and formally gave me his mule. I tied the animal to a barbed-wire fence and have neither seen her nor Rivers since.

General Wood told me the other day in Washington, that Rivers' conduct during the battle was most extraordinarily commendable. He must have gone back and got the mule, for General Wood said that he rode mounted up and down the firing line, and did mighty good work in encouraging the men and keeping them cool. It is interesting to note that McCormack and Rivers were the only men in the regiment who wore the United States Army blue uniforms, and it is probable that they were, because of these uniforms, selected as especial targets by the Spanish sharpshooters. I don't know this to be true, I simply guess at it.

At the time I saw General Wood in Washington, this book was practically completed. He asked me to add this reference to Rivers. I add it with pleasure.

Some regiments of regular infantry were ahead of us, and the superiority of the Rough Riders, not only over volunteers, but over most regulars, was never better illustrated than it was that day. During the march from Daiquiri to Siboney, probably one-half of the men in the regiment preceding us dropped out from heat prostration. Our path through the Cuban jungles was literally lined during most of the distance by poor fellows in blue, who had fallen by the wayside and lay there helpless and alone, gasping for breath. We lost not one man from exhaustion who did not succeed in rejoining us before we went to bed that night.

There was an exhibition of grit on this march that deserves mention. One trooper had had his legs crushed between the bumpers of two cars on the way from Tampa to Port Tampa. He had only partially recovered when this march began, but he insisted on going with the regiment. On the way he fell out from exhaustion, and the men with him thought that he would die. He was, of necessity, left by the wayside with some exhausted ones from other regiments. Before the next day's battle was half over, he crawled slowly to the front and fired his full share of shots before the fighting ended.

One of the most astonishing things I saw in Cuba occurred on this trip. A regular soldier, belonging, I think, to the Tenth Infantry, suddenly discovered that his period of enlistment expired that day at five o'clock in the afternoon. We had perhaps completed half our march when he made this discovery. Without hesitation, and at the beginning of the campaign, he demanded his discharge from his commanding officer, turned over such of his equipment as belonged to the Government, and left the United States Army then and there. His departure was accompanied by a chorus of jeers from his own comrades, and as he answered them, he fell in the path of Captain Capron.

Capron collared him as if he had been a yellow dog, and passed him down to the long line of Rough Riders which stretched behind. I don't know what happened to him after he passed out of my sight, but I know that before he had disappeared, there was very little clothing on him, and he was very properly bleeding.

There is no country on the earth more beautiful than that through which we passed. For a large part of our way we were almost embowered by the rising Cuban jungle on each side of our path; for several miles we marched through a cocoanut grove where the palms towered on an average more than a hundred feet above our heads; we crossed several handsome streams and went through the dry bed of one river. The Spaniards had announced that we could never march from Daiquiri to Siboney, without building elaborate bridges, but we found that all of the streams were easily fordable.

Nothing is thirstier than a long march, except a battle. As we crossed one of the streams, the water looked so cool, clear, and delightful that Colonel Wood stopped and told us to be careful.

"You can fill your canteens here," he said, "if you don't foul the water yourselves."

So, we stopped on stepping stones, and we hovered on the edges, and we hung ourselves out on overhanging boughs, and we filled our canteens. And just as we got them filled, we heard a great splashing around a curve upstream, and a large section of the Tenth Cavalry (coloured) came into view. They were swimming in the river.

We emptied our canteens.

After that the march was long and weary. By no means as large a proportion of men dropped out of our regiment as had dropped out of the regular regiment that preceded us, but still twenty or thirty fell by the wayside. Along towards the end of the march—after we had come across the railroad tracks, and were momentarily expecting to see Siboney—the men began to grumble a little bit. Darkness had fallen, and marching was difficult. The curious lumpy roots of the scrub palmettos grew constantly across our path, and walking was not joyful. When a man called back "hole," we were all unhappy until we had seen some other fellow fall in, and thus knew that we had passed it.

Humorous sentries were posted high above us on the railroad embankment to our left, and they cried out ribald cries about imminent Spaniards and sudden death that was likely to strike us in the next thicket. Those last miles were worse than fighting. Finally, it was well after ten o'clock, we began to find the campfires of the regiments which had already reached Siboney,

At last, we went into camp in the very heart of the now famous little village. In front of us were the railway tracks, and beyond them the sea. Some transports had come up from Daiquiri and were vomiting their men into the surf from which they scrambled up to us, drenched and disheartened.

Shortly after our arrival Major-General Wheeler sent for Colonel Wood and General Young.·

CHAPTER 5

The First Shot

The 24th of June had well begun before this conference between Generals Wheeler and Young and Colonels Wood and Roosevelt was ended.

Before the day had finished, nine of the men in the regiment were dead on a Cuban hillside, scarce six miles away, and thirty-two were lying in hastily improvised hospitals, sore wounded.

I was not actually present at this conference, but Richard Harding Davis was, and he says in his book, and says privately, that General Wheeler had reconnoitred the trail that afternoon with some Cubans, and found that the enemy were intrenched at Guasimas, which, Davis says, is at the apex of two trails only three miles from Siboney, but which is really more than five miles away from that strange little Cuban town.

Before the rain came that night, despite our weariness, some of us started to explore. Troops were still being landed through the surf. Two warships lay in the slight coastline indentation which is dignified by the name of bay, and played their searchlights on the landing place. Probably no more picturesque sight was ever presented to the eye of a newspaper correspondent than was before me and half a dozen of the Rough Riders when we went down to the edge of the ocean for a swim. The canteens of the regiment were empty, and I was thirstier than I have ever been before in my life, and the men of the regiment must have been worse off than I was.

They had been carrying their heavy arms and equipment during the long march from Daiquiri, while I had borne only a blanket, in which I had wrapped my photographic films and my camera. The blanket, by the way, belonged to Stephen Crane. Mine had fallen a victim to the skeleton pier. We took our little bath. We stripped for it as boys do who go into the Erie Canal to swim, and thus saved ourselves from attracting attention, because the man who had clothes on, unless he was just getting out of one of the landing surf boats, would have appeared unusual. Probably two hundred American soldiers were there in the surf, helping the newcomers to disembark, and they were quite as God made them.

I shall not soon forget the wet look of the water in the sea. We all wanted to drink it. While we were standing there talking about it and discussing the thoughts which must come to shipwrecked sailors on rafts who see "*water, water everywhere and not a drop to drink,*" one of the Tenth Infantry came along with six or eight canteens on his shoulders. He asked us if we wanted a drink. We did.

"Well, here you are," he said, and handed a canteen to Dr. Church.

The doctor took it. He took one swallow. He handed it sorrowfully back.

"Never mind," said he. "I will go thirsty."

The canteens were filled with that same sweet Spanish wine which the Rough Riders had learned to dread at Daiquiri.

We had returned to camp before the men had cooked supper. Colonel Wood asked me join the regimental mess, and I was filled with exceedingly great joy. But the men were handicapped by lack of water. The Spaniards had cut the pipes which were supposed to bring water from the hills, and Colonel Wood had given the strictest orders that no member of his regiment should drink the water which was being given out freely in the Cuban shanties of the town. His wisdom in taking this course is plainly shown by the fact that not one member of the Rough Riders developed a case of fever dating from that day, although the regular troops who were encamped thereabout began to come down with it within forty-eight hours. From the beginning of the campaign to its very finish, Wood's medical knowledge and regard for sanitation saved the men of his command from many evils to which the soldiers of other regiments, even among the regular troops, were often exposed.

Finally, and it was fully midnight, the details of men who had been sent for water came back from somewhere with an ample supply, and the cooking which had been delayed by the lack of it began to go merrily forward. We were hungry—officers and men alike—and the gleaming campfires, against which the figures of the sturdy cooks were strongly silhouetted in the inky blackness of the Cuban night, seemed especially inviting. There was probably not one man in the regiment who was not licking his chops in anticipation, as he looked on.

From a photograph by William Dinwiddie.

Building Palm Shelters.

But the luck of the Rough Riders deserted them then. We were in Cuba at the beginning of the rainy season, and had every reason to expect the worst kind of weather. For some reason, God had been good to General Shafter and had let him land his troops under smiling skies. Nothing that nature could do to help him be a good commanding general had been omitted by an all-wise Providence, up to that time, and we had been able to get along fairly well. But suddenly, while we were waiting for our supper to be cooked, the first rain which had descended since we landed in Cuba began to fall. It was not what we know as rain in the North. It was a deluge. It was such a downpour as we have never heard of in the United States. It put out the campfires and we suffered accordingly. Those of us who were too tired to wait for it to stop before we went to sleep, missed our suppers. That was a serious matter for some of us who had not had breakfast or dinner, and who did not have breakfast the next day. But it was Cuba.

Just back of Siboney rises another of those abrupt hills which are so frequent along that part of the Cuban coast. Over this hill runs one trail and along the valley at its side and to the right of it runs another. General Wheeler ordered General Young and three hundred and sixty-two men of the First and Tenth Cavalry to pass up the valley trail, and ordered Colonel Wood and his five hundred and seventy-four men to go up the hill trail. They were to meet where the trails met and merged into a wagon road to Santiago at Guasimas.

The Cuban scouts had reported the presence of Spanish sharpshooters in the jungle along the trails, and had announced that a body of Spaniards were strongly entrenched just beyond where the roads met. So, it is well to say here that the battle which followed was not technically an ambush, although it is true that the American troops met the Spaniards before they had expected to. Still, as they were marching through an enemy's country, and were taking every possible precaution, it is scarcely fair to say that they were actually surprised. The night in Siboney was probably the most uncomfortable one which most of the members of the regiment had up to that time experienced.

It was fully midnight before they were ready to sleep, and the terrific downpour had soaked the Cuban upper soil until it was of the consistency of breakfast oatmeal, bound together and rendered doubly disagreeable by the wire grass. Our men had only their dog tents, and their cheap ponchos or rubber blankets were slight protection to them against the penetrating mud. In addition to this, no one thing which the underbred and unmilitary Cuban officers in charge of troops there at Siboney could do to render sleep in our camp impossible was omitted.

Reveille was sounded at 3.15.

The camp of the Rough Riders presented a weird sight in the early morning darkness. Campfires had been left burning all night, and the figures of the cooks at work around them looked like busy demons. I had tried to sleep during the night on the porch of a Cuban shanty, with two or three officers. My fitful slumber was disturbed by the voice of Buck Dawson, chief herder in the Rough Riders' pack-train. Buck's remarks were not less weird than his appearance, and that was absolutely unearthly. Two of his mules had come over and knocked at the door of that Cuban shanty with their hind feet. He was arguing the matter with them.

Colonel Wood and Colonel Roosevelt did not lie down to sleep that night at all. When rooming came, they were still wandering busily around in their long yellow "slickers" or rain coats. Wood looked worn and haggard, and his voice was cracked and hoarse. Roosevelt was as lively as a chipmunk, and seemed to be in half a dozen places at once. There was tremendous trouble in getting the mule-trains packed, and the mess kits ready for transportation.

Dawn had fairly broken—and broken is the right word to describe the coming of the Cuban dawn, for the change from darkness to light is almost as quick as the crack of an egg—and Wood's exasperation over the slowness of the men was a cheerful sight to witness. Finally, he announced to the packers and cooks in stentorian tones that if they were not ready in ten minutes, he would abandon them. They were ready.

And so, as the first heat of the Cuban day began to beat down upon the side of that precipitous hill, the Rough Riders commenced to crawl slowly up it like great brown flies. The trail was miserable. I marched in advance of the regiment, and many times had to pull myself up by clinging to rocks and shrubs. The men behind me with their guns and blanket rolls must have had a much harder time than I did. We were forced to halt for rest half a dozen times during the ascent of this six or seven hundred feet. By the time we had reached the summit, we were all at least as tired as we had been the night before, when we lay down to take our unsatisfactory sleep.

From that summit as beautiful a view was presented to us as had been shown to the little group of Rough Riders the day before, when they raised the flag on Mount Losiltires. There were transports and warships in the little bay at the bottom of the hill, and every level spot of ground in sight was covered with. the camps of our troops. Delicate bugle calls floated softly up to us like blasts from fairy trumpets, and the squalor of the Cuban town at our feet was gilded into glory by the morning sun. When that same day's sun was setting, another group of Rough Riders looked down at the same scene, and some of them saw it through a haze which approaching death had spread before their eyes.

From this point our march to the front was through one of the most beautiful countries that I have ever seen. We went very rapidly—so rapidly, indeed, that there came unheeded protests from the exhausted men. L Troop was, as it had been the day before, at the head of the column. We marched in single file, and Captain Capron was just behind me. Richard Harding Davis, who was suffering from sciatica, had borrowed a government mule, and made a picturesque sight as he went before us, preceding Captain McCormack as a matter of necessity. McCormack was also mounted on a mule, and if Davis had not ridden ahead of him, the column would have stopped, for McCormack's mule would only go at all when it could follow the animal Davis rode. Colonel Wood sent two Cuban scouts to reconnoiter before us.

They must have kept well in advance, for we did not see them again that day. The colonel, of course, rode ahead of all of us, while at first Colonel Roosevelt remained in his place in the middle of the line.

We had advanced less than a mile from the brow of the hill, when Wood ordered Capron and his troop to go forward as an advance guard. The trail had here narrowed down to a mere bridle path, bordered on each side by dense thickets. Those of us who knew what the Cubans' report had been on the night before, looked sharp when we heard coming from these thickets the plaintive call of the wood cuckoo. This call had been used as a signal by the Spaniards when our marines landed at Guantanamo, and we thought it indicated the presence of sharpshooters. Colonel Wood and McCormack both spoke to me about it, and both peered anxiously into the thickets when the call came, but there came no following rifle shot.

After this episode had occurred five or six times, we ceased to heed the cuckoo calls, thinking that they were really bird voices, but a Spanish prisoner on the hospital ship *Olivette* told me that the progress of the Rough Riders was reported in detail to the Spanish commanding general by pickets who passed this call along, and that the sharpshooters who were posted along that trail only refrained from shooting in order to allay our suspicions and induce us to march unthinkingly into the cul-de-sac which they had prepared for us farther on.

I have no doubt that the Rough Riders in the ranks had been told that they would meet the Spaniards before the day was over, but the statement had made little impression on them. While we were in Tampa, we had waited so long for orders to move that the war had come to seem a dreamy kind *of* myth to us; when the navy bombarded Daiquiri, not an answering shot had been fired; on the long march from Daiquiri to Siboney the men had seen no Spaniards and had seen no signs of Spaniards. They had *never* seen a Spaniard. I doubt if most of them actually realised that morning that there were any Spaniards on the island. As I have said, they had been told that they would meet the Spaniards before the day was over, but it was as if you were told, when you got on a railroad train, that you would have an accident before you reached your destination. You have never seen a railway accident, and while you know there are such things, still you take very little stock in the announcement that has been made to you.

The Rough Riders took no stock at all in the story that they would meet the Spaniards.

No words can describe the desolation of the country through which we were now marching: A land which has always been a wilderness is not one-half so dreary as a land which has been under cultivation, and been abandoned.

In a year a tropical wood will make inroads which a Northern forest would not make in a generation. The plantations along our route, victims of the revolution which had raged in Cuba for three years, ware desolate and overgrown with scrub and creepers. In places, erstwhile cultivated fields had been filled with a twenty-foot growth, which towered higher than our heads and arched completely over us. It was as if we were marching in a tunnel with green walls. No words can describe the oppressiveness of the heat which made us gasp and sweat in these places. Frequent haltings for rest were unavoidable. On both sides of us, barbed-wire fences hedged us into the bridle path.

By and by we came to a place where, at the right of the trail, a deserted mansion stood. We could just catch glimpses of it through the bushes. A palm tree had grown in its very middle and, lifting its roof, had cast it aside in ruins. Just here Colonel Roosevelt, who had come forward and was riding in the group at the head of the main column, and behind L Troop, picked up two shovels and fastened them to his saddle. What the colonel intended to do with the two shovels is unrecorded history.

It was perhaps five hundred yards beyond this point that a Cuban scout is alleged to have informed Captain Capron that the Spaniards were in force ahead of us. For myself, I do not believe that any Cuban scout did any such thing, or any other thing, except to double back to Siboney and return to his companion long before we reached a danger point.

Colonel Wood had warned Captain Capron that, at a certain point, he would come across the dead body of a Spanish guerrilla, who had been killed the day before by Cubans, unless the Spaniards had removed him, which was improbable, and if they did not find this corpse, Capron would, a little farther on, see a campfire. Woodbury Kane came back and simply told Colonel Wood that the enemy had been discovered, and Wood does not know now whether they found them out through the presence of the dead guerrilla, or through the presence of the campfire.

We halted.

Colonel Wood gave the order of "Silence in the ranks." We could hear the men send it to the rear along the line, and then someone saw lying a little way back, and over at the side, the dead body of a Cuban. I have been told that this Cuban was one of our scouts, but I do not believe it, for I examined his body myself, and know that he had not been killed that morning. There was no visible wound on his body, and, if I judge his nature by that of the other Cubans whom the army learned to know, I am forced to believe that he must have died a natural and peaceful death. He certainly was not the Spanish guerrilla.

Notwithstanding the order of "Silence in the ranks," the men still failed to be seriously impressed by the situation. As a matter of fact, it did not occur even to me, who was somewhat on the inside of affairs, that we were about to go into a fight. I made a trip back along the line as a matter of form, so that I might get something to write about, and I found the men lolling on the grass with their guns lying carelessly beside them. Some of them had started to take off their blanket rolls, as they had done during previous halts for rest, but they were stopped by their officers. They were not talking of war, and they were not thinking of war. The heat was probably more dreadful now than it had been at any other time, and they discussed that. A private of B Troop said:

"By God! how would you like a glass of cold beer?"

Drawn by W. Frank Myers.   ROOSEVELT.   MARSHALL.   R. H. DAVIS.   WOOD.
Lieut.-Col. Roosevelt Examining the Severed Wire just before the Battle of Las Guasimas.

The men resented it as a particularly aggravating suggestion, and tossed bits of stick and stone at him. One man blew a putty ball at him. All the way down on the transport, this man had carried his tiny tin blow-gun for the exasperation of his friends, and the wad of putty was in his pocket and the little tin tube was sticking out of the breast of his blue shirt when, a couple of hours later, we found him lying dead on the field:

L Troop was two hundred yards in advance of us. Captain Capron had deployed six men and himself two hundred yards in advance of it.

When I returned to the colonel's group, he was telling a funny story. Nearly everybody except Colonel Wood and Colonel Roosevelt was lying gasping in the grass. Roosevelt came over by me and we talked of a luncheon in the Astor House, New York, with Yr. Hearst, the proprietor of the *Journal*. I was very near to the barbed wire fence. Roosevelt glanced towards it casually. The posts were standing, but the wire was down. He picked up one end of the strand. I noticed that he started as he looked at it.

"My God!" he exclaimed, "this wire has been cut today," and he passed it over to me.

I looked at it.

"What makes you think so?" I asked.

"The end is bright," he replied, "and there has been enough dew, even since sunrise, to put a light rust on it, had it not been lately cut."

Just as he spoke, Surgeon La Motte blundered up the line on a mule, making much noise. Roosevelt jumped after him, and in urging him to keep quiet made more noise than he did. Then came the first shot.

Chapter 6

The First Battle

The six men who went in advance of L Troop were the men at whom the first shot, and the almost immediately succeeding first volley, fired by land forces in the Spanish-American War, were directed.

Tom Isbell, a full-blooded Cherokee Indian, went first at one side of the middle of the road. Captain Capron kept even with him on the other. Private Culver was a few feet behind on the left flank in the bushes, and Bob Pernell was on the right flank in the bushes. Wyley Skelton, Tom Meagher, and Sergeant Byrnes, who had been a member of the New York police force, were spread out about thirty feet apart. Someone had fired a shot in reply to that first one which came shrieking through the bushes, and, as proof of our marksmanship, this little group found a dead Spaniard lying in the middle of the road. I have tried to find out who fired this shot, but I have been unable to do so.

After that Tom Isbell saw a Spaniard, and cheerfully killed him. Then everything opened up. The Spaniards were in force in the bushes, and Isbell went down with seven shots in him from their first volley. Not five seconds elapsed before Captain Capron received his fatal wound.

By this time the men had naturally ceased to advance as boldly as they had started to, and dropped behind what cover they could find. Culver, who was also an Indian, was on his face behind a rock. Sergeant Hamilton Fish rushed up to him in advance of the other men of L Troop, who were running forward into the fracas as rapidly as they could, and said:

"Culver, have you got a good place?"

"Yes," replied Culver.

Fish lay down beside him at the edge of the road and began firing as fast as he could. After four or five shots, he gasped.

"I'm wounded," said Fish.

Culver replied by saying, "I'm killed."

They had been hit by the same bullet, and the cowboy warrior and the dude soldier mingled their blood there in the Cuban trail. Fish died; Culver lived.

The man to come up first, after Hamilton Fish, was Samuel Davis, known to the regiment as Cherokee Bill. He was standing upright when he saw Fish shot, and had only time to look at him a second with wondering eyes, when he went down with a crash himself.

This, very briefly, tells the story of the gallant advance guard of L Troop. They had gone into battle in a strange country. They had in their hands guns which they had never fired before. If they had ever done any fighting, it had been on horseback; but they were now dismounted. They were shooting at an enemy which used smokeless powder, and of which only one man was at any time visible during that first skirmish.

Some of them were college men who had never seen anything rougher than a football game, or a possible prize fight. They had been fired upon by men who shot, to kill and without a second's warning, but not one of them turned his face other than towards the front; not one of them showed the slightest sign of cowardice. Two out of the seven were almost instantly killed, and the other five were badly wounded. But the men who were wounded were glad of their wounds, and the men who died exulted because it was their proud privilege to be the first in the United States Army, during this war, to perish for their country.

In the meantime, back at the point where the little group of officers and Davis and myself had heard the first shot of the war fired, there was great rushing.

This first shot had been fired by the Spanish pickets. Wood rushed forward far enough to become satisfied that it was Spanish, and not American, fire. He then returned to the head of the line and gave the order to "load chamber and magazine." Then he again ordered absolute silence in the ranks. I have since asked him if, while he was standing there, telling us that funny story which I have mentioned, he had been expecting that first sudden shot which so startled the rest of us. He told me that he had been expecting it momentarily for ten minutes, because Capron had told him some time in advance of the evidences of Spanish presence, and had said that while he marched, he constantly expected the attack to begin. He felt as if something might drop upon his head any minute.

Colonel Wood was as cool a man as ever I saw. He gave his orders with the utmost calmness and showed then (indeed it was true of him throughout the battle) not one sign of undue excitement. Colonel Roosevelt, on the contrary, jumped up and down, literally, I mean, with emotions evidently divided between joy and a tendency to run. The barbed-wire fence on the right of the bridle path was intact at first, but some of our men cut the strands with their wire nippers. Roosevelt picked up one of these strands, and looked at it curiously, as he had looked at the strand of the fence on my side of the trail. Wood ordered him to take Troops G. K, and A into the tangle of bushes and creepers on the right, and ordered Troops D, F, and E (Muller's troop in reserve) to deploy into the naturally open field which stretched beyond the tell-tale barbed-wire fence on the left.

Perhaps a dozen of Roosevelt's men had passed into the thicket before he did. Then he stepped across the wire himself, and, from that instant, became the most magnificent soldier I have ever seen. It was as if that barbed-wire strand had formed a dividing line in his life, and that when he stepped across it he left behind him in the bridle path all those unadmirable and conspicuous traits which have so often caused him to be justly criticised in civic life, and found on the other side of it, in that Cuban thicket, the coolness, the calm judgment, the towering heroism, which made him, perhaps, the most admired and best beloved of all Americans in Cuba.

For the next half hour, I lost sight of Colonel Roosevelt, and know what he and his men did only by hearsay. I know that they must have had a terrible time as they beat into that jungle, and I know that while they could not see the Spaniards, the Spaniards could plainly see them, for they had planned each individual's position so that the Americans, when they came, should be in uninterrupted view. It was the worst kind of guerrilla warfare. The fact that our men still failed to realise that the Spaniards were in Cuba, and were shooting at us to kill, is indicated by the other fact that, when withering fire struck Roosevelt and his men, they believed that L Troop had made a blunder and was firing back at them.

This belief was so strong that our men ceased firing into the thickets for fear of killing Capron's troopers, and shouted out to them to stop shooting. A moment later, however, Colonel Roosevelt himself saw Spaniards in front of him and ordered his men to again return the fire. By this time the ground over which his men marched was strewn with the empty shells of Spanish cartridges. Those troops did

The Trail where the Fight began.

not again cease firing for fear that they were shooting into their own comrades. They did not again doubt the presence of the Spaniards, and the Rough Riders realised at last that it was war.

A very few minutes had passed before Colonel Roosevelt saw that it was impossible to carry his men further into the dense jungle, and he turned them to the left and worked back across the trail into more open country. While our men were still in some doubt as to the exact position of the Spaniards, the Spanish had us in absolute range, and shot low and with excellent aim. The firing was rapid beyond anything which had occurred up to the time this turn was made, and our men had to work their way lying flat on their faces. Even then the Spanish bullets struck some. The little episode cost the Rough Riders nine men killed and wounded.

One unfortunate fact in connection with the failure to break through the thicket was that we were, of course, especially anxious to establish communication with General Young's brigade, which was marching up the valley, and which our men could plainly hear on the other side of that impassable thicket. They were evidently as hot at it as we were. Probably fifteen minutes had elapsed before communication was finally brought about, and it then came through the effort of K Troop. Nothing more astonishingly brave occurred during the entire war than the feat of the guidon-bearer who did this. Captain Jenkins had sent him to the top of a bare little knoll, and instructed him to wave his guidon until General Young's men saw it.

The Spaniards were in force just across the valley and within good range of him, and they poured a merciless fire at him. He paid no heed to it whatever, but walked erect and waved his little flag until an answering wave from Young's men told him that his signal had been seen. Then he got quickly down and sensibly scuttled away like a crab. It is interesting to state that this man had once been a candidate for Congress.

Another pleasing episode of this particular point of the battle is related by Richard Harding Davis, in his book on *The Cuban and Porto Rico Campaigns*. (*Vide Richard Harding Davis' War in Cuba & Spanish-American War* by Richard Harding Davis: Leonaur 2021.) He said:

> While G Troop passed on across the trail to the left, I stopped at the place where the column had first halted-it had been converted into a dressing station, and the wounded of G Troop were left there in the care of the hospital stewards. A tall, gaunt young man with a cross on his arm was just coming back up the trail. His head was bent, and by some surgeon's trick he was advancing rapidly with great strides, and at the same time carrying a wounded man, much heavier than himself, across his shoulders. As I stepped out of the trail he raised his head, and smiled and nodded, smiling in the same cheery, confident way and moving in that same position.
>
> I know it could not have been under the same conditions, and yet he was certainly associated with another time of excitement and rush and heat, and then I remembered him. He had been covered with blood and dirt and perspiration, as he was now, only then he wore a canvas jacket and the man he carried on his shoulders was trying to hold him back from a whitewashed line. And I recognised the young doctor with the blood bathing his breeches as "Bob" Church, of Princeton. That was only one of four badly wounded men he carried on his shoulders that day over a half-mile of trail that stretched from the firing line back to the dressing station, under an unceasing fire. And as the senior surgeon was absent, he had chief responsibility that day for all the wounded, and that so few of them died is greatly due to this young man who went down into the firing line and pulled them from it, and bore them out of danger.

In the meantime, I had gone down to the left with Colonel Wood and F and D Troops. The first wounded officer I saw was Captain James H. McClintock, of B Troop. He was leaning propped up against the tree on the backbone of the hill which was as clearly defined and bare as the buttress of a cathedral. Two bullets had met in his lower left leg and I have never seen a man suffer such pain as he did. Months afterwards I saw him, the day after he was discharged from the hospital and from the army with a record of "half-total disability." He seemed to be very cheerful that day at Las Guasimas, and was carefully explaining to Lieutenant Nichols that the place was altogether too hot for any man to stay in who was not obliged to. I shook hands with him and got his name and address, as I did of the other wounded, and asked him if there was anything I could do for him.

"Not a damn thing," said McClintock, "except get out."

Since then he has told me about one of his troopers, who, after McClintock had been forced to lie down by exhaustion, came and lay close beside him. He talked cheerfully to him and tried to keep his spirits up.

"You'd better get out of this," said McClintock. "It's too hot."

"Don't worry, captain," the man replied, "I'm between you and the firing line."

McClintock, touched as he was by this exhibition of the man's devotion, still wanted him to get away. He urged him to leave him. The man refused. Finally, McClintock said:

"I am your captain, and I order you to go; you are doing no good to any but me, here; this is no place for a well man. I order you."

Then the man had to tell.

"I ain't no well man," he slowly admitted. "I'm shot."

"Where?" asked McClintock. "Oh! it's only a scratch."

They lay there in silence for a long time.

The firing began to come from the left. The soldier worked his painful way around until he was again between McClintock and the line of fire. McClintock was too weak from loss of blood, even to speak.

Then a hospital man came and lifted McClintock to carry him back.

"Take him, too," McClintock managed to articulate. "No use," said the hospital man; "he's dead."

Among all the men who faced the unknown perils of singing Mausers, there were no signs of fear. They went into that field of battle almost as they had gone into that transport at Tampa—as if it were a picnic, a summer's holiday among the towering palms. And there was nothing in the aspect of the scene to disabuse them of this idea. They could look down the green slope toward the incline on the other side, and see nothing hostile. Nothing stirred. Not an enemy was in sight. There was no smoke, nor any other visible sign of battle. And yet from nowhere came the shrieking little Mausers, and from everywhere we heard the popping of the guns that sent them. When you combine smokeless powder with a carefully prearranged ambush which hides from view every man who fires it, the fight becomes uncanny. The setting was fitter for a fete champetre than for a battle.

This had its strange effect upon the men, but did not cow them. There were no panic-stricken ones then or at any time during that day, so far as I know, although there was much reason for being panic-stricken: I thought only once that I had found a coward. I stopped a man who was limping quickly back, and asked him why. He threw at me a new oath, in wishing that I might be "double-damned," and raised his carbine over me with the plain intention of beating out my brains.

He then explained that he had torn the sole off one of his shoes and could not go farther forward because of the penetrating thorns which were under foot. Together we found a dead man, and took from one of his feet the shoe. I helped fasten it on the living myself, as I had helped to take it from the dead. The dead man was Marcus Russell, of Troy, N.Y. Who the living man was, I do not know. I only know that, as soon as he had his shoe, he ran back toward where the firing was again, much more rapidly than I could.

I soon rejoined Colonel Wood. No man has ever made a finer spectacle in battle than he did that day. He went well in advance of his own men, and had led his horse into the field. He stood leaning against its sorrel side with what seemed like absolute indifference, and the side he leaned against was the outside. He had taken a natural breastwork into the field with him, but he scorned to use it.

I shall never forget how he looked as he stood there with his face burned to a brown, which was almost like that of the Khaki uniform he wore. His sandy moustache, too, had been grizzled by the sun until it fitted into the general harmony of tone, and he stood there brave and strong, like a statue in light bronze. The Cuban grass reached almost to his waist. There was not a breath of air, and yet the grass about him moved, once, slowly, as if a breeze were blowing it.

At first, I had no right idea of what had caused this, but presently the thought came to my mind that it might be bullets. And then I realised that Colonel Wood, forming, with his horse, the most conspicuous item in the view before the Spaniards, was naturally the target for all the bullets they could shoot.

It was the effect of volleys fired from Spanish trenches and from the bush across the valley that made the grass wave about his feet. I realised it slowly. He knew from the start. That he escaped unscathed, was extraordinary. But that he stood there without the quiver of a muscle, without the tremble of a second's worry, was not less than wonderful. He had left a wife and a family of little ones in Washington, and, of course, he wanted to return to them. The certainty that he would be advanced, with or without honour-winning battles, was absolute. Yet he stood there in the battle which he had sought himself, and never stirred a finger.

And he stood on the outside of his sorrel horse. It cannot be that that man failed to remember that all good things were behind him, where peace and quiet were, and he knew that there were ahead of him only worry and strain and possible death. Men who had already been hit were near him, and he could see their red pools of blood from where he calmly stood. He played the highest stake that man can offer against the honour which he won that day, and if fate did not win her wager, it was not the other gambler's fault.

I watched him—fascinated.

And then I turned away to watch the men whom he commanded. An officer had walked into the field with me and gone back to encourage a wounded man. From across the valley the enemy marked him, and the "*zeu*," "*zeu*," "*zeu*," of the bullets going over his head, and the "*zip*," "*zip*," "*zip*," of the bullets going into the grass at his feet, were as frequent as the raindrops which had beaten on the garret roof above him when he was a baby. He had exposed himself recklessly, but, like Colonel Wood, he escaped without a scratch.

I asked Colonel Wood afterwards about his sensation when he stood on the battlefield in front of his horse.

He said that he was unfortunately situated, because he was almost the only man in the regiment who had nothing to do. All he could accomplish was to make the men believe him to be perfectly cool. As a matter of fact, he said, he appreciated his danger and his mind was filled with regrets over the fact that he had not taken out $100,000 life insurance, for he had no idea that he would survive the battle. He had given his troop officers careful instructions before they went into the fight, and as they went in had assured himself that they understood their orders and were cool enough to carry them out.

This one episode deserves some comment. I was standing by Colo-

From a photograph by William Dinwiddie. Cooking a Cuban Half-ration. Breakfast.

nel Wood, as Captains Llewellyn and Huston passed into the battlefield. Wood stopped each of them, and indulged in airy persiflage, which I thought was irrelevant and unthoughtful at the time. Llewellyn was carrying a pick-axe on his shoulder, for no reason whatever. Huston was carrying a shovel. Wood stopped them both and joked them about their collection of agricultural implements. Then he said:

"What are you going into the fight to do? To dig holes in the ground?"

Neither man could answer. They had picked these things up, as Roosevelt had picked up the two shovels, which he had tied to the pommel of his saddle. They said they didn't know what they had them for, and they undoubtedly spoke the truth. Wood then worked around in a joking way, until he got both these men to repeat to him the orders which they had received before they had started. He explained to me in Washington what I did not understand at Guasimas—that this whole conversation was carried out for the purpose of making them repeat their orders unconsciously, so that he would know for certain that they understood what they were to do.

Before I left Tampa, I had been ignominiously thrown from a fractious horse, and had sprained my elbow. My left arm was not strong enough to hold my notebook, and so I rested it against a palm tree. The fact that Spanish guns were firing at us was impressed upon my mind by the triplicated *"chug"* of bullets striking against this tree. It was too small to offer much protection, and it was the biggest thing in sight. Occasionally I saw in the long grass, as I surveyed the field, an indentation which showed where a man had fallen in fighting for his country, or was lying down in order that he might fight well. Aside from those indentations, and aside from the solemn figures of Wood and another officer or two, outlined above the dun-brown of the Cuban grass, there was nothing to indicate to the visual sense that fighting was going on.

Orally there was much evidence. Richard Harding Davis was over to my right with L Troop, and pumping wildly at the Spaniards with a carbine. I had the only smokeless powder revolver cartridges which were in the army in Cuba. They had been given to me, at Tampa, by Sir Bryan Leighton, of the British Army. They were known as "man stoppers," and I knew that they would not carry more than 400 yards. The Spaniards were at least 600 yards away, and yet I fired cheerfully in their direction. I presume those bullets are lying imbedded in the ground, somewhere between the lines, while I am writing this.

I heard a man crying out. I turned and saw him; I had seen him before, and then he had been firing as fast as his new gun would work. Now he was on the verge of sobs. I ran up to him and asked him if he was hurt.

"Hurt? No," he exclaimed, "but my leg's asleep and I can't get up, and my gun's jammed. Gi' me a gun! Can't ye gi' me a gun?"

It was at about this time that we actually saw the Spaniards for the first time. Although we had forced them to fall back nearly half a mile, they had kept so thoroughly under cover that our men had rarely had anything other than a movement in the long grass, or some suspicious waving of the shrubs and bushes to fire at. One body of about 300 men, plainly panic-stricken, broke from their cover at last and started to run away from us like rabbits. With a wild whoop, the men of D Troop opened fire on them at Captain Huston's orders, and we could plainly see that the aim was good, for half a dozen Spaniards dropped as the first volley was sent into them.

Colonel Wood jumped over from where he had been standing and shouted, with all the force he could put into his voice:

"Don't shoot at retreating men."

But it was the first good chance our men had had at the Spaniards, and the colonel's voice was drowned by the noise of firing. They kept on shooting. He called Trumpeter Cassi to him and had him blow "cease firing" on his bugle. Finally, our men stopped.

Wood lately made this point clear to me in Washington. It puzzled me on the battlefield. When he ordered us to stop firing at retreating men, I thought that he had made a serious mistake. I stood very near to him and saw that the Spaniards were completely demoralised by the beginning of our fire, and saw that after its cessation they quickly rallied. I thought that he had been wrong in ordering our firing stopped at all, and have twice made the statement in print that he made a mistake in stopping this firing.

He has since told me what I did not dream of at the time—that he was expecting a flanking attack from a body of Spaniards who were trying to reach our rear, and that because of this contemplated struggle with attacking men, he did not wish our men to waste their somewhat scanty ammunition on men who were already running away. It is interesting to note that it was a shot from this body which was trying to flank us which afterwards laid me low.

Strange things happen on the battlefield. For instance:

Two wounded men were lying under a tree, waiting for the first-aid men to come and dress their hurts. I went over to them to get their names, and, just as I approached, one of them swung his foot so that it struck the other in the mouth. They had both been shot and the Mausers were shrieking over them. Yet instantly they forgot the battle with the Spaniards, and had one between themselves. Bloody and hot, they clinched, and I presume they fought it out. I went on to another point.

I saw many men shot. They never failed to fall in little heaps with instantaneous flaccidity of muscles. There were no gradual droppings on one knee, no men who slowly fell while struggling to keep standing. There were no cries. The injured ones did not throw hands up and fall dramatically backward with strident cries and stiffened legs, as wounded heroes fall upon the stage. They fell like clods. Two things surprised me about these episodes. One was the strange noise which soldiers in their trappings make as they go down. It is always the same. It is a combination of the metallic jingle of canteens and guns, and the singular, thick thud of a falling human body. I cannot quite describe it, but it will always be in my ears, whenever I think of Las Guasimas.

Even stranger than the sound of the soldier's fall is the "*chug*" of the bullet which strikes him. One would not naturally expect a bullet to make much noise when it hits a man. As a matter of fact, this noise is plainly audible at 100 feet, and I have heard it at twice that distance. It is not a pleasant sound, for after one has heard it once, its significance becomes gruesome. It is not unlike the noise made by a stick when it strikes a carpet which is being beaten.

Still another strange thing is the fact that only the useless bullets seem to sing. Those which fly over your head and which pass you at the side make a queer little noise entirely unlike the whimper of the Minic balls of the Civil War, as it has been described to me.

The Mauser's noise, as nearly as I can indicate it in print, is like "*z-z-z-z-z-eu*." It begins low, goes up high, and then drops, and stops suddenly on the "*eu*." Bullets which strike in foliage combine a curious little "*ping*" with, the "*zip*" of the parting leaves; but the bullets which strike men make no noise at all until they hit them. They go silently, grimly to their mark, and when they hit it, the man is lacerated and torn, or, very likely, dead. There is something which is particularly solemn and awe-inspiring about the death of men upon the battlefield.

Before Las Guasimas, as a newspaper man, I had seen death in many of its most dreadful forms. I had seen men die gently in their beds, surrounded and petted and coddled by anxious friends, and worked over by physicians, who found pretty problems of strange microbes to solve while they were dying. I had twice seen death in railroad accidents, once at St. Thomas, Canada, and once in Wales. I had seen the death of a maniac, whose distorted mind, in dying, craved only to kill another. I had seen the death of a murderer suicide, who cast himself into hell from the elevated railway structure in New York. I had seen the death of two criminals on the scaffold, and another in the electric chair, and I had learned to look at death, as a newspaper man does—as an interesting thing to watch—and write about.

But I had never seen any death like that of those men who dropped in the long grass, on the hill of Las Guasimas. I almost forgot, for a moment, that I was there to see things which I must afterwards describe. I had never seen that regiment until the day before, but I felt that every man who was hit was my personal friend, and there was nothing professional in the interest which I took in each one of them.

Nothing had ever, and nothing ever will again, impress me as did the silent patience, the quiet, calm endurance, with which those men—heroes all—accepted their suffering, and nothing has ever seemed grander to me, more beautiful, or more sublime, than the deaths of some of them. Rough men they were, who had come out of the West to fight; but if a great church organ had been pealing on that hillside, if softened lights had been falling on those faces, through stained-glass windows, devoutly patterned, if the robes and insignia of the most solemn and holy of all the rites of all the churches had surrounded them, I could not have been more impressed than I was when I looked down into the rusty swaying grass of that Cuban hillside, and saw the dirty, sweaty faces, the rough and rugged clinched fists, the ragged uniforms of our American soldiers—dying.

CHAPTER 7

Death and Suffering

There may be those who will think that, in devoting three chapters to the Battle of Las Guasimas, I am giving it too much space. I have heard it called a skirmish, but, if it was a skirmish, then I wish never to see a battle. It was of paramount importance in the war, and it was of special interest to the people who read this book. For it was almost wholly a Rough Riders' battle. The only other men engaged were the few troops of the First and Tenth Cavalry, and their loss was very small.

At about the time when I was shot, Colonel Wood ordered all of his men forward, stretched out in a long line which was ridiculously thin for the work it had to do. The body of retreating men whom he had forbidden his soldiers to fire on had turned, as I have said, and poured a bitterly galling fire at the Rough Riders. When they saw our men still hurrying toward them, despite their recurring orders, they turned and ran again. Young's brigade was doing effective fighting on the right, and the Rough Riders had about half a mile to carry on the centre and on the left, before the Spaniards must give up their strong positions. We had worked down into the shallow valley, and had reached the beginning of the slight ascent on its other side.

The ground was almost entirely open now, and our men were absolutely exposed to the fire of the Spaniards, while they were still well hidden by the trees and in an old building which had at one time been used as a distillery. This was very properly considered to be the Spaniards' most important position, and both Colonel Wood and Colonel Roosevelt turned their particular attention toward it. The bullets poured in even faster than they had before, and at a rate which, Major Brodie tells me, has not been equalled in the history of warfare. The strength of our regiment had been sadly depleted by the loss of the men already killed and wounded, and an uncanny number of Mauser bullets found their American billets, as our men broke and charged on the old distillery.

It had been predicted in Washington, by the regular officers around the War Department, that the great and serious difficulty of a regiment like the Rough Riders, would be that they would not wait for the command to fire, but would shoot as each individual thought best to shoot. Regular army officers, indeed, in Washington, at Tampa, and the day before at Daiquiri and Siboney, had expressed the gravest doubts as to the usefulness of the Rough Riders. They had said that they would lack discipline. As a matter of fact, when they made this terrible charge, they showed better discipline than the regular troops showed, I am told, at the charge on San Juan Hill a few days later. There was very little scattered firing. The men invariably waited for the command, and obeyed it by firing volleys. On one occasion, when the noise of Spanish rifles was so great that L Troop could not hear its officers shout, Lieutenant Day had to pass down the line, striking his men with his hat, in order to make them know what he wanted.

It was in the charge toward the old distillery that Major Brodie was wounded. Up to that time he had shown himself to be absolutely fearless, and had failed to seek cover, even when it was at hand. The bullet hit him in his outstretched forearm, and its terrific force was indicated by the fact that it spun him about like a top before he fell in a heap. It is curious that no matter where a man was hit by a Mauser bullet—even if the wound was in some part quite remote from vital, like the wrists or fingers, or feet—he always went down quick and limp, as a very wet rag might fall.

Frequently men who were, a couple of minutes later, quite strong enough to stand up and walk, or even go back to their work on the firing line, went down in this way when they were shot. I have heard surgeons discuss it, and they say that it is due to the tremendous nervous shock which such a high-speed projectile communicates from the point of impact to the uttermost limits of the body. All nervous force is, for the moment, paralyzed, and the muscles become absolutely limp.

Colonel Wood described to me Brodie's action at the time he was shot:

> Brodie had not the least idea that he could be hit by a mere Spaniard. I shall never forget his expression of amazement and anger as he hopped down the hill on one foot with the other held in the air, before he fell. He came toward me, shouting: 'Great Scott, colonel, they've hit *me!*'

It was plain to see that he considered the wound an unwarrantable liberty.

Colonel Roosevelt's escape from injury was not less remarkable than that of Colonel Wood, which I have already described. Like Wood and Brodie, he scorned cover, although he insisted that his men should protect themselves as well as they could, and, at one time, when he was leaning against the side of a palm tree, with his head nonchalantly resting against its bark, a bullet struck close by his cheek, and filled his eyes with dust and splinters.

Champneys Marshall was shot through his sleeve and through his shirt; Greenway was shot through his shirt across the breast; Colour-Sergeant Wright was blistered three times on the neck by close passing bullets, and, after the engagement, found four bullet holes in the flag he carried. A strange wound was that of Thomas W. Wiggins, whose cartridge belt was hit. The Mauser must have clipped just along the top of his cartridges, so as to touch the pin fire, for half a dozen of them exploded, and his lower legs were well-nigh shot to pieces by his own bullets. After he was wounded, he went off into a series of faints, but, between them, he continually called to Captain McClintock offers of help.

Elmer H. Hawley went into battle smoking his pipe like a chimney. He stopped smoking when a bullet took the bowl off.

In an interview, after Colonel Roosevelt returned to New York, he told these stories:

> At Las Guasimas, as brave a man as there was, was Tom Isbell—the Indian. He was shot four times, but continued fighting. Corporal George H. Seaver was shot in the hip when we were in a pretty hot corner. After a minute, he sat up; we propped him behind a tree, and gave him his rifle and canteen. He continued firing until we charged forward and left him. I supposed him to be mortally wounded, and had him sent to the hospital, but to my surprise he turned up in camp a week or two later, having walked the five or six miles from the hospital.
> Another man, named Rowland, a cow-puncher from Santa Fe, was shot in the side. He kept on the firing line until I noticed the blood on him, and sent him to the hospital. He returned to the front in about fifteen minutes and stayed with us until the end of the fight. He was then sent to the rear hospital and told that he must be shipped North. He escaped that night, and

walked out to the front to join us, and was by my side during all the Santiago fighting.

Richard Harding Davis tells of Lieutenant Thomas, after he was wounded. Davis and others started to carry him into the shade. He was in terrific pain, and his cowboy companions had stopped the flow of blood only by means of rude tourniquets made of twigs and handkerchiefs, but he protested loudly that he wished to be carried to the front. Davis records the remark which he made just before merciful unconsciousness gave him ease, he begged:

> For God's sake take me to the front. Do you hear me I order you; damn you, I order—we must give them hell; do you hear? we must give them hell. They have killed Capron; they have killed my captain.

The most astonishing wound received in this war, or in any other war, was that of David E. Warford in the battle of Las Guasimas. The bullet hit him in the outside of the right thigh, and, striking the bone, caromed up. For some unaccountable reason it then went across his body, through his intestines, and then down through the left thigh, where it made a wound of exit precisely opposite to its wound of entrance on the other thigh. Thus, Warford was supposed to have been shot through both thighs when the surgeons found a wound of entrance on his right thigh and a wound of exit on his left thigh, until they discovered that there were no wounds at all on the inside of his thighs. The extraordinary trick of the bullet was only figured out after Warford had been taken to the hospital ship.

Another amazing wound was that received by Norman L. Orme. No one knows who shot Orme, for his wound was made by a bullet from a Remington rifle, and it is not supposed that any of the American or Spanish troops were armed with Remingtons. The bullet made eight wounds in him. This was owing to the cramped position in which he held his gun when he was shot. The shot first passed through the left forearm, making two wounds, then through the left upper-arm, two more wounds, then through the body, two more wounds, and then through the right upper-arm, making the last two of the eight.

An interesting little point told to me by Captain McClintock is that Clifton C. Middleton had gone to him before the battle began and announced that he, Middleton, would certainly be shot before it was over. "I am sure to be wounded," said Middleton. "All my people were killed in their farmhouse by Indians, and I shall die the same way." He was shot, but was not killed, I think.

It would be unfair to omit from this chapter a paragraph about the superb work of the surgeons. Surgeon Church, especially, distinguished himself. Before I was shot, I saw him running along with his surgeon's packet on the very firing line, and attending promptly to all the wounded he could find, without paying the least attention to his own safety as he did so. In one case, where the fire was so hot that every man in the neighbourhood was lying flat on his face to avoid it, Church knelt at the side of a wounded man and made himself a shining mark for Spanish bullets without hesitation.

And here I have an opportunity of paying a slight tribute to one of the bravest men I ever knew. His name is George W. Burgess. Burgess was with D Troop and enlisted in Oklahoma. No one detailed him to do first-aid duty during the Battle of Las Guasimas, or at any other time. He has the quiet blue eyes and the thin straight lips of the gentleman *desperado* whom Bret Harte wrote about. I don't believe that anything on earth could frighten him, nor do I believe that, in any emergency, his voice would rise above a calm and quiet drawl. Before I fell into the long grass, I saw Burgess standing up when others were lying down, and running along the firing line with his brown red-crossed first-aid pouch.

Sometimes he would stop and take a shot at the Spaniards, "just for hell," as he said, but most of the time he was busy with men who had been wounded and were lying in dangerous places. There was one man in this battle who took advantage of his first-aid pouch to stay in the rear where comparative safety was, and wasted much good time in too elaborately dressing the wounds of men who had been braver than himself. Burgess made his red cross an excuse for placing himself in extraordinary dangers. He was the first man to come to me, and the other day he gave to me the little flask from which he had administered the ammonia which restored me to consciousness.

Ammonia Flask.

I know that when he stood over me looking kindly down and telling me that he did not think it was worth his while to dress my wound, because he and the surgeons considered that it could not be otherwise than mortal, the bullets were flying about him as thickly as they ever flew about anyone. I can remember distinctly how the volleys sounded as they swept over my face, and I know that I, who was lying down, shrank and shivered as they shrieked their devilish little songs, while Burgess stood there calm and quiet, and told me softly and sympathetically that he was extremely sorry for me.

He added, with something of contempt, that it was a damned shame that I was only a correspondent. Then he started on a run for another wounded man who was nearer to the front than I was, and who was probably lying under a hotter fire than I was. Not two minutes had elapsed before he came back to me, still running, and asked me if I did not want to be carried to the shade.

I had had a sunstroke when I was a boy, and I had been hoping that I might be spared another one, although I greatly feared it. It seemed to me that as long as I had a Mauser bullet in me, it would be nice to die respectably of my wounds under the shade of a tree that I could see as I lay, instead of staying out there in the blistering long grass and dying of sunstroke. So, I told Burgess that I should be very glad to be taken to the shade.

He took me there.

Afterwards when I found that he was suffering from an intensely painful case of water on the kneecap, I wondered at his strength.

He dropped me under the shade of that tree as if I had been a hot potato, and muttering wild and Western oaths, he sped desperately to the front, which had in the meantime advanced many yards.

That was the last I saw of Burgess until the battle was over. He was a brave man.

And while the heroic work of our soldiers ceased when the battle ended, the heroic work of our surgeons and their assistants went on all that afternoon and all that night. The field hospital was established at about the place where Hamilton Fish had been shot. The regiment moved on to camp, but its wounded were taken back to form a little group under the sheltering shade of a mango tree there in the wilderness. Captain McClintock lay near where I lay, and Major Brodie sometimes lay, sometimes sat, and sometimes walked painfully about us, nursing his shattered arm. I do not think that anyone was there except the Rough Riders, but some of the wounded from the First and Tenth Cavalry may have been brought up.

I was taken away from this hospital very late in the afternoon. Most of the others lay there all night, and when dawn came, a little row of eight dead men who had been carried from among them lay stark and ghastly on the slope of a knoll to one side. It is, perhaps, well here to refer once and for all to an extremely disagreeable subject.

The land crabs and their attending horrors, the Cuban vultures,

Captain McClintock wounded at Las Guasimas.

wrought terrible mutilations on our dead that day, and after succeeding battles, and there is no doubt that several of our wounded were killed by them while they lay waiting for treatment.

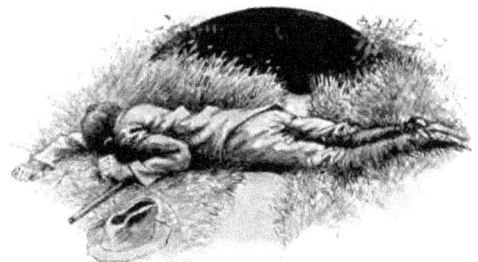

There were probably twenty of us in that field hospital. It had not even a tent to cover it, but the men were well sheltered beneath the spreading branches of the mango tree. A few had blankets to lie upon, but most of us were protected from the wet grass only by the canvas halves of shelter tents.

Up to this time, the men had stood their suffering with cool patience and without comment, but now there were a few whose nerves were so strained and racked that they could no longer control themselves, and they groaned uncannily. Some terrible operations were performed in that little hospital in the woods. "Bob" Church was there, and the other surgeons, and they were working with an energy that could have been born only of desperation. Church, I remember, had cut the sleeves out of his shirt, and his arms were as red as if they had been dipped in claret. Indeed, all the surgeons were literally soaked in blood. I remember that Church kneeled close to me at one time and my hand touched his trousers. It came away with a bright red stain. The medical staff was straining every nerve to prepare the wounded for the journey to Siboney.

I described in *Scribner's Magazine,* for September, 1898, an episode which occurred at this time. A couple of months later I received a letter from a man who was there when I was, which said that he remembered no such incident. It seemed almost too pretty to be true, and for a time after I had read his letter, I doubted my own memory and thought this might have been one of the vain imaginings which continually beset me in those hard hours. Since then, however, I have seen Captain McClintock in New York. He was very near to me that day, and he remembered the incident as well as I did. I shall, therefore, describe it briefly here.

We had been doing what we could to keep our spirits up. Most of us were badly hurt, and cheerfulness was difficult to bring about. Death stared some of us in our faces, and other men were contemplating amputation of their arms or legs with what courage they could summon. We were doing very little talking. I was simply waiting for the end.

With a suddenness that startled all of us, someone began to sing:

My country, 'tis of thee,
Sweet land of liberty,
Of thee we sing.

McClintock and I joined in:

Land where our fathers died,
Land of the Pilgrims.

The strangely trembling song went on. It had its quivering interruptions of pitiful groans, and some of those who sang, sang jerkily, because they were in mortal pain. But we were a doleful little group of hurt Americans, off there under a tree, in the midst of the Cuban solitude, and nothing seemed so dear to us, just then, as the homes which we might never see again and the country which some of us had left behind forever. Probably no song was ever sung more earnestly; certainly, no words were ever uttered which cost more effort to some of us than those did.

By and by I noticed that there was one voice which faltered and lagged behind. Indeed, I did not hear it until all the rest of us had finished with the line:

Let freedom ring.

Then slowly, strugglingly, and faint, it went on:

'Land—of—the—Pilgrims'—pride—
Let freedom—

And that last word was a man's last word. And one more son had died as died the fathers.

CHAPTER 8

After Las Guasimas

After the battle came the reaction. Human nerves which had been screwed up to the point which those of the Rough Riders had reached and held during those terrible hours when they were in that long grass and among those bushes, must, of necessity, relax and leave their owners weak. The regiment marched about two and a half miles forward and to the left of the spot where the battle had begun, and went into camp. It wasn't much of a camp. The morning's work had tired them too completely—officers and men alike—to let the idea of establishing an elaborate camp seem reasonable. Wood and Roosevelt were glad enough to relax discipline to some extent, and they did not force the men to put up their shelter tents.

Those who wanted to, lay in the shade and took long, grateful whiffs of the hot air, which seemed cool in their inaction after the terrible exertions of the morning. As a matter of fact, most of the men had no shelter tents to put up. Their blanket rolls had been discarded with a charming disregard of what would come, during the march from Siboney to Las Guasimas, and during the fight that followed. Some of them were found again, but a good many of them were appropriated by the Cubans, who appeared in numbers as soon as the danger of being shot had ended. To see a Cuban with a Rough Rider's blanket, which he solemnly swore had been in his family for generations, became so usual that it attracted no attention, and to see them in the tunics of our soldiers (which they announced had been theirs before the war began) became as common as to see them in their own ragged and disreputable clothes.

Many stories were told of the robbing of the dead and wounded by our allies that day, but concerning their truth I know nothing. I only know that after that day our men were prone to regard a Cuban with that same delicate consideration and pleasure with which they looked on land crabs. In view of this almost universal sentiment of dislike and suspicion, it is greatly to the credit of our troops that there were not more collisions between them and the soldiers of Cuba Libre. There was certainly more or less good reason for this feeling. It probably had its beginning in the boorish lack of courtesy which had been shown by the officers of the Cuban Army to the officers and men of the American Army the night we reached Siboney.

Of course, the first thing which was done after the battle was to look after the wounded, and see that the dead were found and protected from the ravages of land crabs and vultures. This was accomplished with all possible expedition. The little field hospital had been established back on the trail at about the place where we had first met the Spaniards. Dr. Bob Church was in charge. Dr. La Motte, the senior surgeon, was not there then, and the chief burden of the whole awful situation fell on the ex-football player. Nothing could have exceeded his bravery on the field, and nothing could have exceeded his patience, skill, and delicacy in caring for the men back there under the mango tree. He did not forget in his hurry to be kind. We had all been told that both Roosevelt and Colonel Wood were dead. I remember with vivid distinctness the breath of relief we drew when Church assured us that this was not the case.

While I was lying on the field after I had received my wound someone had asked me for my name and address, thinking that my death was a matter of only a few moments. I was so dazed by the effect of the shot that I could not think of it for a moment, and told them that I did not know, but that Colonel Wood did. The man who had asked me—I did not know him nor have I since been able to find out who he was—learned my name from someone else, and a few moments later, just as the final attack was being made on the old distillery, he told Colonel Wood that I wanted to see him.

That, of course, was silly, for I was too sick to want to see anyone. But Wood's big heart did not see the absurdity of it, and he sent me a pleasant message, saying that he was sorry that I had been shot. This was brought by an officer, whose identity I have also been unable to establish. I didn't care about anything just then, and remember trying to turn over, and wearily wishing that people wouldn't bother me. Later, though, and just after we had heard that the colonel was not dead, Wood came to me, and stooping over, said:

"Hello, Marshall! How are you now?"

I was suffering the tortures of perdition and told him so.

I shall not forget the kind look of solicitude on his face as I slowly drifted into unconsciousness after I had spoken. When I regained my senses a few moments later, his pleasant face was still bending over me.

"I was awfully sorry that I couldn't go to you when you asked me to," he said. "I tried to, but it was the turning point of the battle."

The idea that I had sent for him and that he wanted to come to see me while the infernal fight, which I had seen the most of, was in progress, seemed so amusing that I laughed at it, and he laughed too.

"Won't you have a drink?" he asked.

There had been no stimulant other than aromatic spirits of ammonia on the field, and when the colonel held a little four- or five-ounce vial of Scotch whiskey to my lips, it seemed to me that it was the finest thing in all the world.

A moment later he was holding that same little bottle up for Mc-Clintock, and I heard McClintock say between the pain gasps:

"By God! that's good!" And so, it was.

The men were brought to join the little group there on tent-cloths and blankets. There was not a single stretcher in the regiment. As a matter of fact, there were not even enough tent-cloths and blankets to handle the wounded on, for I distinctly remember seeing Privates Burgess and Love of D Troop—the same men who had carried me to the shade—trying to bear a wounded man on a narrow board. Once or twice, he rolled off and fell in the grass, greatly to his own exasperation and the sorrow of the bearers. I managed to get a stretcher, through the kind offices of Stephen Crane.

He and Richard Harding Davis had come up to me immediately after I was wounded. I am told that they were the only other newspaper men in the fight. Crane not only took my story of the fight down to the coast for me, but described my misfortune to George Coffin, Acton Davies, and Charles McNichol, who were on one of the *New York Journal's* despatch boats. They brought up a stretcher which may have belonged to the government, but which I think was the *Journal's* property, and took me down to the hospital ship *Olivette*.

Most of the wounded men who were taken to the field hospital, perforce remained there for the night. Captain McClintock was too weak from loss of blood to make his removal possible. He tells me that the wounded lay there during the long darkness and sang songs, as they had sung "*My Country, 'tis of Thee*," before I was carried away. Sleep was pretty nearly out of the question, for the moans of those in awful pain and the ravings of the men who had been rendered delirious by suffering or by drugs, were incessant.

The utter inadequateness of the force sent to the front that day to fight its way forward and at the same time protect its own rear; was shown by an episode near the field hospital. Lieutenant-Colonel Brodie told me of it the other day in Washington. Brodie was walking up and down nursing his wounded arm. The regiment had gone on to camp a mile and a half away, and the wounded were left there in the woods with a small guard. One of them lay at Brodie's feet. His eyes were on the ground level.

"Great Scott, Major!" he said to Brodie. "There come a lot of Spaniards."

Brodie looked in the direction he indicated, but could see no one.

"Get down here," said the wounded man, "and you can see them through the bushes and grass."

Brodie got down, and saw them. There certainly was a body of two hundred men or more who had approached within a few hundred yards of our pitiful little hospital, and were well in the rear of our regiment. Fortunately for us they were Cubans. But they might quite as well have been Spaniards, as far as any means of prevention that were in our power were concerned. If the Spanish forces had executed a flanking movement on us that day, they could have doubled us up, despite the magnificent fighting qualities of our men. There were four thousand of them against our nine hundred.

A corporal and seven men were left to guard the hospital. There was good reason for this, for the Spanish sharpshooters, which afterwards infested that part of the country so thoroughly, had already begun their work and were firing at our wounded and at our surgeons and our hospital men. There were seven alarms during the night, and one of them was caused by a shot from a sharpshooter, who hit someone. I cannot find out who his victim was. The other six were caused by land crabs, which were there by the hundreds of thousands, and which, when they scuttled through the sundried grass and leaves, made a noise quite loud enough to be reasonably accredited to careful men, creeping up. The corporal in charge was brave. He did not know whether or not the whole Spanish Army was stealing on us there in the dark, yet he took his seven men and went out as bravely against the unknown terrors of the Cuban wilderness as if those men had numbered seven thousand.

And here it is well to say a word about those Spanish sharpshooters. That they disregarded all the rules of civilized warfare and ordi-

The Battlefield of Las Guasimas.

The old distillery is seen on the hill in the background to the left.

From a photograph by William Dinwiddie.

nary, straight humanity, in firing on our surgeons and wounded and into our hospitals, that day and on succeeding days, there is no doubt whatever. I cannot believe that they could have been regular Spanish soldiers. Our hatred for the Spaniards as a common enemy should not make us forget that they were brave men in fight, and brave men are not likely to do such things. An explanation which most of the officers of the American Army down there afterwards heard from the Spaniards themselves, and which some of them told to me, does not seem unreasonable. The jails in Santiago were full of military prisoners. The city had long been the abiding place of large bodies of Spanish troops, and these troops were discontented because they had not been paid and were not well. Offences against army law, both serious and petty, were common among them. Many soldiers were locked up.

When our army came, and when the Spanish commanding officers saw that there was likely to be a lack of food in Santiago before they whipped us and drove us away—which they undoubtedly thought they could more or less easily accomplish—these prisoners became a problem. It was finally decided to give them rifles and ammunition and tell them to get out, kill as many Americans as they could, and never come back to Santiago under pain of death. The prisoners appreciated the situation. They had a wholesome and natural longing for freedom on any terms. They took the rifles and the ammunition and got out. A few of them escaped to parts of the country where they did not come in contact with our troops until after the surrender, but most of them were released at places where they had either to run the chance of being shot by their own countrymen or take the risk of being shot by Americans. They found that our lines were much less closely guarded than were the Spanish lines, and they worked their way into them.

A few of them gave themselves up to our officers and told what they knew of the Spanish situation. But by far the greater number of them, either from that love of country which animates the meanest souls, or from the belief that we were a set of bloodthirsty and merciless ruffians who would kill them with torture if they fell into our hands (a belief which was carefully fostered by the Spanish press in Cuba and which was really generally held by the average unintelligent, uneducated Spanish soldier), refused to surrender themselves or to give us information, and took their positions in the trees along the trails within our lines, and cleverly concealing themselves with leaves and bushes, proceeded to prey on whoever came within their range.

Shots were fired at us as I was being carried down the trail to Siboney, I am told, although I did not realise it at the time. James Creelman's litter-poles were twice penetrated by bullets as he was being taken to the rear from El Caney, and at least six wounded men were killed at one time or another. So bold were these scamps that they actually got close enough to the hospital near General Shafter's headquarters later in the campaign, to send several bullets through the canvas of its tent. So far as I can learn, no organised effort was ever made to drive them away from the trails along which our wounded men were continually being carried and our well men constantly passing to and fro.

Up to the very time of the surrender, and during the truce, these men kept up their hellish guerrilla warfare on our troops, and many a man carries a wound today or fills a grave in Cuba, who never would have been shot if they had been driven out. Of course, our men did what they could in a casual way, to kill them. Individual soldiers, finding themselves fired upon, fired back, and became mightily suspicious of all those branches in the trees which they saw moving in any way which was not warranted by the breeze which blew as they approached, but they made little impression on the Spanish sharpshooters.

If I am to believe the reports which I have heard, there could not have been less than two hundred of these men. Once in a while one of our men would pot one of them, and he would fall from his tree all spread out like a killed crane, with his concealing branches still tied to him. But the evil was really only wiped out with the surrender of the Spanish Army. It is impossible not to feel a sort of qualified admiration for the rough bravery of these chaps who were within an enemy's lines and entirely cut off from the possibility of getting food or other supplies from their own army, but it is equally impossible to feel anything other than unspeakable horror for the spirit which induced them to fire on our wounded and into our hospitals, in open disregard of the dictates of humanity and the neutrality of the Red Cross flag and badge.

They make you think of the Spaniard who killed Lieutenant Ord. Ord and his men had captured a rifle-pit. A Spaniard was lying in this trench, badly wounded but still firing. One of Ord's men did not see that he was wounded and was about to kill him. Ord knocked his gun up and told him not to fire at a wounded man. The wounded man took deliberate aim at the American officer who was trying to save his life and blew his brains out. It is needless to say that the men of

Ord's command killed the Spaniard with the butts of their rifles. They did not give him the honour of dying as a soldier wants to die—from bullets.

As Friday night had been the most terrible night in the field hospital, so Saturday night was the worst night at Siboney. The men whose experiences I have described at the field hospital had not all been carried down to Siboney before midnight of Saturday. Probably half a dozen of us had been taken out to the hospital ship *Olivette*, which was slowly cruising up and down, over the sickening swell of the Caribbean Sea. Major Appell had tried to let her ride at anchor, but had found that the motion was much less distressing to us when her screw was turning.

It was along toward evening when the last of the men who had been shot the day before, but were still able to walk, came limping into Siboney. Some of them struggled painfully down the precipitous path which led from the crest of the cliff to the little group of shanties underneath, but most of them had found that the valley road was easiest, and had come in by the way which General Young's forces took in going to the front.

There were so many of the wounded, and of those who were just beginning to come down with fever, that it was impossible to give even shelter to all of them. There were so few surgeons and hospital men that the problem of medical attendance was absolutely unsolvable, and noon of Sunday had come before the last of the sufferers had received attention.

At midnight, the bright moonlight shone upon a gruesome scene. The sick and wounded were lying everywhere. The silence would have been complete had it not been for the whispered talking of the surgeons, and an occasional groan from some man in agony. Little *piazzas* fronted most of the huts. One of those, which had been turned over to the *New York Journal* by the Cubans for a headquarters, was the gathering place for most of the suffering Rough Riders. Brewer, who had gone to Cuba to establish a post-office, and who afterwards died of yellow fever, had piled his mail bags on one end of this hut's *piazza*.

They made capital beds, and were covered by sleeping men. The sleepers had twisted themselves into all sorts of grotesque positions to fit their uneven resting places and their aching limbs. By the door, like a pale-faced sentinel, was Arthur Crosby, in a rocking-chair. His head and arms were swathed in bloodstained bandages and his agony was violent. In the brim of his hat there was a little hole which showed where the bullet had passed before it tore off his cheek, perforated the palm of his left hand, and then buried itself in his chest. Just how one bullet could have made this wound is a pretty problem, and Crosby does not know. He probably had the back of his hand against his chin, as he was lying in the grass, when he was shot. He had been one of the lucky few to whom had been given cot beds when they reached the hospital, but the agony of a recumbent position had been so great that he had gladly swapped his bed for a rocking-chair, and there he sat through all the dreadful night, his face convulsed with agony, but never groaning and never making one complaint. He was one of the Rough Riders.

Not far from Crosby lay Sergeant Basil Ricketts. He had a bullet in his thigh. No man ever endured pain with greater fortitude than Ricketts showed. Personally, I can never forget him, for before he was wounded, he made one of the men who carried me from the sun into the shade. It is interesting to speak here of an episode in the life of his father, General Ricketts:

During the War of the Rebellion, he was hit by one of the old Minie balls, in nearly the same place which the Mauser bullet afterwards found in his son at Las Guasimas. Mrs. Ricketts was staying at a hotel just within the Union lines. She heard that her husband was wounded, and that night went out to find him. He was lying on the field, not far from the Confederate outposts. The surgeons were bending over him and explaining to him that it would be necessary to amputate his leg. Mrs. Ricketts protested, but the surgeons told her he would die from loss of blood or gangrene, if the leg were not taken off.

"If he were in a Northern hospital," they said, "we might save his leg, but down here, where good nursing is impossible, we cannot think of risking it."

"I will stay and nurse him," Mrs. Ricketts declared. With water from the canteens of dead men, she laved his wound all that night; when morning came, the Union troops had found it necessary to fall back, and she was left with her wounded husband in Confederate territory. They were captured, and with seventeen other Union officers put into a single room in Libby prison, where Mrs. Ricketts was the only woman. The Confederates often offered to exchange her, but she had told the surgeons that she would stay and nurse her husband, and stay she did. For six months, she worked there, saving not only her husband's life, but the lives of many other Union officers.

Basil Ricketts took his wound as the son of such parents might be expected to take a wound. One of the sergeants of the Rough Riders had served under General Ricketts, and was the first man to come up to Basil after he had been shot.

"I'm hit," said Ricketts.

The old sergeant leaned over him and saw that he was taking it calmly.

"God almighty," said the sergeant, "wouldn't the general be tickled if he could see you now!"

After Ricketts returned to New York, he suffered terribly from fever, and for a long time lay in St. Luke's Hospital in a room not far from mine. I have never seen him since the war, but nurses and doctors alike continually told me of the plucky way in which he endured his pain.

Not far away from Ricketts lay Lieutenant Devereaux, of Colorado Springs. Next to McClintock's, his wound was the most painful that I knew of during the campaign. The bones of his forearm were literally ground to powder. Later he was taken out to the *Olivette*, and he spent much of his time in an armchair in front of my stateroom.

The surgeons made a mistake in thinking that the bullet had gone down instead of up, and put him through the most dreadful agonies of probing. He said never a word, but took his pain as a man should take it, quietly and without protest. The same great surgeon who carved me up, and thereby saved my life, worked over Devereaux in New York, and saved his arm. Dr. Robert Abbe occasionally pulls from his pocket, even now, a battered bit of steel. This is the bullet which he took from Lieutenant Devereaux.

Over in the corner, on the inside of the shanty, lay Burr McIntosh. The troubles which he had with sweet Spanish wine had not been enough for him. He was the first man to go down with yellow fever, and its first stages were that night convulsing him with pain and leading his mind off into the unknown paths of muttering delirium. McIntosh has now recovered, and it is fair to tell some details of what his wandering brain dwelt upon during that uncanny night.

He had in mind the production of a play called the *War Correspondent*, and a part of his costume was to consist of a high pair of russet leather cavalry boots. With an eye to the value of theatrical effect, he had purchased these boots before he left New York, and taken them to Cuba with him. It was his plan to wear footgear on the stage which had actually been stained by Cuban mud, and, if possible, to see to it that, during the campaign, some real blood fell upon those boots.

From a photograph by William Dinwiddie. Making Camp after the Battle of Las Guasimos.

From the moment of his landing in Cuba, envious glances had been cast upon them by troopers whose shoes were going the ruined way of army shoes in Cuba.

They were stolen the first day. That night he got them back. The next day, before the start to Siboney, another man purloined them and he recovered them after much detective work, just before the yellow fever caught him in its scraggy arms. As he lay there, the precious boots were lovingly gathered beneath his head. He talked of them incessantly. Home, friends, ambition-all were subordinate in his delirium, to the yellow boots. In the middle of the night a shadowy trooper appeared, ghostlike, from nowhere. He carefully picked his shoeless way among the wounded men and steered a course for McIntosh. When he went out, the yellow boots were closely clasped beneath his tunic, and McIntosh, his head now on the floor, raved on about them.

The story of that night in the hospital might be much prolonged, but I could only write a repetition of such anecdotes. The men lay there and suffered, the surgeons worked, 'midst blood and groans. The only light in the main building came from a bottle which some thoughtful Cuban had half filled with native fire-bugs. Sometimes a chap would enter with a blazing brand from a neighbouring campfire and cast a flickering, ghastly glow about him; and so, the night dragged on until the sudden Cuban dawn.

After Wood was made Governor of Santiago province, he went out to look over the old battle-ground. The strongest testimony to the fierceness of the fire he found in the condition of the trees (and this was six months after the battle had been fought). At the point where the Spaniards first opened on us, the forest looked as if a conflagration had swept it. The trees had been absolutely killed by the terrible hail of bullets which had been poured into them; while our men were advancing through them.

The Rough Riders were not comfortable in their new camp. They had thrown away most of their tents and blankets, and the weather had turned bad. They began to realise what the rainy season in Cuba means. Those who had tents, put them up, but they offered little protection against the tropical downpours, which beat the canvas to earth and sent streams of water down the little slopes actually strong enough to sweep mattresses and blankets out from under tents, unless they were anchored down by the recumbent forms of sturdy troopers.

The camp was within two thousand yards of the Spanish trenches, but not a shot was fired.

It would have been worse than foolish to have sent the regiment forward into another fight just then, when everything was considered, yet the men were anxious to go. By this time the Rough Riders had "got their mad up." During the first battle they had killed Spaniards as a matter of business, but the devilish work of the sharpshooters on their wounded, and the thousand and one discomforts growing out of the campaign—worse discomforts than the hardiest cowboy among them had ever suffered on our plains—had exasperated them to the point of frenzy, for they longed now to kill Spaniards because they hated them.

El Caney was off at the right, in the distance, and El Poso, where some of them were to meet their deaths in a few days, was well to the left. The men were very curious about El Caney. It was understood to be a Spanish stronghold, and it was supposed that it would be the next point that the regiment would attack. As a matter of fact, it was Lawton's and Chaffee's men that fought there, but after their fight some Rough Riders visited it. Captain Huston and Benjamin Harney were in the party.

Harney, by the way, is the sculptor who missed a chance to enlist in the regiment in the States, and who was so anxious to join it that he followed it to Cuba for the purpose. He figured that by the time he got there enough men would have been killed and wounded to make room for him. He landed in Cuba on Saturday night, and his unpiloted trip from Siboney to where the Rough Riders were encamped was full of perils from sharpshooters. When he got there, he found that he had been right about there being room for him. He was almost exhausted by his long and dangerous tramp, but he was fully rewarded when he heard the ringing cheer which the men sent up for him when they found how far he had come and what he had come for, and when he was gladly accepted and enlisted as a member of the best volunteer regiment that ever fought in our army or any other army.

Afterwards, in writing home, he said, first, that he had plenty of material for sculpting, and second, that the stone fort at El Caney, which he had just visited, was an absolute slaughter pen. Its walls were literally kalsomined with the blood of dead Spanish soldiers. It will be remembered that this fort was the one which surrendered to Mr. James Creelman of the *New York Journal*. Creelman was shot while it was being done, but he gained distinction as being the only newspaper correspondent to whom a hostile force had ever surrendered a fortification.

The camp was on the right of the main road leading to Santiago, and had no pleasant features that I have been able to learn. The tents were pitched in a hollow instead of on high ground, which was plentiful thereabouts, and the men suffered accordingly, not only when the rains descended as I have described, but from malaria and other fevers. Every day four or five Rough Riders went out over the trail to the hospital at the rear. Wood and Roosevelt had been mighty good to the men at San Antonio and Tampa, as well as on the transport, and after they landed in Cuba, but it was in this camp that the men began to really appreciate the stuff of which their commanding officers were made. Whatever the men had to go without, they went without themselves. They would take no better shelter than their men had, and they would eat no better food than was offered to the men to eat.

There were thousands of tons of rations out in the bay on the transports, but they were disembarked and brought up the trail so slowly that the Rough Riders were only allowed one-third rations. It was understood that the officers should have something a little better than this, and they had carried with them to the front a few delicacies like canned tomatoes. But Wood and Roosevelt would touch none of them. Within a couple of days, it was the rule among the Rough Riders that the officers would accept nothing which the men could not get. What poor dainties did come in the regiment's way went to the sick and not to the officers' mess. This, perhaps, explains, in some slight measure, the devotion which the men showed for their officers later in the campaign.

There were one or two exceptions to this rule of complete consideration, but I only mention them because if I did not it might be thought that I did not know of them. In so large a body of men as were the Rough Riders, there are certain to be some fellows who lack the finer points. There were some in the Rough Riders, just as there were one or two men who were not brave. I shall not speak of them again, because the general spirit of the regiment was so fine and whole-souled and valorous, that it deserves to go down in history as an organisation practically without flaws.

At first, some of the officers and men built shacks which they thatched with palm and banana leaves. This was very nice till night came on, when tarantulas and other callers took to dropping from the greenery of the roofs. These little episodes were rendered doubly disagreeable by the fact that the men could not light lights—not even matches—in order to make search for the invading vermin. To make a light was likely to be fatal. The Spaniards, in their trenches, were watching for the foolish ones who did it, and their temerity was always followed by a shot, if not a volley. The Spanish sharpshooters who had their eyes on the Rough Riders during these trying days and nights were really sharpshooters. They could easily wing a man across the short space which separated them, and they often did. During the constantly recurring night rainstorms, which were always accompanied by the most vivid and disconcerting tropical lightning—a kind of flash which is totally unknown and totally indescribable to the people North—they frequently hit men.

The long nights in the trenches were not pleasant. They were half-full of water after the rains. Many and many a man has told me that he stood up to his knees in the Cuban rainwater while he was waiting for the Spaniards to shoot at him. One man—I think it was the sculptor, Benjamin Harney—tried to keep out of this water one night by kneeling on a little mound in the trench. When morning came shining rosily over the hills, he looked at the mound. He found that he had been kneeling on a Spanish soldier's grave, and that the corpse had stuck a hand out of the edge of it as if in protest at the desecration.

These few days had no cheerful features. In this camp the men had momentarily expected battle orders, their quarters had been uncomfortable; tarantulas, vermin, and other disagreeabilities, had made sleep at night almost impossible. During the days the men had slept in such shade as they could find when it was not raining, and had done their best to keep dry and save their small properties from floating off in the floods when it was raining. Their rations of one-third allowance of bacon, hardtack, and coffee without sugar, had not been sufficient to keep their physical strength up, and their spirits drooped accordingly. This unfortunate condition was aggravated among the smokers of the regiment—and what member of the Rough Riders was not a smoker?—by the lack of tobacco. It was at this time that a little two-ounce package of smoking tobacco which some man had come into possession of in a way which history has forgotten, was auctioned for forty-seven dollars and fifty cents.

A dramatic episode occurred. A Spaniard was captured in a tree. He was not one of the sharpshooters, for he had no rifle. But he was armed with a revolver and wore the uniform of the Spanish regular, so that he was legitimate prey of war. He was captured by a Cuban, who turned him over to the Rough Riders. In his pockets they found many incriminating papers. He was, almost without doubt, an officer of some rank, for there were documents of an official nature in his clothes which would hardly have been entrusted to a private soldier. He said he was a Cuban who had been captured by the Spaniards and forced to put on a Spanish uniform, and maintained that his only wish was to rejoin the Cuban Army. No one believed this, but because of his statements he was finally given back to the Cubans by Captain Luna, who had him in charge.

He might much better have said nothing about the Cubans, and left himself in American hands, for the Cubans took him up to a hill to the left of where the Rough Riders were encamped, and cut him to pieces without mercy and in spite of the protests made by two or three American private soldiers who were present. When American officers, who had been summoned, arrived, they found the Spaniard dead.

On the evening of June 30th, the regiment went to El Poso, which the Spaniards had been forced, by our artillery fire, to evacuate.

They did not reach this last point until late at night. It was, indeed, long after eleven o'clock before they were really in the place which had been assigned to them as camp—an assignment which the following day's events proved to be either criminally careless or inconceivably stupid.

I may, perhaps, be excused for saving the story of the burial of the dead in the Battle of Las Guasimas for the end of this chapter. It was the burial of the first dead in the army, during the Spanish-American war. It was significant, and it was grim, and it was pitiful. I do not suppose that there ever was a regiment in which the men, as individuals, had a higher regard for each other. The mere fact that another man had been accepted as a member of this carefully selected organisation gave you a certain respect for him. You knew what you had been through yourself.

The men loved one another, as strong men love those who have passed through some trials with them already, and are considered completely competent to pass through other trials with them.

Yet when the burial of the dead came, not more than half of the men in the regiment went out to see the ceremony. Tired, tired, tired! No men were ever more thoroughly worn out than they were when they made their primitive camp on that Cuban hillside over to the right of where Hamilton Fish was killed.

Colonel Wood had ordered a detail in which all the troops were represented, to dig the grave the night before. These men were proud of their task, and they were anxious to perform it, but they were too terribly tired to do it well. Eight dead men were lying in a gruesome row near the field hospital under that mango tree—a tree which should be surrounded by a bronze railing and held as an exhibition for future generations of Americans who are interested in what our men did in Cuba in those summer days of Eighteen Ninety-Eight.

These were not all the dead, but they were the ones who were laid away on Saturday morning in that first crude grave.

Tired, dead tired, were the men who dug it. They were too tired to dig separate graves for their hero comrades. But what they could, they did. They began the work on that unlucky Friday night. How near they were to the point of complete exhaustion is shown by the fact that it was not finished until the middle of the following morning.

At eleven o'clock, officers' call was sounded. All men in command of troops were told that the funeral services over the men who had fallen the day before would occur in half an hour. No one was compelled to go. Neither officers nor men turned out because they were told to. Many of the men were busy on other tasks connected with the new camp, and all had plenty to do in cleaning guns and getting themselves and their equipment ready for the next battle.

The ceremony was brief.

"*I am the Resurrection and the Life, saith the Lord,*" Chaplain Brown repeated, and so on, through the Episcopal service. He knelt and prayed by the trench. The men knelt too, and as they doffed their campaign hats, the Cuban sun beat down as fiercely on them, and on the men in the trench before them, whose battles were finished forever, as it had the day before on all of them when the fight began. Someone threw a heavy clod into the trench. The men rose, and their deep bass voices joined in "*Nearer, my God, to Thee.*" It was as impressive as the singing of the patriot's hymn had been in the field hospital.

It is useless for me to tell how those men lay there; they were without coffins, and their only shrouds were the uniforms in which they had nobly died. The Cuban soil was shovelled over them. The chief bugler stood upon the mound and blew the mournful notes of "*taps*," and the ceremony was finished. Their living comrades marked their grave with stones and bits of wood. The names of the men that slept there were written on the wood.

Now, eight months after the war ended, even these markings have been obliterated. Someone has erected a tombstone, which reads:

Where the Rough Riders waited in the Quivering Heat before the charge of San Juan.

> To the
> MEMORY OF
> EIGHT
> UNKNOWN SOLDIERS.

The stone was not officially erected, and the names of the soldiers are not unknown. By and by, when the authorities get around to it, proper tombstones and a monument will be erected. General Wood has already planned for it.

The body of Hamilton Fish has been taken from Cuba since that day, and brought North to be interred at Garrison's, New York. Captain Capron was buried on a hillside near the seashore. His grave is marked by a neat tombstone erected by Colonel (now Major-General) Wood.

The men marched off, leaving their dead alone in their glory behind them. The strange new routine of regimental life was taken up, and new thoughts and wonderings of what the future held for them busied the minds of those who were left, but after that battle, and after that burial, no man in the regiment was quite the same. The Rough Riders had passed through their baptism of fire, and passed gloriously, but they had paid a terrible price to Fate.

CHAPTER 9

The Beginning of San Juan

I must start by saying that I did not see any part of the three days' Battle of San Juan, and that what is written here is written from what I have been told by men who did, and from what I have read. I have taken considerable trouble to see that every statement is accurate, however, and am convinced that there are few, if any, mistakes in this account.

As everyone knows, the battle started on the first day of July. General Wheeler and General Young were both ill, so General Sumner took command of the cavalry division, in which the Rough Riders were included, in the Second Brigade. This promoted Lieutenant-Colonel Roosevelt to the colonelcy and to command of the regiment, for Colonel Wood became a brigadier-general, and took command of General Young's brigade.

The regiment had moved to El Poso the previous day, and were encamped on that picturesque little farm which the Spaniards had evacuated. Nothing can describe the filthy state in which the retreating soldiers had left the place. "If Cuba is unhealthy, this is what makes it so," said General Sumner to a foreign *attaché*. "New York City would breed yellow fever germs faster than a horse can run, if it were left in such a state as this. When they eliminate unnecessary dirt from Cuba, they will eliminate yellow fever."

But the fevers which began to make many a man in the Rough Riders ache and shiver, were not caused by the filth. The days were incredibly hot and the nights were chilly. From the valleys on both sides of the hill where the regiment was encamped white mists full of the miasma of malaria rose every night to fill the air until the next morning's sun dissipated them, and these mists sent many men to hospital. They added greatly to the beauty of the situation, however, although it is not probable that the Rough Riders were as deeply interested in that as they were in the quinine which was scarce and which this detail of the beauty made necessary.

The order to move forward toward Santiago along the San Juan trail was given the night before to Colonel Roosevelt, who had reveille sounded at three in the morning, for his troops were supposed to be on their way at four. There was a good deal of suppressed excitement among the men. The feeling of security that had preceded the Battle of Las Guasimas was replaced by a feeling of wonder and, in some cases, apprehension. The general orders which had been given to their commanders spread among the men with great rapidity, although it is, of course, the military intention that such things shall he known only to the men who must of necessity be confided in. There was no longer any doubt in the minds of the Rough Riders that there were Spaniards in Cuba and that the Spaniards had guns, and that the guns would be loaded and fired, and that they would be fired for the purpose of killing the soldiers in the American Army.

I do not wish to give the idea that the Rough Riders were afraid the night before San Juan, for I do not believe that this regiment could have found any set of circumstances which would have made it, as a body, feel afraid. But I do mean that the Rough Riders had learned to take war seriously. They had only to close their eyes to see the battlefield of Las Guasimas where they had so busily passed that morning of the twenty-fourth of June. And in the visions which they thus called to their minds they saw it dotted with prostrate comrades who were not lying down in order to facilitate their own aim at their enemies, but were lying down because they had been hit by Spanish bullets.

They could see wounded men all bloody and they could see dead men. They knew that just before the battle those men who were wounded and those men who were dead had felt just as they had felt—had not believed that they would be wounded or dead. And the Rough Riders who brought these pictures to their eyes when they closed them knew that the next day there was going to be another battle and had every reason to believe that after it was over there would be a new list of hurt and killed. And they knew and considered carefully the fact that it was not at all impossible that their own names should be written on it.

So, they wondered and gossiped among themselves as to who would be hit. And instead of saying scornfully, "Aw, them Spaniards won't fight," and, "*Dagoes* can't shoot, anyhow," they polished up their rifles which they had now learned how to use, and they did what they could to prepare to fight ably and manfully against a foe for whom they had achieved a very considerable respect.

It would not be right to say that the men were not sorry to see Colonel Wood taken away from the command of the regiment, but that they were all extremely well pleased over Colonel Roosevelt's promotion is certain. And they could feel that way without hurting anyone's feelings, for they could congratulate Colonel Wood on the fact that he was now a brigadier-general, both by word of mouth and in their minds.

While they had been learning to respect the Spaniards, they had continued to lose their respect for Cubans. The Cuban officers were very largely responsible for this themselves, for they kept up the same policy of boorish indifference to the comfort of the American troops which had distinguished them and surprised us the night we landed at Siboney. And the Cuban soldiers had shown a great tendency to appropriate the property of our soldiers in blue. The sight of American blankets in the possession of Cubans who could not explain where they had got them had ceased to excite surprise, and ugly stories were afloat among the men, of Cuban vandals who had rifled the pockets and bodies of the dead and wounded at Las Guasimas.

For some reason or other the Rough Riders, particularly, had conceived violent doubts of the courage of our Cuban allies, and when it was announced that General Chaffee in his attack upon El Caney would be supported and assisted by a large body of Cuban troops, loud derisive cries were heard in the camp of the Rough Riders. I do not know how Chaffee's men felt about it, nor how General Chaffee himself felt about it, but I am inclined to believe that he had been infected with the same doubts. For he went ahead and prepared for battle exactly as if there were to be no brave and doughty legions of Cuban warriors to help him win, and, later, he went ahead and won just as if there had been none. Exactly as if there had been none, for there were none.

That is, the Cuban troops were in the position which had been assigned to them, but they forgot to fire their guns and they forgot to advance on the enemy. Which indicates that bad memories, as well as dirt and fever, are among the constitutional misfortunes of· this downtrodden race.

Who planned the position which was given to the Rough Riders on the morning of the 1st of July, I don't know. It indicated a strange disregard of the safety of the regiment which had already shown itself to be one of the best fighting machines that a modern army had ever held. The regiment was halted in the yard of the El Poso farmhouse, and then Grimes's battery was wheeled into position just a little in front of it. Grimes's battery had no smokeless powder. Every shot it fired was followed by a cloud of smoke large enough to furnish a good target even to such inaccurate gunners as the Spaniards.

To the unthinking men in the ranks of the Rough Riders, the presence of the guns was a great comfort. I have heard it said by English officers of eminence, that if it were not for the comfort which the sight and sound of big guns give to the soldier armed with a rifle, and for the terror which the sight and sound of those same big guns inspire in the minds of the enemy, it would not be worthwhile to take artillery on the field except where there were heavy fortifications to be reduced or a siege to be conducted. For statistics show that artillery is by no means proportionately fatal to the enemy with small arms. In other words, the cannon are there for moral effect while the rifles are there for man-killing purposes. The same English officers greatly appreciate the moral effect, however and have full belief in the necessity of artillery.

The moral effect of Grimes's battery was strong in the Rough Riders, and filled the hearts of them with glee. Grimes's battery fired about nineteen shots before the Spaniards answered. When the answer came it was directed with excellent aim at the cloud of smoke which hung over and around the American guns, and was, itself, fired with smokeless powder which gave the American guns no target.

Our first shot was fired while the men were eating breakfast. They could plainly see a Spanish blockhouse, and when they observed that either the first or some succeeding shot had struck this blockhouse, they gathered in little groups and they shouted wild western and college yells with the same enthusiasm which afterwards carried them up San Juan Hill. The rejoicing of the Rough Riders over this shot was at the height of its intensity when the first Spanish shell was fired in answer.

They heard the shot fired and then they heard for the first time in their lives the awful shriek of a shell's flight. They could not see it, but the growing sound of its advance seemed to come toward them so slowly that they looked against the sky eagerly and anxiously as if they should see the black ball in relief against it. Like the passage of a mammoth sky-rocket, hissing and howling like a fiend of the air, this first Spanish shell came to freeze the grins on the faces of the Rough

Riders and to stop midway their screams of excited delight over what our shells had done.

Then the shell exploded with a report which is not like any other report. And when it exploded, it was in the midst of the Rough Riders and, as its smoke cleared away, it exposed to view two dead men, and seven wounded men with a kind of wounds which was new to the regiment. These were not the clean-cut Mauser holes which had marked the unfortunates at Las Guasimas. They were great jagged rents torn into the quivering flesh by rough-edged fragments of broken steel. And there was no more laughter. And there were no more shouts. War was grim again. More of their comrades were lying dead. The second battle had begun. The Spaniards were really shooting to kill.

It was the first time and the last time, during the campaign, that there was anything like a stampede among the Rough Riders. It was the first time and the last time, during our war with Spain, that they ever yielded an inch to Spanish shots of any kind. But this shell was so unexpected and so dreadful, that the men did not wait for the word of command. They ran scurrying away from the position which they had been ordered to occupy over the edge of the hill to the right, where they showed their newly acquired respect for Spanish gunnery by keeping cover until about half-past eight o'clock. The first shot from the American battery had been fired at six-forty, and the Spanish shell had shrieked its way into their midst at exactly seven o'clock.

Lieutenant-Colonel Brodie asks me to mention Private Hollister, of A Troop. He was one of the men struck by the shell at El Poso. He was badly torn, but he partially recovered from his wound, through his pure grit. But he recovered from his wound only to die of typhoid fever.

While they were at El Poso, a funny episode was the strange manoeuvre of the First Cavalry. It moved past them with great enthusiasm. It had only a disconcertingly short distance to go before it struck the Spanish outposts, and the Rough Riders knew this. They supposed, of course, that an attack on the foe was intended by the movement. Promptly on time, and exactly at the place where the Spaniards were supposed to be, the First Cavalry ran into them.

The Rough Riders were waiting for a battle royal, and more or less expecting that they would soon be involved themselves. But with a promptness which was only equal by the rapidity of their advance, the First Cavalry retired again to some unknown point, and the night

The Shell at El Paso.
Thus Spanish shot killed two and wounded seven Rough Riders.

grew still and peaceful, and the First Cavalry had marched up the hill, and then marched down again, as did the King of France in the nursery rhyme.

It was nine o'clock before they received their orders to go forward. They had watched many regiments pass along the trail before their turn came, and they shared the experiences of the others when they finally debouched into it. They found it as the others had, muddy, overcrowded, and badly managed. The whole army was moving forward in a line not much wider than the one which the Rough Riders alone had found so inconvenient when they marched up to Guasimas.

I mention this, because the army had been inactive for seven days, and had had ample time to prepare for that advance by cutting new trails through the jungle, so that they could have entered the field in half a dozen or a dozen places, instead of in only one place, on which it would have been madness on the part of the enemy if they had not had their guns trained for days. General Chaffee recognised this, and spoke of it. But General Chaffee was not in command, so the Rough Riders started down that trail, as other regiments started down that trail, and when ten o'clock came they entered the zone of Spanish fire as other regiments had and did enter the Spanish zone of fire that day. And they could not reply any more than others could reply. And they were wounded and killed helplessly and steadily as the men of other regiments were.

And, with the other troops who were marched needlessly and stupidly into that death trap, they suffered through the madness which sent up a military balloon at a place where the entire American Army in Cuba must needs march under it or near it, and catch the terrific fire which the Spanish gunners of course directed at so admirable a target.

They were crossing a creek when they first felt the fire. The water was about two feet deep, and many men were hit while they were wading in it. There was considerable danger that the wounded men who fell in it would be drowned instead of dying pleasantly of their wounds as it is intended that soldiers shall die, and the men who had first-aid packages and who were looking after the wounded as well as they could, had their hands very busily employed.

Colonel Roosevelt rode mounted to the right, and when he saw the terrible slaughter that the balloon was bringing to the men who followed the route marked down for them, he took his men out of it and around to the right so that they avoided the worst of it, perhaps. The regiment finally halted while it was standing in the creek. The men of D Troop were waist deep and more in the water. The Spanish shells were whistling weirdly overhead and the blundering gas-bag was still there, as if it had been a signal shown to let the Spaniards know the position of our men.

For half an hour the Rough Riders stood waiting there. Many of them had to keep their positions in the creek, and it is not fun to stand for half an hour in water, with the tropical glare of the Cuban sun beating down upon your head, and its no less stifling reflection beating up into your face and against your body from the water. If you add to these discomforts the continual arrival of shells fired by hostile men, which ripped and tore the life out of your comrades, while you looked impotently at their suffering and wondered how long it might be before you were hit yourself, you will find that happiness is far distant and agony very near.

Yet the irrepressible good spirits of the Rough Riders did not desert them even here. They would have been very much more in evidence if the men had been able to shoot back—if the pleasing consciousness that they were giving Spain as good as she sent had been theirs; but still they laughed and joked and grimly guyed each other.

Their next move was to the woods—the front from which they later charged with their gallant colonel at their head and drove the Spaniards from San Juan Hill. This march covered a distance which I have heard estimated at half a mile and which I have heard estimated at three miles. Probably the first figure is nearer right than the second. It is particularly surprising and not especially pleasing to the writer of a book like this to find that no two men see things alike in wartime. My own remembrance of things I saw at Guasimas is as different from the remembrance of other men who saw the same things at the same time as the difference between these two estimates of distance, and the remembrance of a third man sets both myself and the other chap at fault.

But all writers of battle history agree that the most frequent errors of those who see battles are on the side of exaggeration. At any rate, whether this march was long or short, everyone agrees that the weather was terrifically hot, and that the Spanish fire was hotter. The country was either clear or covered with low bushes which offered the men no protection whatever, and many of them went down here as they had gone down at Las Guasimas. It seemed harder: to be shot here, for not yet were our men able to fire a single answering shot at the Spaniards who were sending those Mausers singing into their ranks. So great was the execution done in this short time, I am told, that the bandages of the first-aid men were wholly exhausted before the men actually reached the front.

The Rough Riders, through Colonel Roosevelt's own good sense, and not through any merit of the orders under which he was acting, avoided the worst place that the American Army found that day. They were not among the troops who poured through the opening from that fatal trail down which most of our helpless men went into the plain where the Spaniards had studied out the range and only had to send their unanswered bullets into the mass of soldiers who were huddled there in a confusion which could have only been avoided by not sending them there at all.

He took his regiment well over to the right to about the point in the line which it had been intended that he should occupy, but he did not take them by the route which he had been instructed to follow. When he got them there, he placed them in the woods as well as he could. He made his men lie down while he stood up or rode around on his horse. He took every chance there was, while he allowed his men to take as few as possible. He did many things to add to their love of him before they proved it by following him up the hill. But he could not give them the one privilege which they wanted more than they wanted anything else. He could not then give them the order to fire back at the enemy which was killing them as pot-hunters kill wild rabbits.

But by and by he gave them all the chance they wanted.

CHAPTER 10

The Charge of San Juan

The middle of the day had passed before the men got their chance. And here it is interesting to go over again that little list of Rough Rider records, which I have already mentioned once or twice, but which is now getting so long that it deserves to be spoken of again.

The Rough Riders were the first regiment to be organised of all the volunteers.

They raised the first flag raised by the United States Army in Cuba.

They fired the first shot fired in anger by the army in Cuba, and they lost the first man shot by the Spaniards.

And now comes the last and best of their record performances. They led the army in the charge up San Juan Hill.

They lay there where Roosevelt had led them, still taking the fire from the Spaniards and still unable to return it, that 1st of July, with as good grace as any troops could have shown under such depressing and disheartening circumstances. Every once in a while, someone among them was shot. It was one of the men who was wounded there who made a remark as his comrades started away, which is likely to go down into the history of the utterances of wounded men.

"Scorch, boys! Scorch!" he said. "My tire's punctured."

The situation was, perhaps, the most exasperating that troops can be called upon to endure. Several regiments were ahead of the Rough Riders, among them the Ninth Regular Cavalry. This regiment is made up of coloured men. I counted its Lieutenant-Colonel—Hamilton—among my dearest friends, and was with his regiment more than I was with any other during the days preceding our departure from Tampa. I know those negro troopers to be brave men, and, indeed, they proved themselves to be among the best soldiers in the United States Army, later that same day.

Colonel Hamilton was killed in the charge up San Juan Hill, and

Charge of the Rough Riders at San Juan Hill.

his men lost very heavily. They were black heroes, every one of them. But they lay ahead of the Rough Riders and did not attempt to go beyond their orders, which were to lie there and wait for someone to tell them from General Shafter to go ahead. That Colonel Hamilton was as brave a man as Colonel Roosevelt, and as brave a man as any man ever was, I do not doubt for a moment, but his regular army training did not stand him in good stead that day.

He had been a soldier all his life and he did what a soldier is supposed to do—he did what he was told to do. He had been told to wait. Colonel Roosevelt understood the necessity of obeying orders as well as Hamilton did, but Colonel Roosevelt had not been turned into a fighting machine by years of discipline, and he thought for himself when his superior officers failed to think for him. Colonel Hamilton did not. So, Colonel Roosevelt was the hero of San Juan Hill, although the opportunity for heroism had been before Colonel Hamilton just as long as it had been before Colonel Roosevelt. Hamilton, doubtless, saw the necessity for the charge as soon as Roosevelt did, but he waited for some superior to see it too. Roosevelt waited a reasonable time for his superiors to see it, and then he went ahead on his own hook.

I did not see Colonel Roosevelt that day, of course, for I was lying wounded out on the hospital ship *Olivette* off Siboney. But I can call to my mind a picture of him which I know is accurate.

His face was streaming with perspiration and streaked with honest dirt. His famous teeth were prominent and bared constantly by those nervous twitchings of his face which always accompany whatever he says. They were, probably, very often and very grimly closed that day—those teeth—and it is certain that in the excitement of it all he bit his words off with more abruptness and determination than he usually does. And that is saying much. For Roosevelt always talks as if he were trying to give each word a farewell bite before it leaves his mouth, and ends it suddenly with snap. His hair hung in wet wisps down his forehead.

Most of the officers in Cuba had their hair cut as short as possible. Roosevelt wore his a little longer than usual. He had on no jacket, and his shirt was soaked with sweat. He did not wear cavalry boots, but had on russet shoes which had wholly taken on the colour of the Cuban mud, and ordinary cavalry leggings such as are served out to the troops at thirty-one cents a pair. His riding breeches were of khaki, which, when it is clean, is a pretty soft brown. But his were not clean.

They were wet and they were covered with great spots of Cuban mud and other dirt.

It is unlikely that he had taken them off the night before at all. But they were no dirtier than his campaign hat, which was full of holes cut by an obliging trooper for the ventilation of the colonel's head. From the back of it a blue bandana handkerchief with white spots hung down to shield his neck from sun. This the colonel always wore on his hat after the first battle, where he had it tied around his neck. It was the battle flag of San Juan, and I doubt if any man who was at San Juan Hill will ever be able to see one like it without wanting -to cheer. Roosevelt had sewed his shoulder straps to his shirt, but one of them had come off and the other hung loosely flopping at one end in imminent danger of being lost as the colonel's wiry shoulder jerked nervously.

I know just how he stood there as he turned to his men and shouted, "We'll have to take that hill," and how they shouted it back along the line, "We'll have to take that hill," and everyone took the colonel's words up and cried, "We'll have to take that hill."

And then they took it.

In front of Colonel Roosevelt's command, as I have said, was the Ninth Cavalry. Hamilton did not move them. Roosevelt, finding them in his way, shouted:

"If you're not going up, get out of my way, for I am." They made no signs of advancing, so he mounted and rushed into their rear, shouting to them to make way for the Rough Riders. The surprised darkies did not know what to make of this unexpected whirlwind which was pushing and shoving its way through them, but they parted and let it pass. After it had gone by, the coloured men fell in with their officers at their head and were the second regiment up the hill. Hamilton was killed in the charge.

The officers of the Ninth felt, at first, a little chagrined at what Roosevelt had done, and were inclined to criticise him for it, but this feeling soon gave way to one of honest and outspoken admiration for the man who had had the nerve to set military rules at defiance and whip the enemy in spite of his own superior officers. With the Ninth went two companies of the Seventy-First New York, a regiment of gallant men who have been criticised as the men in the ranks really do not deserve to be criticised, because some of their officers flunked.

Roosevelt went mounted, waving his sword in the air. I fancy he looked a good deal more like the pictures of fighting men charging,

A Gun in Grimes's Battery.

It was a shot from this gun that drove the fatal Spanish shell into the midst of the Rough Riders

than officers very often do. He must have made the kind of a sight that would have delighted the eyes of any of the famous painters of battle scenes. If Detaille or Meissonier could have seen him, they would probably have felt that they had seen the one thing that they had been longing all their lives to see.

The ground was uneven and he had to pay some attention to his horse, which slipped and stumbled several times before he reached the barbed-wire fence which, at last, forced the colonel to abandon him. Roosevelt would have preferred to go up that hill on foot instead of riding up on his horse, for several reasons. Chief of these is the fact that he was the only mounted man on the whole field, and was, therefore, a bright and shining mark for Spanish bullets. Now no man likes to take an unnecessary risk, no matter how willing he may be to expose himself to such danger as legitimately belongs to him in the course of duty. It is not likely that Colonel Roosevelt enjoyed the realisation that he was the very biggest target on the whole field of battle for Spanish bullets to be aimed at.

Nor was it at all pleasant to have to watch his horse's steps and urge him and encourage him when he wanted to look around, as he could have looked around if he had been walking instead of riding, to see how his men were acting and whether they were following him as rapidly and as closely as he could have wished. But Roosevelt has always been known as a man of lightning thought, and before he mounted at all that day, he realised in a flash that a leader on horseback, brandishing his sword and going like the devil up that hill, would be easier for the men to follow, and more inspiring to them, than a leader walking, who could only go as fast as they could, and who would very likely be so winded by the physical exertion of climbing that he would be unable to shout his orders so that they could be heard.

It has been said that Roosevelt's horse was shot under him that day. This is a mistake. Several officers' horses were shot while their owners were mounted on them before the day was over, but Roosevelt's was not one of these. The animal was hit by a piece of a shell, but the wound was very slight. He is now enjoying well-earned rest and pampered luxury in the colonel's stables at Oyster Bay, Long Island.

The barbed-wire fence was a bad place. It stopped Colonel Roosevelt and it stopped the men who were coming after him. Before that they had straggled along separately and slowly. They could not dash. The hill was too rough, and they were too tired, and the weather was too hot for them to make a wild rush and get there quick. They went up slowly and laboriously. It was mighty hard work—it would have been mighty hard even if the men at the top of the hill in the trenches had not been poring steel death messengers down at them with desperate earnestness.

The ascent they were making was not military. They had no right, according to the ideas of tacticians, to go up that hill as they did, so long as they were not backed up by artillery. But they struggled along without any military formation until they reached this barbed-wire fence. The first men who had wire nippers cut it as quickly as they could, but the pause had been long enough to allow other men to come up, until they were bunched there, and this offered the Spaniards a better chance for shooting than they had had before. They took advantage of it. There were as many men of our regiment hit in that huddle there as were hit in all the places else on the hill put together.

As soon as Roosevelt, now dismounted, had passed the barbed-wire fence he said the only harsh thing which he said to his men during the entire campaign. He turned around and shouted back at the crowd who were toiling along after him:

"If any man runs, I'll shoot him myself."

It hurt the men to hear him say such a thing, for there was no one there who had the slightest thought of running. They felt better a moment after when he added, tactfully:

"And I won't have to shoot any of my own men either," but he was sorry he had said anything of the kind, and they were sorry they

had heard him, although they all realised that when a man is labouring under such excitement as Roosevelt was at that moment, it is impossible for him to pick and choose his words as he would if he were in a drawing-room, or even in a military camp.

At any rate, of course, no one ran and so Roosevelt did not have to shoot anybody.

Perhaps it is not quite accurate for me to call this part of the battle the "Charge up San Juan Hill," for this hill was not properly a part of San Juan Hill. It was a little preceding hill, and between it and San Juan Hill proper was a slight depression containing a shallow pond of water. At the top of this first hill were some large sugar kettles, so the regiment named it "Kettle Hill," so that in speaking of it they could differentiate between it and San Juan Hill.

Here the Rough Riders put in what was, by all odds, the hardest part of their fighting, and lost far more men than they did after they began to ascend the eminence after which the battle is named. The bullets flew like bees around those kettles and like bees they were very busy. But they were not gathering honey. They were spilling blood. Not less than a dozen of the Rough Riders went down here, and several were killed outright. It is said that the fire slacked up slightly after our men reached the top of this first hill, and that the Spaniards began to evacuate their main trenches without waiting for us to come farther.

I could easily devote a chapter to the little incidents which happened at this very part of the charge. But I will limit myself to one.

Captain "Bucky" O'Neill was killed. He had led his troop with great gallantry so far. It will be remembered that he was the Rough Rider who so bravely risked his life at Daiquiri in an effort to save the drowning troopers of the Tenth Cavalry, who had fallen off the skeleton pier.

O'Neill's death was thus described by his first sergeant.

"O'Neill directed us to march at intervals of twelve feet.

"'There will be fewer of you hurt.'

"We went north and then down into the sunken road. It was terrible hot down there, but it was much worse when we got in the open field. Bullets from the blockhouse and from the trenches swept down upon us constantly. We came to a barbed-wire fence; it looked as if it were going to stop us, because for some reason none of us who reached it first had wire nippers, but we beat it down with the butts of our carbines, and scrambled over the prostrate wires.

"Then we lay down and fired, but O'Neill stood up straight, and told us not to get rattled, but to fire steady, and kill a Spaniard every time we shot. Then we made a rush. Troop K came up behind us, and we lay down again to fire, but O'Neill walked cheerfully up and down the line talking to us. Lieutenant Kane cried out:

"'Get down, O'Neill. There's no use exposing yourself in that way.'

"O'Neill turned and laughed, and said:

"'Aw-w! The Spanish bullet has not been moulded that can hit me!'

"And then one hit him in the mouth and killed him."

Roosevelt led his men down the little descent at the other side of Kettle Hill, still waving his sabre and shouting encouragingly at them. Just as they approached the edge of the little pond something—either a bullet or a piece of shell—struck him on the back of the hand and made a slight wound. That moment Roosevelt was the happiest man in Cuba. He was mighty glad of the wound and, incidentally, probably, mighty glad that it was no worse.

He waved his hand proudly in the air so that the men who were near enough to him could see the blood, and shouted:

"I've got it, boys! I've got it!"

Then he turned to a wounded man who was not far away, and cried, laughingly:

"You needn't be so damned proud."

Through the water of the pond, he waded with great strides. Once he stumbled and almost fell, but recovered himself quickly and kept on. By this time the inspiration of the Rough Riders' charge had infected the whole army, and half-a dozen regiments were springing forward all along the line. The Spaniards saw this and were frightened. There was never, for a moment, any doubt as to the ultimate outcome of the fight, for the Americans greatly outnumbered their adversaries; but there probably was never a place where in so short a time so many bullets fired at so few men, as were poured down at the Rough Riders during their charge. But they never flinched.

I have been told by a Spanish officer that the Spaniards were so lost in their surprise that they forgot to fire, but if any forgot to fire, we did not miss their bullets. Our men were able to get along without them. The whole thing, however, seemed incredible. By this time the men had separated again as they were at first, and each man was picking his own route without making any pretence at keeping alignment or doing anything but get up that hill, firing a shot occasionally when he felt that he could afford the time to stop and shoot, which was not often.

The work was slow—painfully slow. By this time the combination of heat, exertion, and excitement had made the men feel as if they had already done a pretty hard day's work. They struggled and puffed. Once in a while one of them would "get it." The effect of the bullets on that upward slope was curious. Sometimes—when a man was hit in an outstretched arm, for instance, or in the extreme outer shoulder, he would whirl part of the way around before he fell. But fall he would, and since I have seen men fall with Mauser bullets in them, I shall never feel that anyone else I see go down really does the task completely.

The shock of such tremendously high-speed projectiles seems to completely paralyze the motor nerves—the nerves which transmit the impulse of contraction and expansion from the brain to the muscles—and thus every muscle becomes instantaneously and completely limp. The men went down, literally, like wet rags. Some of them regained their control over their muscles almost at once, and got up again, either to go on toward those spitting rifle-pits at the top of the hill, or else to drop back again to the ground from the pain of their wounds. Not one wounded man, so many people who were there have told me, even in his agonies, tried to walk or crawl back towards the rear.

The men took their wounds as cheerfully at San Juan as they had taken them at Guasimas. I have talked with the two first-aid men who probably did more work among the Rough Riders that day than any others, and they tell me the same story of "no complaints" from the wounded. Never in any battle in any land could the men involved have shown a more admirable spirit. Never could they have shown an eye more single to the accomplishment of their duty and more blind to their own pains and hardships.

Up, up, up, they went—slowly, painfully, straining every nerve, cracking every muscle. The sun beat on their heads and made them faint, but valour beat in their hearts and made them strong. It may be because I had been with the Rough Riders when I met my own disaster that I feel so strongly on the subject, but it seems to me this moment as if I would rather have seen that regiment, crawling like warlike ants up that hill from which the little deadly spikes of fire were sending death at them, than to have seen any other sight in all the world.

John Foster, of B Troop, was the only American soldier who came near enough to the Spaniards to make a hand-to-hand fight necessary. He killed one with the butt of his rifle.

The trenches at the top of the hill were literally full of dead enemies. They had had all the advantages of position and intrenchments, but notwithstanding reports to the contrary, they were greatly outnumbered, and knew from the beginning when they saw our men starting in swarms out of the woods that the battle could have only one result. It does not detract from, but rather adds, to the glory of the fighting done by our men to give the devil his due, and say that the soldiers of Spain showed a dogged courage and grim determination to kill as many Yankees as they could as they hopelessly fired, fired, fired, from their trenches up there—a bravery which was only exceeded in its glory by the dogged persistence of our own men who went up against them.

The objective point of Roosevelt's charge was a blockhouse. Its nasty little loopholes had been spitting fire at him and killing his men during the entire weary, dreadful climb. There were five troopers with him when he reached it. Most of the Spaniards who had occupied it had been killed. All of the others, except one, had run over to the right when they saw our men getting so near that hope was gone. But this one Spaniard stayed where he was, and with a grim, set face, continued to fire. Someone called on him to surrender. He answered with another shot. Roosevelt's revolver was in his hand. He raised it with deliberate aim and killed the Spaniard. Afterwards he said that he was sorry the man had not been an American.

"It was a pity to kill so brave a man as he," he said.

But the work was not over. On the next hill of the little chain, over to the right, the Spaniards who had run away from the one which Roosevelt now held, were with the men who had been there all the time in the trenches. They must be driven back. A little conference was held, and Roosevelt said he would take that hill too. It was agreed that this further advance could only be made at the expense of many lives, and there were those among our officers who did not think the game was worth the candle. Roosevelt was not a half-way soldier any more than he had been a half-way police commissioner, or any more than he is now a half-way governor. He made up his mind to finish the job he had so well begun, and turned to the men who were around him.

"Who'll follow me?" he demanded.

With that he jumped out. For a moment it looked as if the Rough

Riders might have had enough, for only five men sprang in behind him. Three of these fell at once. Roosevelt stood there with but two living followers. He went back.

"I thought you would follow me," he said, terribly grieved.

"We'll follow you to hell," someone cried out. "We didn't hear you, colonel."

He sprang out once more and there were three hundred men behind him this time.

The spirit of the Spaniards was gone. The terrible Americans were after them again. The task was not a hard one. They fled in terror.

And Roosevelt and his men were on the position which they occupied until the end of the fighting.

From a photograph by William Dinwiddie. *Asleep in the Shade on the Railroad Leading to Santiago.*

CHAPTER 11

The Men Who Died

There are few men in William O'Neill's troop whose eyes do not fill when they think of him. O'Neill was the biggest, handsomest, laziest officer in the regiment. His good-nature knew no bounds. He tried to keep up a strict military discipline among his men, but they did more to keep it up than he did, simply because they knew he wanted them to, and because they knew that he would never be harsh enough to them to demand it. They had the greatest desire to make his troop the model troop of the regiment, and despite the free and easy, open-hearted way in which O'Neill commanded it, it was certainly one of the best. He was always known as "Bucky."

No man had ever felt more certain that he would not be killed, or even hurt in battle, than O'Neill did. Kenneth Harris, who was O'Neill's bunk-mate, says that the captain had decided to remain in Cuba after the war was over. Poor captain! he did remain in Cuba, but not in the way he intended to.

No man could have been more unselfish than O'Neill was. He did everything for his men and very little for himself. He rather hated to have them salute him than otherwise. He always dreaded the possibility of taking advantage of his rank.

Nothing could have been finer than the way he jumped off the skeleton pier at Daiquiri in his efforts to save the drowning troopers. He risked his life without a second's hesitation, and laughed about it afterwards. He was always saying that nobody could kill him, and said that he couldn't drown any more than he could die by Spanish bullets. He didn't drown.

When we got to Siboney, on that never-to-be-forgotten night of June 23rd, it rained, as I have already said in another chapter. All the men were tired. The cook of O'Neill's troop was especially worn out, and Bucky seeing it, went up to him and told him that he didn't want any supper, and should not eat it if he cooked it.

"Why?" asked the amazed trooper.

"It's a damn shame to ask you to cook," said Bucky; "you're too tired."

Captain Bucky O'Neill had the best supper in Cuba that night.

Later, after he had lain down with Harris under their dog tent, he went somewhere, and dragged out a canvas wagon cover. It was raining pitchforks, and Harris' bedding was soaked. Harris protested at O'Neill's using the few moments of possible sleep in this way. O'Neill arranged the wagon cover so that it kept Harris perfectly dry, and replied:

"Don't imagine that I do it on your account, you irritable brute, and stop swearing or I'll put you under arrest. I want to keep the bedding dry, that's all."

Then he disappeared again. When he returned, he shoved something like a pillow under Harris's head. It was, probably, a small cushion from one of the naval launches. Harris kicked again, and Bucky said:

"Shut up, you incorrigible scoundrel. I've got one myself. Now go to sleep."

Harris reached over in the dark, and felt a coiled cartridge belt and a canteen under O'Neill's head.

It is said that he was known as "Bucky" because there never was a game so hard that he would hesitate to "buck up" against it.

Bucky combined his gambling propensities and his patriotism one day in a remark which will, probably, go down into history. Someone was saying that the Spaniards greatly outnumbered us, and that it was a terrible gamble to send our troops into the fever-stricken country against them.

"Is it!" said Bucky. "Who would not gamble for a new star in the flag!"

But Bucky's belief in his own luck was serene and unchangeable. He had so many times escaped death at the hands of border ruffians, that it was perfectly natural for him to stand up while others were lying down at San Juan, and to shoot when they called upon him to take cover.

"The Spanish bullet has not been moulded that can kill me."

Then it was, as I have said before, that a Spanish bullet, which had been moulded, struck him in the mouth and killed him.

He was born in St. Louis in 1860. He was graduated from the National Law School at Washington. He wanted to go into the army, and was appointed a paymaster, but his commission did not come along soon enough to suit his impatient nature, and he went to Arizona. He became a successful newspaper man, conducting the *Arizona Miner,* the *Phoenix Herald,* and *Hoof and Horn,* with profit. He gave up journalism when he was elected judge of Yavapai County. He served three terms as sheriff of this county, and was known as its best armed man, and readiest shot.

At this period, he was Bret Harte's ideal of Western *desperado.* No matter how hopeless the circumstances might be, he never permitted his voice to rise above a quiet drawl, and his calm blue eyes showed never a suggestion of excitement. He was the kind of man who might shoot another if it seemed at all advisable, but if he had ever been called upon to do it he would have done it coolly and with perfect courtesy. "I beg your pardon, but I've got to kill you," might very well have been his formula.

Three times he was a Congressional candidate, but he was always on the wrong side of the political fence and was always badly beaten. Finally, he was elected Mayor of Prescott. When they came to count up the votes, they found that his rival had received only one.

O'Neill afterwards admitted that he had cast that himself.

"I could see," said he, "that the poor fellow was going to feel right bad if he didn't get any vote at all."

"When the war broke out, he got his troop together so quickly that President McKinley sent him a personal letter of thanks.

He left a charming wife behind him, and during the days before his death, while the men were lying in the trenches, cut off from mail communications with anywhere, he wrote to her every day.

"I never failed to yet when I was away from home," he said, "and while I feel pretty certain that she'll never get the letters, I'm going to write 'em just the same."

So much has been written about Hamilton Fish that, perhaps, I have no right to devote much space to the death of this brave young New Yorker here. Fish always craved excitement and always managed to get it in some way, and the manner in which he sought it, particularly when he was at home in New York City, was sometimes criticised. But no one ever said, in my hearing, that "Ham" Fish was ever worse than thoughtless and impulsive. He harmed no one but himself, and was the idol of his acquaintances. He made an ideal soldier, and went to his death with cool and cheerful heroism.

He was one of the few men I have ever known of who expected to be killed before they entered their fatal battles. Fish felt perfectly certain that he was going to die. The morning of the fight he insisted on having an especially good breakfast, because he said that it would be his last breakfast. He had toted a can of tomatoes all the way from Daiquiri to Siboney, and his bunkie was inclined to be economical in the eating thereof.

"Oh, let's have some more," said Fish, "it's my last breakfast."

He was transferred to L Troop the night before the regiment sailed from Tampa because he wanted to fight under Captain Capron. They were not twenty feet apart when they were shot. Capron made him sergeant of the squad from Muskogee, Indian Territory. Those fellows loved him.

Mason Mitchell paid a pretty tribute to him, when he told of his love for animals. Anything that breathed and was dumb, appealed to the very best that there was in him. At San Antonio, he was given one of the worst animals in that collection of wild and wicked brutes. This beast was unbroken, and had been shunned even by the most expert cow-punchers in the outfit. Day after day Fish worked at him with unvarying and patient kindness. At first the animal threw him, but by the time they said goodbye to each other, when the horses were left behind at Tampa, he would follow Fish around like a dog, and Fish was beginning to teach him tricks. In the meantime, the animal's disposition had not changed in the least toward other men. He was quite as vicious with everyone but Fish, as he had been at the start.

Just before we started up the hill, he threw away a new pair of shoes, saying that he would never need them anymore. He had some extra underwear, too, and an extra shirt. These he gave to some of his companions, remarking cheerfully, as he did so, that he wouldn't need them after the battle, for dead men did not often change their clothes.

I have already said that his body has been removed from Cuba, and now lies at Garrison's, New York.

During the stay at San Antonio, Fish saw a crowd of men surrounding two fighting dogs. He slouched surlily in and stopped the fight. One of the dogs was badly hurt, and he took him to his tent. There he bandaged his wounds, and gave him his own supper.

While I am writing of the men who died, it pleases me to briefly mention the patriotism of the father of one of them. He was E. G. Norton, of Eustis, Florida. He had two sons, Edward and Oliver, in B Troop. Ed. was a corporal; Oliver, who had been a medical student in

Chicago before he joined, was killed. His father heard of it and at once sent down to Santiago his son, Gould G. In the letter which he sent with him, to Captain McClintock, he said:

"This is my third son. I send him to you to take the place of my son Oliver, who was killed. It is religion with the Nortons to serve their country."

It is needless to say that E. G. Norton was a Union soldier.

Gerard Merrick Ives, of Troop K, was one of the men who were left at Tampa. He was taken sick there with typhoid, and brought North to New York, where he died. He was the son of the sculptor who made the famous statues of Sherman and Trumbull, now at Washington.

Out in Fort Sill, Oklahoma, a little woman received a parcel five or six weeks after the Battle of Las Guasimas. In it were all that she will ever see again that Captain Capron, her gallant husband, carried into that memorable fight. The parcel contained a dirty grey campaign hat and a pair of shoulder straps. Both were bloodstained. They were wrapped in such torn fragments of paper as could be found near the field hospital where he died, and around the whole a piece was tied with a strand of Spanish wire.

The dead on the field of San Juan were buried almost where they fell. The field is dotted with little tombstones, erected by General Wood, and as Governor of Santiago he keeps a patrol constantly on the field to look after them, night and day.

Chapter 12

After the Fighting was Over

With the days in the trenches which followed the day of the charge, the fighting ceased. Whether our men had "got enough" or not, they had had all there was to be had, and they had fought as hard, and fought as well, and fought as fearlessly, as the most sanguine of them expected the regiment to fight when that regimental cry was invented in San Antonio.

The days in the trenches up to the time of the surrender were weary ones. There was the same old succession of tropical rains and burning suns. There was digging to do, and there were sanitary pains to take which made the men wish that the monotony of armistices would cease, and the variety and excitement of battle begin again. No one was ever, for a moment, comfortable except by accident. The rations were scanty and bad. If the men had coffee, they had to beat the beans up on stones with the butts of their revolvers or with other stones so that they would cook. Tobacco was not to be had at any price, although there was plenty of it out on some of the transports.

Grinding their Coffee.

All kinds of rumors were afloat. It was said that the Spaniards were being starved out, and that they could fight no more; indeed, the news that came to the men from occasional refugees was sufficiently definite on this subject of starvation to make it certain. The men had

From a photograph by H. R. Fullerton.

Troopers at Mess at Montauk.

fought with the Spaniards, though, and had achieved a wholesome respect for them which made them think that all the truces and all the talk of surrender were used to cloak a Spanish trick of some kind, and they had little belief that the active fighting of the campaign was over.

Already the news of Shafter's famous telegram to Washington had been told and retold in the camp. He did not worry and fret about his "thin lines," and tell the President that he might have to retire five miles on the morning of July second, just after our army had made one of the most gallant and successful charges in the history of warfare, without the knowledge of the private soldiers.

It is rarely a commanding general's fortune to hide his feelings or his plans from the men beneath him. No matter how carefully he guards his secrets the men in the tents are likely to be discussing them before the ink on the paper to which he has committed them is dry. And it was so with Shafter. The men in the ranks of the Rough Riders knew that he was worried and that he thought seriously of retreat. It was the men who had made the fight, it was the men who had bled and died in it, and it was the men who were not afraid. The thought of going back after what they had won, filled them with distress and shame. They had been the sufferers at the start, and if anything, worse than what had already happened should come again, they would a second time be sufferers. It was at this time that the private soldiers in the Rough Riders began to feel like jeering when the name of the major-general commanding was spoken in their hearing—a feeling which still exists in the hearts of most of them.

I have been told that I have no right to criticise General Shafter, because I did not see the things for which I have criticised him in private and on the lecture platform. I was lying on the hospital ship when most of them occurred, but I was not lying on the hospital ship when he left the artillery and the ambulances at Tampa—I was there. I was not on the hospital ship when he disregarded the advice and the carefully laid plans of the navy, and landed at the wrong place—I was there.

I was not lying on the hospital ship when he sent the whole American Army ashore over a pier which could have been boarded in two hours but wasn't—I was there and went over it myself. And because I was on the hospital ship during the events that followed, I know, perhaps, more about them than I would have known if I had been at the front. My acquaintance in the army and among the correspondents who were watching the army, was very large, and because of the fact that I was wounded and obviously out of the business of the transmission of news, my acquaintances spoke very freely to me.

It may be that they spoke more freely to me because the doctors thought that I was dying, and so they may have felt that they could unburden their minds to me and give themselves relief through me, without danger, on the theory that I would presently die, and dead men tell no tales. But, at any rate, they did come to me and they did tell me what was going on, and I know they were not lying to me.

Man after man poured tales of Shafter's incompetence and Shafter's intense and unalterable egotism into my ears, and I worried a out the American Army. And I had cause to worry. There were transport captains who came aboard the *Olivette* and said that they had tons of provisions on their ships and could not get orders to take them off. At the same time news from shore told of the terrible sufferings of the troops for lack of food. There were surgeons and hospital men who came aboard and told how the hospitals on shore were handicapped by lack of medical supplies and orders which would enforce good sanitary conditions.

On the *Olivette* we did not suffer—we had a surplus that they were welcome to. Right here it is well to pay a little tribute to Major Appel, who commanded the hospital ship *Olivette*, on which I was as comfortable as any man could be in that climate, with a big hole in him and a part of his spine smashed up and thrown into the Caribbean Sea. Appel was not dearly loved by the men under him and was, unquestionably, a martinet in some ways. But what he needed, he got, and I fancy that he got it because he did not propose to let his superior officers handicap him at the expense of the wounded men on his ship.

It is certain that through his efforts and the generosity of Mr. W. R. Hearst, the owner and editor of the *New York Journal,* who brought over, in some of his boats, frequent cargoes of ice and other supplies from Jamaica for the sufferers on the *Olivette*, purchased at his own expense and given free, without claims on the government, the men on our boat got along as well as they could be expected to get along in the distressing circumstances which surrounded them.

But what Appel did was very different from what the heads of the hospitals which were more directly under Shafter's supervision on shore were able to do.

And here it is pleasant to place another record to the list of the Rough Rider's achievements. The first case of yellow fever developed during the night of June 25th. Burr McIntosh was the victim. I have already spoken of him in connection with the time preceding the march to Siboney. When we were taken down to the shore, I have told how we were put into a curious little shanty. It should have been burned by somebody's orders, but had been permitted to remain standing despite the fact that Siboney had been known as a yellow fever nest in season. The navy had burned every building at Guantanamo as a precaution against fever infection, but Shafter had let these little shanties stand.

We were taken into this one. It was afterwards learned that it had actually been used as a yellow fever hospital during previous epidemics, and it is not at all improbable that it contributed the first germs which afterwards infected the whole army in Cuba. McIntosh's was the first case. Many came after it with a rapidity which was not less than startling.

I remember distinctly the day when a correspondent came out and whispered confidentially to me that there was a case of yellow fever ashore, and added that the story of it must be kept deathly quiet. I held it as a secret. But within twelve hours it was no secret, for there was not one case but a dozen, and the grim story of suffering and death from foes other than the Spaniards began to be telegraphed to all parts of the world.

There was only one man who rose to the occasion after the military situation became such that any man could rise to it. Of course, before the Spaniards surrendered it would have been useless to talk about the withdrawal of our men from this dreadful danger that trembled threateningly over them in each of the miasmatic mists that rose by night; that shook its dreadful yellow fists at them from every thicket; that clasped their necks with baby arms when they helped the children of the Cuban refugees to go back home from El Caney; that threw out grasping tentacles from every building that had been allowed to stand after the arrival of the invading army.

But after the surrender came and the war was over, at least in that part of Cuba, there was no disposition on the part of the commanding general to take the troops away from the menace of the fever. The shanties at Siboney from which the plague had, in all human probability, started, were burned at last on the order of General Miles, but still the army was uselessly held there to suffer and to die, at the mercy of a foe whom bullets would not reach as they had reached the vanquished Spaniards, and which fought unceasingly—by night, by day, without alarms, but always there and always winning victories.

It was at this point that the record-making genius of the regiment again appeared and induced Colonel Roosevelt to violate all military rules. He had violated them once before when he led the charge at San Juan, and that had turned out well. Perhaps he had gotten into the good habit of doing the thing which was obviously right without waiting for the sign from superior officers who were obviously wrong. At any rate, at this point, on his own responsibility, he sent to General Shafter the following, and now famous, letter, which was dated August 1st:

> Major-Gen. Shafter:
> Sir—In a meeting of the general and medical officers called by you at the palace this morning, we were all, as you know, unanimous in view of what should be done with the army. To keep us here, in the opinion of every officer commanding a division or a brigade, will simply involve the destruction of thousands. There is no possible reason for not shipping practically the entire command North at once. Yellow fever cases are very few in the cavalry division, where I command one of the two brigades, and not one true case of yellow fever has occurred in this division, except among the men sent to the hospital at Siboney, where they have, I believe, contracted it.
> But in this division, there have been 1,500 cases of malarial fever. Not a man has died from it; but the whole command is so weakened and shattered as to be ripe for dying like rotten sheep when a real yellow-fever epidemic, instead of a fake epidemic like the present, strikes us, as it is bound to if we stay here at the height of the sickly season, August and the beginning of September. Quarantine against malarial fever is much like quarantine against the toothache. All of us are certain, as soon as the authorities at Washington fully appreciate the conditions of the army, to be sent home. If we are kept here, it will, in all human probability, mean an appalling disaster, for the surgeons here estimate that over half the army, if kept here during the sickly season, will die.
> This is not only terrible from the standpoint of the individual lives lost, but it means ruin from the standpoint of the military efficiency of the flower of the American Army, for the great bulk of the regulars are here with you. The sick list, large though it is, exceeding 4,000, affords but a faint index of the

debilitation of the army. Not 10 *per cent.* are fit for active work. Six weeks on the North Maine coast, for instance, or elsewhere where the yellow-fever germ cannot possibly propagate, would make us all as fit as fighting cocks, able as we are and eager to take a leading part in the great campaign against Havana in the fall, even if we are not allowed to try Porto Rico.

We can be moved North, if moved at once, with absolute safety to the country, although, of course, it would have been infinitely better if we had been moved North or to Porto Rico two weeks ago. If there were any object in keeping us here, we would face yellow fever with as much indifference as we face bullets. But there is no object in it. The four immune regiments ordered here are sufficient to garrison the city and surrounding towns, and there is absolutely nothing for us to do here, and there has not been since the city surrendered. It is impossible to move into the interior.

Every shifting of camp doubles the sick rate in our present weakened condition, and, anyhow, the interior is rather worse than the coast, as I have found by actual reconnaissance. Our present camps are as healthy as any camps at this end of the island can be. I write only because I cannot see our men, who have fought so bravely and who have endured extreme hardship and danger so uncomplainingly, go to destruction without striving, so far as lies in me, to avert a doom as fearful as it is unnecessary and undeserved.

   Yours respectfully,·

           Theodore Roosevelt,
        Colonel Commanding First Brigade.

This had the desired effect. Just as the other officers had followed Roosevelt at San Juan in the attack on the Spaniards, they now followed him in the equally well considered effort to retreat from the fever. Roosevelt's letter was scarcely cold when the following "round robin" was sent in:

> We, the undersigned officers commanding the various brigades, divisions, etc., of the Army of Occupation in Cuba, are of the unanimous opinion that the army should be at once taken out of the Island of Cuba and sent to some point on the Northern sea-coast of the United States; that it can be done without danger to the people of the United States; that yellow fever in

the army at present is not epidemic; that there are only a few sporadic cases, but that the army is disabled by malarial fever to the extent that its efficiency is destroyed, and that it is in a condition to be practically entirely destroyed by an epidemic of yellow fever, which is sure to come in the near future.

We know from the reports of competent officers and from personal observations that the army is unable to move into the interior, and that there are no facilities for such a move if attempted, and that it could not be attempted until too late. Moreover, the best medical authorities of the island say that with our present equipment we could not live in the interior during the rainy season without losses from malarial fever, which is almost as deadly as yellow fever.

This army must be moved at once, or perish. As the army can be safely moved now, the persons responsible for preventing such a move will be responsible for the unnecessary loss of many thousands of lives. Our opinions are the result of careful personal observation, and they are also based on the unanimous opinion of our medical officers with the army, and who understood the situation absolutely.

J. Ford Kent,
Major-General Volunteers,
Commanding First Division, Fifth Corps.

J. C. Bates,
Major-General Volunteers,
Commanding Provisional Division.

Adna R. Chaffee,
Major-General Volunteers,
Commanding Third Brigade, Second Division,

Samuel S. Sumner,
Brigadier-General Volunteers,
Commanding First Brigade, Cavalry.

Will Ludlow,
Brigadier-General Volunteers,
Commanding First Brigade, Second Division.

Adelbert Ames,
Brigadier-General Volunteers,
Commanding Third Brigade, First Division.

Leonard Wood,
Brigadier-General Volunteers,
Commanding the City of Santiago.
Theodore Roosevelt,
Colonel, Commanding Second Cavalry Brigade.

The Associated Press despatch from Santiago which followed this presentation said:

Major M. W. Wood, the Chief Surgeon of the First Division, said:

> The army must be moved north, (adding, with emphasis), or it will be unable to move itself.

General Ames has sent the following cable message to Washington:

> The Hon. Charles H. Allen, Assistant Secretary of the Navy: This army is incapable, because of sickness, of marching anywhere, except to the transports. If it is ever to return to the United States it must do so at once.

To a correspondent of the Associated Press General Ames said:

> If I had the power, I would put the men on the transports at once and ship them North without further orders. I am confident such action would ultimately be approved. A full list of the sick would mean a copy of the roster of every company here.

And so, the army was started North. Providence alone knows when it would have been started if Roosevelt had not sent his letter. Its condition certainly would not have been so plain to the authorities at Washington who were depending on Shafter for their news of it, if Roosevelt had not acted. And so, I say that the Rough Riders again added to their record, when Roosevelt sent in his letter.

CHAPTER 13

Last Days in Cuba

I am afraid that the chapter which has preceded this has been a dull one. The deeds of the Rough Riders were so fast and furious while fighting was going on, and their whole conduct was so free from the conventionality of military usage that to include military reports and letters in the story of them seems almost like describing the process of making iron girders in a story of a fire, because there were some used in the construction of the burning building.

The men were living their strange lives, working hard and getting little comfort from their work. When the armistices and truces were on, they loafed about the trenches and kept as cool as they could, which was not very cool. When the armistices and truces were off, they struggled with the situation as well as they could struggle with it, and sometimes they took a shot at some impertinent Spaniard who made the serious mistake of putting his head up within range.

Not a day passed but some one of them complained in the morning that his bones ached, and said it with such a pitiful expression of rolling yellow eyeballs that his comrades could not fail to know what was the matter with him. It was generally about five hours after these first complaints that it was necessary to carry the man away to the hospital, often raving with fever—yellow fever, of course.

Notwithstanding the feeling of contempt which the Cubans had earned for themselves in the minds of the Rough Riders, and the general desire to jeer whenever a Cuban uniform, or the poor pretence at one which was prevalent, came into sight, the men were filled with sympathy for the poor half-starved refugees and reconcentrados who came to them for help and food.

A great many refugees who had fled from Santiago when the city was warned that it would be bombarded, had gathered at El Caney. They had found little that was better there than that which they had

From a photograph by H. E. Fullerton. *The Famous Regimental Colors.*
They were the first to be raised by the army in Cuba and were the first to go into battle.

known in the places they had come from, except the food which the poorly provisioned American soldiers had been able to give them. There was nothing that was systematic or effective in the efforts made to relieve their distress at first.

A deep gash in a ridge was cut by the road leading to El Caney. This gash was held by the Rough Riders. Thousands of Cuban refugees passed along the road on their return to Santiago, after the surrender. The men had not more than half rations, but when they saw the poor Cubans coming up this trail, they forgot at once their contempt for the race and their own hunger. They gave away their half rations with a reckless indifference as to what the morrow might bring forth. As a matter of fact, the morrow brought forth exactly what it might have been expected to—nothing. The men suffered greater privation through their own generosity at this time, than they had at any time before through the failure of the Commissary Department to furnish them with supplies.

They not only gave away their rations, but they offered such personal assistance as they could to the weakened women and famished children among the refugees. Many and many a woman, and many and many a child, was literally carried through all that territory included within the Rough Riders' boundaries. This work of assistance was headed by "Happy Jack" of Arizona.

Finally, Dr. Bob Church heard of it, and ordered it stopped. He realised that the Cubans were likely to transfer fever germs to the American troops if such close contact was permitted. He assured Colonel Roosevelt that he would not answer for the health of the men if they persisted in helping the Cubans. For the first time in his life "Happy Jack" gave evidence that he realised the existence of religious things. He said to Colonel Roosevelt:

"God wouldn't let a fellow catch yellow fever while he was doing a good turn for them kids."

Of course, at this period many of the men were in the hospitals and suffering dreadfully. There were mistakes in connection with the Cuban hospitals, as there will probably always be mistakes in connection with all things human. The Rough Riders suffered through these mistakes, as other soldiers suffered. Complaints of their misfortunes reached Colonel Roosevelt. A man went up to him diffidently one day, and saluting, said:

"I beg your pardon, colonel, but I have just come from the hospital; I wasn't very sick and so I got along all right, but there are those among our boys down there who are suffering terribly, and I do not think that they are getting proper treatment. I beg pardon, sir."

It had been understood for a long time that Colonel Roosevelt did not want to hear complaints. It was his theory that the men who were under him had seen enough of life, and rough life, too, so that they did not need to be finding fault. Hence the man's timidity. But on this occasion, it was not necessary to be timid. Roosevelt turned to him quickly and thanked him for telling him the story. Then he went quickly to the hospital.

He was rather a rough-looking character by this time. The one shoulder strap which had been hanging by a single thread at San Juan was lost now and there was nothing on him except his riding breeches, with their yellow stripes, to show that he was an officer.

"How are the boys getting along?" asked the colonel.

"Who are you?" said the surgeon.

Whereupon, Colonel Roosevelt waxed exceedingly wroth and made remarks which would not have helped him in his gubernatorial campaign if he had repeated them while he was stumping New York State.

"I'm your superior officer, sir, Colonel Roosevelt; stand at attention, salute, and take your hat off." This is an expurgated version of what the colonel said.

The surgeon lost no time in getting his heels together and buttoning up his open shirt.

After that one visit, there were no more complaints concerning the way the Rough Riders were cared for in that hospital.

The virtual end of the war came when the American flag was raised on the palace at Santiago. The Rough Riders were not among the troops which were sent into Santiago to be present at the ceremony; they remained in the field. They were among the thousands who stayed on the crest of the ridges which had been won at the cost of so many lives. As far as the eye could reach, the straggling line of uniformed men stretched off into the distance. Conspicuous among the blue uniforms of the regular troops were the brown duck suits of the Rough Riders. The hills of San Juan, and the other eminences commanding Santiago, swarmed with happy, cheering men.

The Rough Riders were not only the most conspicuous of the soldiers, but they were the heroes of the occasion; the other troops did them high honour. The First Illinois Volunteers began the cheering for them. After the first three times three had been given, Private

Colonel Roosevelt Visiting Colonel Turner, of the First Illinois Regiment, U. S. V.

Hughes, of the Rough Riders, called for another three times three for Colonel Roosevelt, the man who had led the charge up San Juan. The whole army replied with one great voice. A mighty roar went up and Colonel Roosevelt was happier than he had been since the moment when that bit of shell struck him on the back of his hand. He waved his hat with the famous blue polka dot handkerchief attached to it in acknowledgment of the tribute, and in his turn, called for three cheers for the army. They were given with enthusiasm so great, that the troops in Santiago heard them.

The beginning of the end came in Cuba on the 7th of August. It is a matter of speculation in the regiment whether the marching orders it received at San Antonio, on May 28th, or the marching orders it received near Santiago, on August 7th, were most loudly cheered. Reveille was sounded very early in the morning, and the regiment broke camp with a skill acquired by much practice. It marched to the railroad and took train to Santiago, reaching there at 1 p.m.

At the Santiago station, the troops fell into parade formation and marched like veterans; each troop was preceded by its little flag, bearing the troop letter and the number of the regiment, and made a sort of triumphal progress through the conquered Spanish city.

Colonel Roosevelt rode at the head of the regiment on the same sorrel horse which had been wounded at the charge of San Juan. He was an extremely happy colonel; his round-robin had worked, and his men were being sent away beyond the reach of the ghastly yellow arms which the fever spectre had stretched out toward them. They were leaving Cuba with a record on which there was not one smirch; they had played their important parts in every engagement in Cuba; they had missed nothing which was worth doing, and they had done nothing which was worth missing.

The man who had gone to Cuba as the commander of the regiment, had earned his promotion to a brigadier-generalship and had received it as soon as he had earned it. This was pleasing for many reasons. The men loved Wood as well as they loved Roosevelt. Roosevelt's friendship for Wood was honest and sincere, and he was glad to see him elevated; and besides, with Wood's elevation came Roosevelt's rise to the head of the regiment, which the public had named after him. He himself, while braving every danger and taking every desperate chance he asked his men to take, had escaped unscathed. A small scar on his left hand was the only mark of battle he was taking home with him, and he had not dodged a single bullet.

These reflections were pleasant to the colonel. He knew, as he rode through those Santiago streets, that, partly because of his efforts, the most extraordinary regiment in the army had been organised and equipped as no other volunteer regiment was equipped; he knew that that regiment had raised the first flag raised by the army in Cuba; had killed the first Spaniard killed by the army in Cuba; had lost the first man lost by the army in Cuba; had led every battle fought by the army in Cuba, and he knew that his own personal efforts were responsible for the fact that the army in Cuba, its work well done, was going North again to escape the one enemy it could not fight—the fever.

Is it a wonder that Teddy Roosevelt showed his teeth as he rode through Santiago! I have known him and seen him as Civil Service Commissioner, as Police Commissioner, as he went into his first battle, as he was inaugurated Governor of the State of New York, and yet I doubt if I have ever known him at a moment more satisfactory than that which I am now recording.

The regiment marched down the Alameda, skirting the water front, to the dock where the transport *Miami* was moored. The men were worn out, and their steps lagged as they turned toward home with a weariness which had not shown in them when they turned toward the enemy. They were haggard and ragged and hungry. A few new Khaki suits made bright yellow spots in the dull brown monotony of ragged duck uniforms. They were the punctuation marks of the story of trial and hardship which the clothes of the Rough Riders told as plainly as their faces did, and told much more plainly than their quietly enduring lips did when they reached the North and home.

It is not necessary to speak of the ghastly gaps in their ranks, which made the strong troopers wince as they looked at them.

The official story of the men who had died and were wounded in battle is told in the regimental roster which ends this book. The complete official story of the men who died in hospital—they were as brave as their comrades who were shot—cannot be told, because the records of the War Department have not been completed. Only seven living men were left behind in Cuba. These were Second Lieutenant Wm. Tiffany, of Troop K; Corporal Edgar Schwarz, of Troop G; and Privates Wm. E. Hoyle, of Troop E; F. G. Whalen, of Troop A, and F.G. Page, of Troop D. The men who left were sorry for the comrades who remained behind, but they were wild with joy over their own chance to get away.

Most of their tents and all their baggage had fallen prey to the marauding Cubans, who had ever followed our troops, so that they embarked in their skins and in their uniforms; they carried little else away from Cuba with them, except their arms and what ammunition they had not already been called upon to devote to Spanish enemies.

The embarkation was quick and easy. The regiment by this time had learned the trick of machine work and those little difficulties and delays which occurred in its early history no longer handicapped the men. From Santiago, Colonel Roosevelt sent this final message:

> We shall take home with us a record of which we have reason to be proud; we leave behind us a few Rough Riders who are too feeble to be moved, but we had a larger percentage of soldiers killed in battle than the percentage of loss by fever and disease.

Chapter 14

Home Again

The regiment came North in two sections. First were the men who, disappointed, disgruntled, and unhappy, arrived in Jersey City, August 10th, from Tampa. They were the men who have been spoken of as wearily waiting, hoping earnestly for orders to really go to the front, which never came. They came North on trains, and on these trains were such members of Troops C, H, I, and M as were strong enough to come. When they arrived, they were as hungry as they had been on that morning when they reached Tampa. Then, as now, they had been provided with insufficient rations. Then, as now, they had become the victims of the railroad company.

Their numbers had been sadly depleted by all kinds of sickness, and they were heartsick over their failure to go to Cuba, as well as bruised and worn by the terrific journey up from Tampa. They brought with them as many of the eleven hundred horses and mules, which had been left in their charge, as remained to be brought, and their minds were full of the discouraging fact that, during the war with Spain, they had only cared for animals. When they reached Jersey City, they had been without proper rations for more than twenty-four hours, and life seemed very dreary to them. Some factory girls divided their luncheons with them.

Five days later, a different sight entirely was enacted at Montauk, L. I., when the six troops who had really gone to Cuba, sailed in on the transport *Miami*. Their arrival was a scene of triumph. Unlike their equally brave comrades who had been forced to spend the war days among the sand flies and crackers of dismal Florida, they had actually been to war. Whatever fighting there had been to see they had seen. Many of them had felt the sting of Mauser bullets, and many others who had gone South with them remained there sleeping in rude graves on Cuban battlefields, mute evidences of the regiment's heroism.

Six troops were there. New York had been waiting for them, and preparing to receive them for many days. The deeds of daring which the Rough Riders had credited to themselves had been recorded by a thousand printing presses within the metropolis, and the stories read by seventy million eager eyes. The war was over. New York's own Seventy-First Regiment had fallen the victim of four or five incompetent and unpleasant officers, and come back to pass quietly into an ignominious oblivion, which was to be interrupted occasionally only by the shrill shouts of scandal. New York's Sixty-Ninth had had no opportunity to distinguish itself.

So, New York turned out to welcome the Rough Riders. They were not of New York, but New York was emphatically for them. Roosevelt, who was one of New York's favourite sons, had been promoted to their Colonelcy, and his name was whispered constantly as that of the man who would win, at this, the beginning of one of the State's most exciting gubernatorial campaigns.

It was long before daylight when the *Miami* pulled into the harbour, out there at the end of Long Island, but he did not find the men who were there to receive her, napping. The harbour was dotted with the white hulls of welcoming yachts, and as her name was signalled to the shore, these set up a deafening scream of welcome from their steam whistles. One or two, even, fired greeting guns.

For a long time, the troopship lay there in the harbour, waiting for orders from shore. All the morning, the yachts plied ceaselessly in discreet circles about the transport, and busy little steam launches ran as near to her as the health officers would permit, so that friends could shout merry messages to those on the *Miami*, and they could send ecstatic words of happiness back. Besides the six troops of Rough Riders, the *Miami* carried the four troops of the Third Cavalry, with General Joseph Wheeler and Lieut. Joseph Wheeler, Jr., as well. It was about noon, August 18th, and wild cheers from the waiting soldiers on shore marked the approach of the *Miami* towards the dock.
The gull-like yachts drew in more closely. The hustling little launches sputtered nearer than they had been permitted to go before.

A band on board struck up, "*When Johnny comes marching home again,*" and the cheering became general as the cables from the great steamer were made fast to the stanchions on the pier. When the gangplank was finally put down, everyone was cheering. The bluecoats on shore were yelling with an enthusiasm which they had not shown

From a photograph by H. R. Fullerton.   Colonel Roosevelt and his Staff at Montauk.

since they had reached Montauk. The civilian friends of the men on board were yelling with an enthusiasm which they had never known before, and the Rough Riders themselves were yelling with that enthusiasm which can only be appreciated by the soldier who has been away fighting, in a foreign land, against death in all its forms.

After the first three cheers, the men on board took up their cowboy yell, and from the *Miami* there rang out, as there had rung out at San Antonio, in Florida, and in Cuba, that bit of doggerel rhyme, which meant so much.

Rough, tough, we're the stuff,
We want to fight and we can't get enough,
Whoop-ee.

With the first glimpse of Roosevelt on the bridge of the ship, the crowd on shore went mad. He was the one paramount military hero of the war. He was the man on horseback in the politics of the State. He was Roosevelt. When "Teddy and his teeth" came down the gangplank, the last ultimate climax of the possibility of cheering was reached. He was bronzed by the Cuban sun, and his uniform was, worn out, and stained by the trials of the campaign. But he was happier than Theodore Roosevelt ever had been before, or probably ever will be again. He had come home to step into the superb inheritance which he had earned in Cuba.

A moment after Roosevelt had stepped upon the gangplank, General Wheeler ran forward, and taking him by the arm, came down with him. The Rough Riders who had been at Tampa had begged for the poor privilege of doing guard duty on the dock while their more fortunate comrades in arms stepped ashore, and they had great difficulty in keeping the soldiers and civilians alike, who were gathered on that dock, from rushing forward. When they saw the famous old Confederate cavalry commander and the famous New York hero walking down together, their enthusiasm knew no bounds, and their great desire was to pick them up and bear them on their shoulders. Crossed bayonets alone prevented this. From the dock itself, from the ground beyond it, and from the roofs of the freight cars standing on the tracks, ten thousand cheers went up.

General Young and his staff were on the pier, and were the first to greet the two famous soldiers. Just behind them, and close up to the guard line, was Mrs. General John A. Logan. She had been the very first to recognise Roosevelt when he appeared on the bridge of the ship, and was the first to rush forward and clasp his hands in both of hers as he stepped on the dock.

Roosevelt's men followed him down the gangplank in double file, with the company officers at the head of each troop, and if the cheering diminished as they came, it was only because the throats of the men who cheered had already become hoarse, and not because their heads were less full of enthusiasm. Individual greetings were shouted to many of the men by friends, some of whom had come from beyond the Mississippi to give them welcome that day.

The shouts of the crowd were only silenced when a soldier answered the cry:

"How are you, Sullivan?"

"I'm well, thank God," said Sullivan, "but more than half of my troop were left behind among the dead and sick at Santiago."

One man took off his hat to cheer again, but his voice was husky, and now as the spectators watched the ragged unshaved veterans march down that gangplank, they all uncovered, and this silence was more impressive than their preceding cheers had been. Fathers, mothers, brothers, sisters, sweethearts, and wives were in that crowd, and some of them looked in vain for the faces that they longed to see.

So, at the end, the landing of the troops at Montauk had a tinge of sadness cast over it, in sharp contrast to the exuberant joy with which it had begun.

The period the regiment passed at Montauk was, in some respects, like the days at San Antonio. Only at San Antonio the work of drill and discipline was constant. The men were expecting fight in those days and wanted to be prepared for it. At Montauk they had had their fight and wanted to forget it. They chose various ways of bringing about forgetfulness. I have seen newspaper stories to the effect that the Rough Riders were hard drinkers. As a matter of fact, they drank no more than other soldiers. There were plenty of available "canteens," or drinking places, at Montauk, but the proportion of Rough Riders who patronised them was no greater than the proportion of men who patronised them from other regiments.

One man, who lost his popularity in the regiment by doing it, wrote an article for a Chicago paper, saying that the men of the Rough Riders were likely to forget those safeguards which, in civilized communities, are supposed to surround the ownership of personal property. He was very properly thrown into the guard-tent for writing the story.

The general spirit of the men was more accurately caught during this period by a *New York Sun* writer, than by anyone else. For that reason, I shall take the liberty of quoting his article in very nearly its entirety. It was published in the *Sun* of Friday, September 16th. It follows:

"With their return to such parts of civilization as they originally hailed from, the Rough Riders will probably get back their given names, and they who have for the last four months answered to the general name of "Buddy," or the more specific cognomens of "Mike," "Reddy," "Pudge," "Pop-Eye" and the like, will once more, not without a feeling of strangeness, hear themselves greeted as Harry, James, Charley, Will, or whatever other name was bestowed on them at baptism.

"Almost the first thing that happened to the Rough Rider upon enlistment was to find himself the recipient of a name, very informally presented, according to no set rule, which might cling to him during the entire campaign, or might be replaced in the course of time by a sobriquet which some event would fasten upon the wearer. In this class belongs "Slimpnthx," which is the nearest expression possible with letters to the pronunciation of the very remarkable monosyllable designating a trooper who distinguished himself at Las Guasimas. After the first rush forward, when the Rough Riders were fighting frontier fashion, this particular private was heard between the sounds of the guns to repeat to himself in unwearying iteration a formula of words which, altogether meaningless at first, became simply a jumble of sound as the words came faster and the tone grew louder.

"Finally, it reached the vocal consistency of the word quoted above. Those near the utterer of the mystic tones opined that he was saying his prayers in Greek. He did not, however, appear to be in a panic, but cheered himself on with the strange word, for the faster and louder he shouted the more fiercely did he fight. When the battle was over several curious companions waited upon him with the intention of finding out the secret. Each had a try at repeating the sound, but the originator of it failed utterly to recognise it.

"Never said such a thing in my life," he declared. "You fellows have been listening too hard to the song of the Mausers."

"But the others insisted and kept on essaying the exclamation, until finally a light broke in upon the trooper, and he burst out laughing.

"Well, that's one on me," he said. "I remember now that I was repeating a set of words when I went into the row. I'd heard that it was a good thing to keep one's mind off himself in time of danger just to say over and over again some formula. I was afraid maybe I'd be rattled, so when the bullets began to sing I tried to remember some rhyme or something, and the only thing that came into my head was, 'Six slim, slick saplings,' If ever you fellows tried that at school you'll know it's no snide of a piece to speak over and over, even when everything else is peaceful. I guess I got it pretty well mixed up, but by the time I got fairly into the fight I must have forgotten to stop saying it. I know my tongue feels kind of tangled yet."

"The explanation was accepted, and the trooper was henceforth known by his self-given nickname. A similar case of battlefield nomenclature was that of "Tarantula Hank," who was fighting valiantly in the trenches until one of the hideous and ferocious spiders came darting along toward him, whereupon he turned and fled, nor could he be persuaded to return until a comrade had smashed the tarantula with the butt of a carbine. "The Rockpicker" is a trooper who, while fighting in the trenches, had his carbine ruined by a Mauser bullet, whereupon, in a wild access of wrath, he rose and begun to hurl rocks toward the Spanish lines with furious imprecations.

"As the nearest Spanish fire was directed from a spot fully a third of a mile away, it is not supposed that he added appreciably to the day's carnage. "Pills," a name which by right belongs to the troop surgeon, was bestowed upon a corporal, who, during a swift advance, was heard to rattle like rain upon a tin roof, a phenomenon afterward explained by the fact that his shirt was full of pill boxes. Later on, those pills were of great value to his troop. Many of the nicknames were conferred in a spirit of derision, their basis lying in contrast. Two men of diametrically opposite type were assigned to bunk together in the same tent, and eventually became sworn friends.

"One was the typical fastidious clubman, the other a tobacco-chewing, cursing, rough-and-ready bad man from the middle West. Immediately the clubman was christened "Tough Ike," and his bunkie became known through the regiment as "That Damn Dude," or for short, "The D.D." "Metropolitan Bill" was a citizen of the far West whose chief claim to being a city man was that he had an aunt living in New York. "Sheeny Solomon," sometimes called "Ole Clo'es," was a red-headed Irishman, 6 feet 2 in his stocking feet. The "Immigrant" was a trooper whose family helped settle New York. "Rubber-Shoe Andy" distinguished himself and won his name on scouting duty by invariably tumbling over something with a great clatter at the very moment when silence was most essential.

"There were three bald-headed men in one troop, known, of course, as the Sutherland Sisters—Sister Jane, Sister Anne and Sister Araminta. A young fellow—and a mighty good fighter, too-proud of his Jewish blood, accepted with perfect equanimity the nickname of the "Pork Chop." In the same troop with him was a private who was probably the mildest spoken man in the army; one evening, however, he got excited over something and was plainly heard by several auditors, whose testimony is unimpeachable, to exclaim: "Oh, thunder!" That settled his case. He was known ever after as "Blasphemy Bill." A Mississippi River gambler, noted for his quiet demeanour, was called "Hellroarer," while the most picturesquely and flamboyantly profane man in the regiment rejoiced in the appellation of "Prayerful James."

"The fun-maker for one troop was a light-hearted Swede, always full of jokes, and because of his propensities and his nationality called the "Weeping Dutchman." "N———r" was a young fellow so white as to be almost an albino. "Beefsteak John" had many times called down the wrath of his famine-stricken comrades by describing to them just how he would like a steak cooked at that particular moment, how it should be two inches thick, delicately brown outside and deep red inside, and how the melted butter should flow over it.

"To a cowboy who arose one night and fled through the camp in his dreams, under the impression that he was being pursued by an army of scorpions, his Eastern bunkie has given the name of "The Wicked Flea," because, as he says, it was a plain case of "no man pursueth," until a sentry collared the fugitive. It goes without saying that at the start all the fat men were called "Living Skeleton," "Beanpole," "Shadow," "Starvation Bill," "Dr. Tanner" and so on, while the thin troopers were generally designated as "Jumbo," "Heavyweight," "Anti-Fat" and the like. Before the return the former list had dwindled to nothing, and the inventive genius of the self-appointed godfathers was taxed to find new names for those who had fortunately preserved their bones, but left most of the covering thereon in Cuba.

"To act as Col. Roosevelt's orderly was an honour to which every trooper aspired. It was not always an easy berth, as the colonel covered a great deal of ground and kept his orderlies hustling, and had, moreover, a habit of noticing everything that was going on. A Rough Rider who was detailed one day to act as the colonel's orderly in Cuba relates that the two of them had ridden to El Caney, where, while his commanding officer was attending to some business, the orderly contrived to acquire by purchase several bottles of Jamaica rum, which he disposed of in a nose bag. the return Col. Roosevelt set a lively pace, as is his habit, and the nosebag began to dispense music.

"*Clink-clink, clinkety-clink, clinkety-clinkety-clink,*" it went.

"Smith," said Col. Roosevelt, pulling in his horse, "what is that noise?"

"Sounds like glass, sir," said the orderly.

"So, it does. Where does it come from, Smith?"

"From my nosebag, sir."

"Indeed! And what have you got in that nose bag?"

"Purchases, sir."

"What?" said Col. Roosevelt, his brow wrinkling.

"Purchases, sir," repeated the orderly, firmly, but trembling in his boots.

"Hm! I should think so," snorted the colonel, and rode on.

The clinking continued. Presently the colonel pulled up again.

"Smith!"

"Yes, sir."

"At the turn of the road there is a tree with large soft leaves. I wish you would stuff some of them into that nose bag. It makes too much noise."

"Yes, sir," said the orderly.

There was a pause and the colonel rode on.

"Besides," he added, with a smile, suddenly turning in his saddle. "Some of those—er—purchases might smash. And you never can tell whom we might meet."

"At the tree the orderly packed the nose bag with leaves, which deadened the sound. Five minutes later they met a general on the road, but the nose bag was safely muffled, and Col. Roosevelt's foresight was gloriously vindicated."

On the 13th of September, the Rough Riders were paid off; they had been in the service almost exactly five months, and so each man received something like five times $15.50. Now $77 is a fortune to any man who has not seen the colour of money for several weeks, and is likely to be received by such with great enthusiasm. It is a question, if the men were happier when they heard of the surrender of Santiago than they were when they were paid off at Montauk.

It was all over before one o'clock; at that hour a committee of embarrassed troopers waited upon Colonel Roosevelt at his tent and asked him if he minded stepping over to a rough pine table, which stood unsteadily on uneven ground. His command was informally drawn up in a square of which this table formed the centre. Upon the table was a curious something, full of knobs and bunches and covered by a horse blanket. Lieutenant-Colonel Brodie happened along just then, and taking Roosevelt by the arm, conducted him to a place in front of the table.

Up to this time Roosevelt had not known what was coming. The breathless silence which pervaded the place and the curious expectant manner of his troopers warned him now that something pleasant was likely to presently occur. His face, already tanned to a deep dark brown, took on the ruddy hue of a Cuban veteran's blush, and he stood there awkwardly, not knowing what to do. There was a pause while he looked about at the men who followed him so bravely at Guasimas and San Juan. H saw that in the eyes of some of them the tears were beginning to start, and while he waited, his own were dimmed with moisture.

From the ranks of M Troop stepped William S. Murphy, who, although he was a private in the regiment, had been a judge in the Indian Territory at the time of his enlistment, and was known as one of the most eloquent men in that part of the West. He took off his campaign hat and presented the colonel with Frederick Remington's famous "Bronco Buster." Murphy had prepared an elaborate speech, which would have done honour to the Indian Territory courts, but he couldn't speak it, and if he had, most of the men in the regiment would not have heard it.

The chaps who had followed Roosevelt through the terrible hardships of the whole campaign, who had endured their wounds without complaining, and who had stood their sickness without once crying out, gave way this day for the first time. There was almost no one in the regiment who was not crying, when Murphy said, with streaming eyes:

> It is fitting that I, one of the troopers from the ranks of your regiment, should try to tell you as well as I can, to what is due the honour given me in making this presentation. It is well known that while you hold your officers in the highest esteem, because of their bravery, gallantry, and ability, your heart of hearts was ever with your men, whether in the tented field or in the trenches before the enemy's lines, or better still, in the

Photographed by H. E. Fullerton just before the regiment was mustered out at Montauk.

The Last Guard.

trenches which your regiment captured from the enemy.

I want to tell you, sir, that one and all of us, from the highest of us to the humblest of us, will always carry with us in our hearts a pleasant and a loving memory of your every act, for there has not been one among them which has not been of the kindest. As lieutenant-colonel of our regiment, you first made us respect you; as our colonel you have taught us to love you deeply, as men love men. It is our sincerest hope, now that we are about to separate, that this bronze 'Bronco Buster' will sometimes make you think of us, as we shall ever think of you.

It was a strange thing to see these strong men, who had, while they were together, been through so much, standing there almost overcome by emotion, when the moment came for them to part. Roosevelt spoke briefly and he faltered often. He said:

Officers and Men: I really do not know how to answer you. Nothing could touch and please me as this has touched and pleased me. Trooper Murphy spoke quite truly when he said that my men were nearest to my heart, for while I need not tell to my officers in what deep regard I hold them, they will not mind my saying, that just a little closer come my men.

I have never tried to coddle you, and I have never made a baby of any one of you. I have never hesitated to call upon you to spend your best blood like water and to work your muscles to the breaking point. Of course, I have tried to do all that I could do for you, as you have ever done all that you could ever do for me. You are the best judges as to whether or not I have succeeded.

I am proud of this regiment beyond measure; I am proud of it, because it is a typical American regiment, made up of typical American men. The foundation of the regiment was the 'Bronco Buster,' and we have him here in bronze. The men of the West and the men of the Southwest, horsemen, riflemen, and herders of cattle, have been the backbone of this regiment, as they are the backbone of their sections of the country. This demonstrates that Uncle Sam has nobler reserve of fighting men to call upon, if the necessity arises, than any other country in the world.

The West stands ready now to furnish tens of thousands of men like you, who are only samples of what our country can produce. Besides the cow-puncher, this regiment contains men from every section of the country and from every State within the Union. This shows us that the West is not alone in its ability to furnish men like you. This gives us double reason to feel proud on this day when we disband.

I have profound respect for you, men of the Rough Riders, not only because you have fighting qualities, but because you also have those qualities which made men recognise you all fighters, and enabled you to be among the first who found the opportunity of getting into the fight. Outside of my own immediate family, I shall always feel that stronger ties exist between me and you than exist between me and anyone else on earth. If your feeling toward me is like mine towards you, I am more than pleased to have you tell me of it.

I realised when I took charge of you, that I was taking upon myself a grave responsibility. I cared for you as individuals, but I did not forget at any moment that it might be necessary to sacrifice the comfort or even the lives of the individuals, in order to ensure the safety of the whole. You would have scorned a commander, who hesitated for a second to expose you to any risk. I was bound that no other regiment should get any nearer to the Spanish lines than you got, and I do not think that any other regiment did.

We parted with many in the fights who could ill be spared, and I think that the most vivid memories we will take away with us will be not of our own achievements, not of our own dangers, not of our own suffering, but will be of those whom we left under Cuban sod and those who died in the hospitals in the United States—the men who died from wounds and the men who, with the same devotion to their country, died from fevers—I cannot mention all the names now, but three of them, Capron, O'Neill, and Fish, will suffice. They died in the pride of their youthful strength and they died for their country, like men who were proud to die.

I should have been most deeply touched if the officers of this regiment had given me this testimonial, but I appreciate it tenfold, as coming from you, my men. You shared the hardships of the campaign with me; when I had none, you gave me of your hardtack, and if I lay coverless, I never lacked a blanket from my men to lie upon.

To have such a gift come from this peculiarly American regiment, touches me more than I can say. It is something that I shall hand down to my children, and value more highly than I do the weapons which I carried through the campaign with me.

Now, boys, I wish to take each of you by the hand, as a special privilege, and say goodbye to you individually; this is to be our farewell in camp; I hope that it will not be our farewell in civil life.

Then the men were mustered out of the service of Uncle Sam. Colonel Roosevelt ceased to be a soldier when his men did. He jumped into one of the camp stages, taking with him Lieutenants John C. Greenway, John A. McIlhenny, Chas. Ballard, and Hal Sayre. They were his guests at Oyster Bay for several days, and on the morrow, Lieutenants David Goodrich and R. H. Ferguson joined them there. A large party of Rough Riders gave him a rousing goodbye at the station and he went away wearing his worn and stained uniform—the same which had carried him through one of the most extraordinary campaigns known in the history of warfare.

During the stay at Camp Wikoff, an effort was made to organise a permanent Rough Riders' Association. Lieutenant-Colonel Brodie was elected president of it, and one or two meetings were held, after the men were mustered out. So many of them departed immediately for their homes that by no means all the members of the regiment have as yet been inscribed as members of this organisation, but it will undoubtedly be eventually put on a firmer basis than it now occupies.

The exodus of the Rough Riders was rapid. The camp seemed dead after they had gone away. Only one remained. This was Lieutenant-Colonel Brodie, who, because of his wounds, had been promoted from a majorship to the second place in command. His chief aim, after he had ceased to be a soldier, was to find a man in the uniform of a second lieutenant, who had sold him a horse the day before. Shortly after he had bought and paid for the animal, another officer walked up to the line where he was picketed, and surprisedly remarked:

"Hello! who tied my horse here?"

Then he took away the horse, which really belonged to him.

Colonel Brody is still searching for the lieutenant who sold the horse to him.

And thus ended the Rough Riders, as a regiment.

CHAPTER 15

In New York

The Rough Riders made almost as much of an impression on New York City as they had made on Cuba, although the carnage was not so great. Discipline forgotten, the articles of war no longer an important consideration, and home in immediate prospect, they started out with what enthusiasm they had at their command—and it was much—to make things as hot in the metropolis as they had been in Daiquiri, on that never-to-be-forgotten time of landing. The officers of the regiment went as one man to the Hoffman House, although it was understood that the Fifth Avenue Hotel would be Colonel Roosevelt's headquarters, because it was the headquarters of the Republican Committee.

Troop H reached New York at midnight, and got lodgings in the Olive Tree Inn, on East 23rd Street. That midnight was a hot midnight for New York City, and it is not likely that the proprietors of the Olive Tree Inn will ever forget the fact that the Rough Riders took lodging there.

Troops K, M, and B paused temporarily in Long Island City. I will not say that the Red Cross people who cared for them there are sorry that they did, but it is unquestionably true that they will never forget the fact that the men of troops K, M, and B paused in Long Island City, and that they were cared for by the people of the Red Cross.

New York was dotted with their brown uniforms early after the first day of the Rough Riders' release. Probably half of them visited Broadway, and the same half later found things to interest them in other parts of New York City. Not one of them had removed his uniform, and so the public readily recognised them. Hundreds of civilians forced their hospitality upon them. Four of them went to the Stock Exchange. They were instantly spotted by the members and were taken to the floor, an honour accorded to few. Whoever was of great financial interest in the building at the time was formally introduced to them, and no one was introduced to them who was not glad to be. The old building on Wall Street resounded for hours with cheers for the regiment, and their presence there really had its decided effect upon business for that day.

An interesting episode of the evening occurred on Broadway. Six of them paused to explain to a Broadway policeman that he didn't dare arrest them because, if he did, they would sick Roosevelt on him. He was considerably puzzled by the strange situation, and was about to rap for assistance when he discovered that one of the invading troopers was his long-lost brother.

He didn't rap.

The other five joined hands about the two reunited ones, and danced a war-dance which blocked Broadway. And so, it went. Wherever the Rough Riders could go, they journeyed, and wherever they journeyed they owned the town.

Troop H assembled at the Hoffman House and had a little celebration at the expense of Captain Curry. It was formally announced that night that $1,000 would be paid for any horse that Sergeant Tom Darnell could not ride.

At the Hotel Imperial, the men of Troop K were gathered, and L Troop held a farewell session at the Grand Union. Very late in the evening, a number of the officers gathered at the Holland House and said their last goodbyes.

And so ended the Rough Riders.

With the dawning of the next day many of them were on the trains, speeding towards their distant homes. Some of the Westerners have stayed East and some of the Easterners have gone West. The regiment is broken up and scattered.

Vale to it.

It was the greatest fighting machine that any army ever held.

Vale.

Roster

THE ROSTER OF THE ROUGH RIDERS.

(1st U. S. VOLUNTEER CAVALRY.)

FROM THE OFFICIAL MUSTER-OUT ROLLS IN THE WAR DEPARTMENT.

Secured for this volume through the great kindness of Hon. R. A. Alger, Secretary of War, and the prompt courtesy of Col. F. C. Ainsworth, Chief of the Bureau of Records, War Department.

FIELD AND STAFF.

NAME.	RANK.	PLACE OF RESIDENCE.	REMARKS.
Theodore Roosevelt	Colonel	New York, N. Y.	
Alexander O. Brodie	Lt. Colonel	Prescott, Ariz.	Wounded in action at La Guasima, Cuba, June 24, 1898. Gunshot right forearm.
Henry B. Hersey	Major	Santa Fé, N. M.	
George M. Dunn	Major	Denver, Col.	
Micah J. Jenkins	Major	Youngs Island, S. C.	
Henry A. Brown	Chaplain	Prescott, Ariz.	
Maxwell Keyes	1st Lt. & Adjt.	San Antonio, Tex.	
Sherrard Coleman	1st Lt. & Qr. Mr.	Santa Fé, N. M.	
Ernest Stecker	Sergt. Major	Los Angeles, Cal.	
Matthew Douthett	Qr. Mr. Sergt.	Denver, Col.	
Clay Platt	Cf. Trumpeter	San Antonio, Tex.	
Joseph F. Kansky	Saddler Sergt	Tacoma, Wash.	

Loss. Promoted.

| Leonard Wood | Colonel. | | |

Resigned.		
Thomas W. Hall......	1st Lt. & Adjt......	Resigned as 1st Lieut. and Adjt., Aug. 1, 1898, S. O. No. 175, A. G. O., July 29, '98.
Jacob Schwaizer......	1st Lt. & Qr. Mr. El Reno, O. T......	Resigned his commission as 1st Lieut., Aug. 4, 1898. Resignation, Sept. 7, 1898.
Discharged.		
Joseph A. Carr........	Sergt. Major.... Washington, D. C......	Discharged at San Antonio, Tex., to accept 1st Lieut. in Regiment, May 19, 1898.
Christian Madsen...	R. Q. M. Sergt... El Reno, O. T......	Discharged on disability Aug. 26, 1898. Disease contracted in line of duty.
Deserted.		
Alfred E. Lewis......	R. Q. M. Sergt......	Deserted from Camp at San Antonio, Tex., on or about May 5, 1898.

HISTORICAL RECORD.

Under act of Congress, approved April 22, 1898, the 1st Regiment U. S. Volunteer Cavalry was organized at San Antonio, Tex., between May 9 and 19, 1898. Troops A, B, and C comprised of men mostly from Arizona, D from Oklahoma Territory, E, F, G, H, and I New Mexico, K New York and the Eastern States, and L and M from the Indian Territory.

The troops were instructed, armed, and equipped until May 29, when, in compliance with telegraphic instructions from A. G. O. dated July 27, 1898, the regiment proceeded by rail to Tampa, Fla., arriving thereat June 3.

June 8. Headquarters Troops A, B, D, E, F, G, K, L (two squadrons), consisting of 30 officers and 580 men, left Tampa, proceeded to and boarded the troopship Yucatan in Port Tampa Bay, and formed part of the first military expedition against the Spaniards in Cuba.

June 22. Arrived at Daiquiri.
June 23. Marched to Siboney.
June 24. Marched to Las Guasimas with 29 officers and 560 men; engaged and defeated the Spanish forces at that place, with the loss of 1 officer and 7 men killed, and 3 officers and 29 men wounded in action.
June 30. Marched to El Poso.

167

July 1. Participated in the San Juan engagement, with 26 officers and 502 men; defeated and pursued the enemy to Santiago. Loss, 1 officer and 14 men killed, 5 officers and 69 men wounded.
July 2 to 17. Duty in the trenches before Santiago when the city and province surrendered.
July 18. Marched to regular camp near El Caney.
August 7. Marched to Santiago, boarded the troopship Miami, and returned to the United States.
August 15. Landed at Montauk Point, L. I., N. Y., and went into detention camp.
August 19. Marched to regular camp, rejoined Troops C, H, I, and M, which remained at Tampa until August 7, and performed regular duties until September 15, 1898, when the regiment was mustered out of service.

TROOP A.

Name.	Rank.	Place of Residence.	Remarks.
Frank Frantz	Captain	Prescott, Ariz.	
John C. Greenway	1st Lieutenant	Hot Springs, Ark.	
Joshua D. Carter	2d Lieutenant	Prescott, Ariz.	Shot in foot and leg July 1, '98. Engaged La Guasima, June 24; San Juan, July 1.
William W. Greenwood	1st Sergeant	"	Wounded July 1, '98. Eng'd La Guasima June 24; San Juan, July 1, & siege Santiago.
James T. Greenley	Sergeant	"	
King C. Henley	Q. M. Sergeant	Winslow, Ariz.	
Henry W. Nash	Sergeant	Young, Ariz.	
Samuel H. Rhodes	"	Tonto Basin, Ariz.	
Robert Brown	"	Prescott, Ariz.	
Charles E. McGarr	"	"	
Carl Holtzschue	"	"	
George L. Bugbee	Corporal	Lordsburg, N. M.	
Harry G. White	"	Richenbar, Ariz.	Absent from July 2 in Governor's Island Hospital, wound in leg, received July 2.

168

Name	Rank	Residence	Remarks
Cade C. Jackson	Corporal	Flagstaff, Ariz.	
Harry B. Fox	"	Jerome, Ariz.	
William Craufurd	"	San Antonio, Tex.	
George A. McCarter	"	Safford, Ariz.	
Rufus H. Marine	"	Flagstaff, Ariz.	
John D. Honeyman	"	San Antonio, Tex.	Wounded in hand on July 2, 1898.
Emilio Cassi	Trumpeter	Jerome, Ariz.	
Frank Harner	"	Prescott, Ariz.	
Thomas Hamilton	Blacksmith	Jerome, Ariz.	
Wallace B. Willard	Farrier	Cottonwood, Ariz.	
Forest Whitney	Saddler	Richenbar, Ariz.	
John H. Wallar	Wagoner	Prescott, Ariz.	Wounded in arm in battle of July 1, 1898. Left arm, slight.
Adams, Ralph R.	Private	Yonkers, N. Y.	
Allen, George L.	"	Prescott, Ariz.	
Azbill, John	"	St. Johns, Ariz.	
Azbill, William *	"	"	
Arnold, Henry N.	"	New York City.	
Barnard, John C.	"	"	
Bartoo, Nelson E.	"	Winslow, Ariz.	
Belknap, Prescott H.	"	Boston, Brookline, Mass.	
Brauer, Lee W.	"	Richmond, Va.	
Bugbee, Fred W.	"	Lordsburg, N. M.	Wounded in head in battle of San Juan, July 1, 1898, slight.
Bull, Charles C.	"	San Francisco, Cal.	
Bulzing, William	"	Santa Fé, N. M.	
Burke, Edward F.	"	Orange, N. J.	
Bardshar, Henry P.	"	Prescott, Ariz.	
Church, Leroy B.	"	Ithaca, Mich.	
Curtis, Harry A.	"	Boston, Mass.	
Freeman, Thomas L.	"	Thurber, Tex.	

TROOP A—*Continued.*

Name.	Rank.	Place of Residence.	Remarks.
Griffen, Walter W.	Private	Globe, Ariz.	
Glover, William H.	"	Liberty, Tex.	
Hawes, George P., Jr.	"	Richmond, Va.	
Haymon, Edward G. B.	"	Chicago, Ill.	
Huffman, Lawrance E.	"	Las Cruzes, Mex.	
Hoffman, Fred	"	Pueblo, Colo	
Hodgdon, Charles E.	"	Prescott, Ariz.	
Hogan, Daniel L.	"	Flagstaff, Ariz.	
Howard, John L.	"	St. Louis, Mo.	
Hubbell, John D.	"	Boston, Mass.	
Jackson, Charles B.	"	Prescott, Ariz.	Wounded in neck in battle of San Juan, July 1, 1898. Slight.
Johnson, John W.	"	Kingman, Ariz.	
Lefors, Jefferson D.	"	Prescott, Ariz.	
Lewis, William F.	"	Congress, Ariz.	
Larned, William A.	"	Summit, N. J.	
Le Roy, Arthur M.	"	Prescott, Ariz.	
May, James A.	"	Safford, Ariz.	
McCarty, Frank	"	Flagstaff, Ariz.	
Mills, Charles E.	"	Cedar Rapids, Ia.	
Murchie, Guy	"	Calais, Me.	
Osborne, George	"	Bungenders, N. S. W., Aus.	
O'Brien, Edward	"	Jerome, Ariz.	Wounded in head by shrapnel morning of July 2, 1898.
Page, William	"	Richenbar, Ariz.	
Perry, Charles B.	"	Perry's Landing, Tex.	Shot in the head July 2, 1898. (John Perry.) Severe.

Paxton, Frank	Private	Safford, Ariz.	
Pearsall, Paul S.	"	New York, N. Y.	
Pettit, Louis P.	"	Flagstaff, Ariz.	
Philip, Hoffman	"	Washington, D. C.	
Pierce, Harry B.	"	Central City, N. M.	
Raudebaugh, James D.	"	Flagstaff, Ariz.	
Rapp, Adolph	"	San Antonio, Tex.	
Sells, Henry	"	Flagstaff, Ariz.	
Sellers, Henry J.	"	Williams, Ariz.	
Sewall, Henry F.	"	New York, N. Y.	
Shaw, James A.	"	Prescott, Ariz.	
Shanks, Lee P.	"	Paducah, Ky.	
Stark, Wallace J.	"	Safford, Ariz.	
Sullivan, Patrick J.	"	Prescott, Ariz.	
Thomas, Rufus K.	"	Boston, Mass.	
Thompson, Jos. F., Jr.	"	Washington, D.	
Tuttle, Arthur L.	"	Safford, Ariz.	
Van Sielen, Frank	"	" "	
Wager, Oscar G.	"	Jerome, Ariz.	
Wallace, Walter D.	"	Flagstaff, Ariz.	
Wallace, William F.	"	" "	Wounded in neck in battle of San Juan, July 1, 1898.
Wayland, Thomas J.	"	Williams, Ariz.	
Webb, Adelbert D.	"	Safford, Ariz.	
Weil, Henry J.	"	Kingman, Ariz.	
Wilson, Jerome	"	Chloride, Ariz.	
Wrenn, Robert D.	"	Chicago, Ill.	
Discharged.			
Garret, Samuel H.	"	Prescott, Ariz.	Honorably discharged the service by order A. G. O. Spec'l order No. 14, Aug. 24, '98.

171

TROOP A—Continued.

Name.	Rank.	Place of Residence.	Remarks.
Discharged.			
Greenwald, Sam	Private	Prescott, Ariz.	Discharged by authority of Secretary of War, at Camp Wikoff, Aug. 31, 1898.
McCornick, Willis	"	Salt Lake City, Utah	Honorably discharged the service Aug. 23, 1898, by order Secretary of War.
Killed in Action.			
William O. O'Neill	Captain	Prescott, Ariz.	Engaged and killed in battle of San Juan, July 1, '98, by gunshot wound in the head.
George H. Doherty	Corporal	Jerome, Ariz.	Engaged and killed in the battle of Las Guasimas June 24, by bullet wound in head.
Boyle, James	Private	Prescott, Ariz.	Engaged in and mortally wounded in battle San Juan, July 1, '98; shot through neck and body; died July 2, '98.
Champlin, Fred E.	"	Flagstaff, Ariz.	Eng'd in battle of Las Guasimas, June 24, 1898; and battle San Juan, July 1, 1898, where he was mortally wounded. Died July 2, '98; shot in the leg and foot by shrapnel, and arm torn off by shell.
Liggett, Edward	"	Jerome, Ariz.	Eng'd and killed in battle of Las Guasimas, June 24, 1898. Shot through the body.
Reynolds, Lewis	"	Kingman, Ariz.	Killed on July 1, '98. Shot thr'h stomach.
Died of Disease.			
Hollister, Stanley	"	Santa Barbara, Cal.	Wounded thigh July 2, severe. Died typhoid Gen. U. S. Hosp., Fortress Monroe, Aug. 17.
Wallace, Alexander H.	"	Pasadena, Cal.	Died of typhoid fever at St. Peter's Hospital, Brooklyn, Aug. 31, 1898.

Name	Rank	Residence	Remarks
Walsh, George	Private	San Francisco, Cal	Died aboard S.S. Miami, Aug. 11, chronic dysentery; buried at sea Aug. 12, '98.
Suicide.			
De Vol, Harry P	"	San Antonio, Tex	While in guard house, Camp Wikoff, died of self-inflicted wound in the head.
Deserter.			
Jackson, John W	"	Jerome, Ariz	Deserted the service at Tampa, Fla., July 7.

TROOP B.

Name	Rank	Residence	Remarks
James H. McClintock	Captain	Phoenix, Ariz	Wounded at battle of Las Guasimas, June 24, 1898. Wounded in left ankle.
George B. Wilcox	1st Lieutenant	Prescott, Ariz	
Thomas H. Rymning	2d Lieutenant	Tucson, Ariz	
William A. Davidson	1st Sergeant	Phoenix, Ariz	
Stephen A. Pate	Q. M. Sergt	Tucson, Ariz	Wounded in right lung before Santiago de Cuba, July 1, 1898. Severe.
Elmer Hawley	Sergeant	Phoenix, Ariz	
John E. Campbell	"	"	
Charles H. Uttling	"	"	
Edward G. Norton	"	"	
David L. Hughes	"	Tucson, Ariz	Wounded in head July 1, 1898, at battle before Santiago de Cuba. Severe.
Jerry F. Lee	"	Globe, Ariz	Shot in head before Santiago de Cuba July 1, 1898. Severe.
Eugene W. Waterbury	Corporal	Tucson, Ariz	
Walter T. Gregory	"	Phoenix, Ariz	

TROOP B—Continued.

NAME.	RANK.	PLACE OF RESIDENCE.	REMARKS.
Thos. W. Pemberton, Jr.	Corporal	Phoenix, Ariz.	
George J. McCabe	"	Bisbee, Ariz.	
Calvin McCarthy	"	Phoenix, Ariz.	
Charles E. Heitman	"	"	
Frank Ward	"	Globe, Ariz.	
Dudly S. Dean	"	Boston, Mass.	
John Foster	Bugler	Bisbee, Ariz.	
Jesse Walters	"	Phoenix, Ariz.	
Frank W. Harmson	Farrier	Tucson, Ariz.	
Fred. A. Pomeroy	Blacksmith	Kingman, Ariz.	
Joseph E. McGinty	Wagoner	Tucson, Ariz.	
Richard E. Goodwin	Saddler	Phoenix, Ariz.	
Boggs, Looney L.	"	"	
Buckholdt, Charles	Private	Kickapoo Springs, Tex.	
Beebe, Walter S.	"	Prescott, Ariz.	
Brady, Fred. L.	"	New York, N. Y.	
Butler, James A.	"	Albuquerque, N. M.	
Barrowe, Beekman K.	"	Tampa, Fla.	
Colwell, Grant	"	Phoenix, Ariz.	
Collier, Edward G.	"	Globe, Ariz.	
Chester, Will M.	"	Oakville, Tex.	
Christiain, Benjamin	"	Norfolk, Va.	
Chamberlin, Lowell A.	"	Washington, D. C.	
Day, Robert	"	Santa Fé, N. M.	
Drachman, Sol. B.	"	Tucson, Ariz.	
Draper, Durward D.	"	Phoenix, Ariz.	
Eakin, Alva L.	"	Globe, Ariz.	

Eads, Wade Q.	Private		San Antonio, Tex.	
Fitzgerald, Frank T.	"		Tucson, Ariz.	
Goss, Conrad F.	"		Tampa, Fla.	
Gurney, Frank W.	"		"	
Hall, John M.	"		Phoenix, Ariz.	Wounded in shoulder July 1st before Santiago de Cuba. Piece of shell not removed.
Hammer, John S.	"		San Antonio, Tex.	Slightly wounded by shell July 1st, before Santiago. Wounded in leg. Knee.
Hildreth, Fenn S.	"		Tucson, Ariz.	
Hartzell, Ira C.	"		Phoenix, Ariz.	
Haydon, Roy F.	"		Prescott, Ariz.	
Henderson, Sibird	"		Globe, Ariz.	
Hildebrand, Louis T.	"		Prescott, Ariz.	
Heywood, John P.	"		Tampa, Fla.	
James, William T.	"		Jerome, Ariz.	
Johnson, Anton E.	"		Prescott, Ariz.	
Keir, Alex. S.	"		"	
King, Geo. C.	"		Bisbee, Ariz.	
Laird, Thomas J.	"		Prescott, Ariz.	
Merritt, Fred M.	"		Tucson, Ariz.	
Merritt, William W.	"		Red Oak, Iowa.	
McCann, Walter J.	"		Phoenix, Ariz.	Stanchion fell upon right side of head, on transport Yucatan, June 21, 1898.
Middleton, Clifton C.	"		Globe, Ariz.	
Misner, Jackson H.	"		Bisbee, Ariz.	
McMillen, Albert C.	"		New York, N. Y.	
Norton, Gould G.	"		Tampa, Fla.	
Orme, Norman L.	"		Phoenix, Ariz.	Shot in left arm and side, June 24, 1898, at Las Guasimas.
Owens, William A.	"		Jerome, Ariz.	
Profitt, William B.	"		Prescott, Ariz.	

TROOP B—Continued.

Name.	Rank.	Place of Residence.	Remarks.
Peck, John C.	Private	Santa Fé, N. M.	
Pollock, Horatio C.	"	Phoenix, Ariz.	
Patterson, Hal A.	"	Selma, Ala.	
Roberts, Frank S.	"	San Antonio, Tex.	
Rinehart, Robert	"	Phoenix, Ariz.	
Stanton, Richard H.	"	"	
Saunders, Wellman H.	"	Salem, Mass.	
Snodderly, Wm. L.	"	Bisbee, Ariz.	
Smith, Race H.	"	San Antonio, Tex.	Shot in stomach, breast, and arms by shrapnel July 2, 1898, before Santiago. Severe.
Schenck, Frank W.	"	Phoenix, Ariz.	
Stewart, W. Walton	"	Selma, Ala.	
Toland, Jesse T.	"	Bisbee, Ariz.	
Truman, Geo. E.	"	San Antonio, Tex.	
Townsend, Albert B.	"	Prescott, Ariz.	
Tilkie, Charles M	"	Chicago, Ill.	
Van Treese, Louis H.	"	Tucson, Ariz.	
Warford, David E.	"	Globe, Ariz.	Shot in both thighs July 1, 1898, before Santiago de Cuba. Severe.
Webb, William W.	"	Prescott, Ariz.	
Wiggins, Thomas W.	"	Bisbee, Ariz.	Shot in right hip at Las Guasimas, June 24, 1898. Bullet not extracted. G. S. left hip.
Whittaker, George C.	"	Silver City, N. M.	
Wilkerson, Wallace W.	"	Santa Fé, N. M.	
Woodward, Sidney H.	"	Kingman, Ariz.	
Young, Thomas H.	"	Phoenix, Ariz.	

Discharged.			
Bird, Marshall M.	Private		Discharged on disability. Fracture of skull and concussion of brain Aug. 8, 1898.
Cronin, Cornelius P.	"	Yuma, Ariz.	Discharged June 13, 1898, on surgeon's certificate.
Crimmins, Martin L.	"		Mustered out to accept commission July 29, 1898.
Goodrich, David M.	"	Akron, O.	Discharged May 19, 1898, to accept commission.
Murphy, James E.	"	Debrio	Discharged Sept. 10th by Secretary of War. Shot in head July 1, 1898, Santiago. Face.
Died.			
Hall, Joel R.	Corporal	Seattle, Wash.	Killed July 1, 1898, before Santiago de Cuba. Buried on field of battle.
Logue, David	Private	Globe, Ariz.	Killed July 1, 1898, before Santiago de Cuba. Buried on field of battle.
Norton, Oliver B.	"		Killed July 1, 1898, before Santiago de Cuba. Buried on field of battle.
Swetnam, John W.	"	Globe, Ariz.	Killed July 1, 1898, before Santiago de Cuba. Buried on field of battle.
Tomlinson, Leroy E.	"		Sent to hospital boat June 19. Fever. Certificate of death dated June 23, 1898.

TROOP C.

Name.	Rank.	Place of Residence.	Remarks.
Joseph L. B. Alexander	Captain	Phoenix, Ariz.	
Robert S. Patterson	1st Lieutenant	Safford, Ariz.	
Hal. Sayre, Jr.	2d Lieutenant	Denver, Col.	
Willis O. Huson	1st Sergeant	Yuma, Ariz.	
James H. Maxey	Qr. Mr. Sergt.	Yuma, Ariz.	
Sam W. Noyes	Sergeant	Tucson, Ariz.	
Adam H. Klingman	"	Flagstaff, Ariz.	
Sumner K. Gerard	"	New York, N. Y.	
John McAndrew	"	Congress Junction, Ariz.	
Eldridge E. Jordan	"	Phoenix, Ariz.	
Wilbur D. French	Corporal	Safford, Ariz.	
Hendrick M. Warren	"	Phoenix, Ariz.	
Bruce C. Weathers	"	Safford, Ariz.	
Frank A. Woodin	"	Phoenix, Ariz.	
Charles A. Armstrong	"	San José, Cal.	
Elisha E. Garrison	"	New York, N. Y.	
William T. Atkins	"	Selma, Ala.	
J. Oscar Mullen	"	Tempe, Ariz.	
Frank Marti	Trumpeter	Jerome, Ariz.	
John A. W. Stelzriede	"	Tempe, Ariz.	
James G. Yost	Blacksmith	Prescott, Ariz.	
Frank Vans Agnew	Farrier	Kissimee, Fla.	
Francis L. Morgan	Saddler	White Hills, Ariz.	
Jerome W. Lanford	Wagoner	"	
Asey, William	Private	Safford, Ariz.	
Anderson, Thomas A.	"	San Antonio, Tex.	

Barthell, Peter K.	Private	Kingman, Ariz.
Bradley, Peter	"	Jerome, Ariz.
Burks, Robert E.	"	Prescott, Ariz.
Byrnes, Orlando C.	"	"
Bowler, George P.	"	New York, N. Y.
Carleton, William C.	"	Tempe, Ariz.
Carlson, Carl	"	"
Cartledge, Crantz	"	"
Coleman, Lockett G.	"	St. Louis, Mo.
Danforth, Clyde L.	"	Flagstaff, Ariz.
Danforth, William H.	"	"
Dewees, John H.	"	San Antonio, Tex.
Duncan, Arthur G.	"	New York, N. Y.
Engel, Edwin P.	"	Phoenix, Ariz.
Force, Peter	"	Selma, Ala.
Gaughan, James	"	Phoenix, Ariz.
Gibbons, Floyd J.	"	Prescott, Ariz.
Goodwin, James C.	"	Tempe, Ariz.
Gardiner, John P.	"	Boston, Mass.
Gavin, Anthony	"	Buffalo, N. Y.
Henson, Ivan M	"	Phoenix, Ariz.
Hanson, William	"	Prescott, Ariz.
Herold, Philip M.	"	Phoenix, Ariz.
Howland, Harry	"	Flagstaff, Ariz.
Hubbell, Wm. C.	"	Nogales, Ariz.
Hall, Edward C.	"	New Haven, Conn.
Kastens, Harry E.	"	Winslow, Ariz.
Marvin, William E	"	Yuma, Ariz.
Mason, David P.	"	Brownsville, Tex.
Moffett, Edward B.	"	Yuma, Ariz.
Neville, George A	"	"

TROOP C—Continued.

NAME.	RANK.	PLACE OF RESIDENCE.	REMARKS.
Norton, John W.	Private	Lockport, Ill.	
O'Leary, Daniel	"	Tempe, Ariz.	
Parker, John W.	"	Safford, Ariz.	
Payne, Forest B.	"	Phœnix, Ariz.	
Pond, Ashley	"	Detroit, Mich.	
Perry, Arthur R.	"	Phœnix, Ariz.	
Ricketts, William L.	"	"	
Roderer, John	"	Prescott, Ariz.	
Rupert, Charles W.	"	"	
Reed, George W.	"	Tucson, Ariz.	
Sayers, Samuel E.	"	Yuma, Ariz.	
Scharf, Charles A.	"	Flagstaff, Ariz.	
Sexsmith, William	"	Yuma, Ariz.	
Shackelford, Marcus L.	"	Jerome, Ariz.	
Shoemaker, John	"	Phœnix, Ariz.	
Skogsburg, Charles G.	"	Safford, Ariz.	
Scull, Guy H.	"	Boston, Mass.	
Sloan, Thomas M.	"	Phœnix, Ariz.	
Somers, Fred. B.	"	Flagstaff, Ariz.	
Trowbridge, Lafayette	"	Prescott, Ariz.	
Vines, Jesse G.	"	Phœnix, Ariz.	
Vance, William E.	"	Austin, Tex.	
Wormell, John A.	"	Phœnix, Ariz.	
Younger, Charles	"	Winslow, Ariz.	
Wright, Albert P.	Sergeant	Yuma, Ariz.	

Discharged—Disability.			
Alamia, John B	Private	Port Isabel, Tex	Dis. acct. epileptic fits per order A. G. O.
Pearson, Rufus W	Sergeant	Phoenix, Ariz	Discharged Aug. 26, 1898, on cer. of dis. signed by Sec. of War, General Alger.
Discharged by Order.			
Grindell, Thomas F	"	Tempe, Ariz	Dis. by tel. order, A. G. O., Sept. 8, 1898.
Hill, Wesley	Private	"	Dis. by tel. order, A. G. O., Sept. 8, 1898.
Scudder, William M	"	Chicago, Ill	Dis. per S. O. 204, par. 52, War Dept., A. G. O., Washington, D. C., Aug. 30, 1898.
Wallack, Robert R	"	Washington, D. C	Dis. July 19, 1898, per par. 27, S. O. 203, War Dept., A. G. O., Washington, D. C., Aug. 29, 1898.
Transferred.			
Rowdin, John E	"	Phoenix, Ariz	Trans. Troop B to C May 7; trans. per S. O. No. 6, dated Tampa, Fla., June 8, 1898.
Died.			
Adsit, Nathaniel B	"	Buffalo, N. Y	Died Aug. 1, at Buffalo, of typhoid fever.
Clearwater, Frank H	"	Brownsville, Tex	Died at Corpus Christi, Sept. 2, 1897, of typhoid malaria.
Newnhone, Thomas M	"	Phoenix, Ariz	Died hospl., Ft. McPherson, of typhoid fever, Aug. 4, 1898.

TROOP D.

NAME.	RANK.	PLACE OF RESIDENCE.	REMARKS.
Robert B. Huston	Captain	Guthrie, O. T.	
David M. Goodrich	1st Lieutenant	Akron, Ohio.	
Robert H. M. Ferguson	2d Lieutenant	New York City.	
Orlando G. Palmer	1st Sergt.	Ponca City, O. T.	
Gerald A. Webb	Sergeant	Guthrie, O. T.	
Joseph A. Randolph	"	Waukomis, O. T.	
Ira A. Hill	"	Newkirk, O. T.	
Charles E. Hunter	"	Enid, O. T.	
Scott Reay	"	Blackwell, O. T.	
Paul W. Hunter	"	Chandler, O. T.	
Thomas Moran	"	Fort Sill, O. T.	
Calvin Hill	Corporal	Pawnee, O. T.	
George Norris	"	Kingfisher, O. T.	
John D. Rhoades	"	Hennessey, O. T.	Wounded in battle of Las Guasimas, June 24, 1898. G. S. leg.
Lyman F. Beard	"	Shawnee, O. T.	Wounded in battle before Santiago, July 1, 1898. Both shoulders.
Henry Magher	"	El Reno, O. T.	
Alexander H. Denham	"	Oklahoma City, O. T.	Wounded in battle of Las Guasimas, June 24, 1898. G. S. left thigh.
Henry K. Love	"	Tecumseh, O. T.	
Harrison J. Holt	"	Denver, Colo.	
William D. Amrine	Saddler	Newkirk, O. T.	
Starr M. Wetmore	Trumpeter	" "	
James T. Brown	"	" "	Wounded in battle before Santiago, July 1, 1898. Severe; right thigh.

Name	Rank	Residence	Remarks
Lorrin D. Muxlow	Wagoner	Guthrie, O. T.	Wounded in battle before Santiago, July 2, 1898. Right foot.
Bailey, William	Private	Norman, O. T.	Wounded in battle of Las Guasimas, June 24, 1898. G. S. leg.
Beal, Fred N	"	Kingfisher, O. T.	
Burgess, George	"	Shawnee, O. T.	
Brandon, Perry H	"	Lancaster, O. T.	
Byrne, Peter F	"	Guthrie, O. T.	
Cesse, Forrest L	"	"	
Chase, Leslie C	"	Kingfisher, O. T.	
Cook, Walter M	"	Enid, O. T.	
Crawford, William S	"	"	
Cross, William E	"	El Reno, O. T.	Wounded in battle before Santiago, July 2, 1898. Leg.
Crockett, Warren E	"	Marietta, Ga.	
Cunningham, Sol. M	"	San Antonio, Tex.	
Calrow, Gerald	"	Boerne, Tex.	
David, Icem J	"	Enid, O. T.	
Emery, Elzie E	"	Shawnee, O. T.	
Faulk, William A	"	Guthrie, O. T.	
Hill, Edwin M	"	Tecumseh, O. T.	
Honeycutt, James V	"	Shawnee, O. T.	
Eppley, Kurtz	"	Orange, N. J.	
Green, Charles H	"	Albuquerque, N. M.	
Hatch, Charles P	"	Newport, R. I.	Wounded in battle before Santiago, July 1, 1898. Severe, left leg.
Holmes, Thomas M	"	Newkirk, O. T.	
Haynes, Jacob M	"		
Howard, John S	"	Boerne, Tex.	
Ishler, Shelby F	"	Enid, O. T.	Wounded in battle of Las Guasimas, June 24, 1898. G. S. right forearm.

TROOP D—*Continued.*

Name.	Rank.	Place of Residence.	Remarks.
Ivy, Charles B	Private	Waco, Tex.	
Johnston, Edward W	"	Cushing, O. T.	Wounded in battle before Santiago, July 1, 1898. Right thigh.
Joyce, Walter	"	Guthrie, O. T.	
Knox, William F	"		
Laird, Emmett	"	Albuquerque, N. M.	
Loughmiller, Edgar F	"	Oklahoma City, O. T.	
Lovelace, Carl	"	Waco, Tex.	
Lusk, Henry	"	El Reno, O. T.	
McMillan, Robert L	"	Shawnee, O. T.	Wounded in battle before Santiago, July 1, 1898. Left shoulder and arm.
McClure, David V	"	Oklahoma City, O. T.	
McMurtry, George G	"	Pittsburg, Pa.	
Miller, Roscoe B	"	Guthrie, O. T.	
Miller, Volney D	"	" "	
Munn, Edward	"	Elizabeth, N. J.	
Newcomb, Marcellus L	"	Kingfisher, O. T.	Wounded in battle of Las Guasimas, June 24, 1898. G. S. right knee.
Norris, Warren	"	Kingfisher, O. T.	
Palmer, William F	"	Shawnee, O. T.	
Proctor, Joseph H	"	Pawnee, O. T.	
Pollock, William	"	" "	
Russell, Albert P	"	El Reno, O. T.	
Sands, George H	"	Guthrie, O. T.	
Schmutz, John C	"	Germantown, Ohio.	
Scott, Cliff D	"	Clifton, O. T.	
Schupp, Eugene W	"	Santa Fé, N. M.	

Name	Rank	Residence	Remarks
Shanafelt, Dick	Private	Perry, O. T.	
Shipp, Edward M.	"	Kingfisher, O. T.	
Stewart, Clare H.	"	Pawnee, O. T.	
Stewart, Cyde H.	"	" "	
Tauer, William L.	"	Ponca City, O. T.	
Thomas, Albert M.	"	Guthrie, O. T.	
Vanderslice, James E.	"	Enid, O. T.	
Van Valen, Alex L.	"	Poughkeepsie, N. Y.	
Wolff, Frederick W.	"	San Antonio, Tex.	
Wright, William O.	"	Pawnee, O. T.	
Wright, Edward L.	"	Guthrie, O. T.	

Discharged.

Name	Rank	Residence	Remarks
James M. Shockey	Corporal	Perry, O. T.	Discharged July 1, 1898, by order of Asst. Adjt. Gen'l.
Arthur A. Luther	Farrier	Pawnee, O. T.	Discharged July 1, 1898, by order of Asst. Adjt. Gen'l.
Page, John F.	Private	Alva, O. T.	Discharged by verbal order of Gen. Wood, August 6, 1898.
Wells, Joseph O.	"	St. Joseph, Mich.	Discharged by order of Asst. Adjt. Gen'l. Aug. 27, 1898.
William S. Simpson	Corporal	Dallas, Tex.	Discharged by reason of promotion into regular army as 2d Lieut., Sept. 3, 1898.

Transferred.

Name	Rank	Residence	Remarks
Schuyler A. McGinnis	1st Lieutenant	Newkirk, O. T.	Promoted to Captain and transferred to Troop I, 1st U. S. V. C., May 19, 1898.
Jacob Schweizer	2d Lieutenant	El Reno, O. T.	Promoted to 1st Lieut. and assigned to duty as Q. M. 1st U. S. V. C., May 19, 1898.
Joseph A. Carr	1st Lieutenant	Washington, D. C.	Transf'd to Troop K, Sept. 5. Wounded, Santiago, July 2, 1898.

TROOP D—*Continued.*

NAME.	RANK.	PLACE OF RESIDENCE.	REMARKS.
Douthett, Matthew	Private	Guthrie, O. T.	Appointed Q. M. Sergt. 1st U. S. V. C. and assigned to duty Aug. 31, 1898.
Freeman, Elisha L.	"	Ponca City, O. T.	Transferred to Troop K, 1st U. S. V. C., May 11, 1898.
Folk, Theodore	"	Oklahoma City, O. T.	Transferred to Troop K, 1st U. S. V. C., May 11, 1898.
Hulme, Robert A.	"	El Reno, O. T.	Transferred to Troop K, 1st U. S. V. C., May 11, 1898.
Jordan, Andrew M.	"	" "	Transferred to Troop K, 1st U. S. V. C., May 11, 1898.
McGinty, William	"	Stillwater, O. T.	Transferred to Troop K, 1st U. S. V. C., May 11, 1898.
Mitchell, William H.	"	Guthrie, O. T.	Transferred to Troop K, 1st U. S. V. C., May 11, 1898.
Staley, Francis M.	"	Waukomis, O. T.	Transferred to Troop K, 1st U. S. V. C., May 11, 1898.
Smith, Fred	"	Guthrie, O. T.	Transferred to Troop K, 1st U. S. V. C., May 11, 1898.
Weitzel, John F.	"	Newkirk, O. T.	Transferred to Troop K, 1st U. S. V. C., May 11, 1898.
Woodward, John A.	"	El Reno, O. T.	Transferred to Troop K, 1st U. S. V. C., May 11, 1898.
Wilson, Frank M.	"	Guthrie, O. T.	Transferred to Troop K, 1st U. S. V. C., May 11, 1898.
Burke, Edward F.	"	Orange, N. J.	Transferred to Troop A, 1st U. S. V. C., July 13, 1898.

Died.

Cashion, Roy V.	Private	Hennessey, O. T.	Killed in battle before Santiago, July 1, 1898. Head.
Miller, Theodore W.	"	Akron, Ohio.	Wounded before Santiago, July 1. Penetrated neck; totally paralyzed. Died July 8.

Deserted.

Crossley, Henry S.	"	Guthrie, O. T.	Dropped from rolls as deserted July 8, 1898.

TROOP E.

Frederick Muller	Captain	Santa Fé, N. M.	
William E. Griffin	1st Lieutenant	"	
John S. Langston	1st Sergeant	Cerrillos, N. M.	
Royal A. Prentice	Qr. Mr. Sergt.	Las Vegas, N. M.	
Hugh P. Wright	Sergeant	"	
Albert M. Jones	"	Santa Fé, N. M.	
Timothy Breen	"	"	Wounded and sent to hospital July 1, 1898. Arm.
Berry F. Taylor	"	Las Vegas, N. M.	
Thomas P. Ledgwidge	"	Santa Fé, N. M.	Wounded and sent to hospital July 1, 1898. Side and head; severe.
John Mullen	"	Chicago, Ill.	
Harman H. Wyrnkoop	Corporal	Santa Fé, N. M.	Wounded in line of duty and sent to hospital July 2. Returned Sept. 4. Leg.
James M. Dean	"	"	Wounded in line of duty; sent to hosp. June 24. Returned Aug. 81. Gunshot left thigh.

187

TROOP E—*Continued.*

Name.	Rank.	Place of Residence.	Remarks.
Edward C. Waller	Corporal	Chicago, Ill.	Wounded in line of duty July 2, 1898. Scalp; slight.
G. Roland Fortescue	"	New York, N. Y.	
Edward Bennett	"	Cripple Creek, Col.	
Charles E. Knoblauch	"	New York, N. Y.	
Richard C. Conner	"	Santa Fé, N. M.	
Ralph E. McFie	"	Las Cruces, N. M.	
Arthur J. Griffin	Trumpeter	Santa Fé, N. M.	
Edward S. Lewis	"	Las Vegas, N. M.	
Robert J. Parrish	Blacksmith	Clayton, N. M.	
Grant Hill	Farrier	Santa Fé, N. M.	
Joe T. Sandoval	Saddler	"	
Guilford B. Chapin	Wagoner	"	
Ausburn, Charles G.	Trooper	New Orleans, La.	
Almack, Roll	"	Santa Fé, N. M.	
Brennan, John M.	"	"	
Baca, Jose M.	"	Las Vegas, N. M.	
Beard, William M.	"	San Antonio, Tex.	
Cooper, George B.	"	Tampa, Fla.	
Conway, James	"	San Antonio, Tex.	
Dettamore, George W.	"	Clayton, N. M.	Wounded in line of duty and sent to hospital July 1, 1898. Abdomen.
Davis, Harry A.	"	Boston, Mass.	
Dodge, George H.	"	Denver, Col.	
Debli, Joseph	"	Tampa, Fla.	
Donavan, Freeman M.	"	Santa Fé, N. M.	
Douglas, James B.	"	New York, N. Y.	

188

Name	Rank	Location	Notes
Easley, William T.	Trooper	Clayton, N. M.	
Edwards, Lawrence W.	"	"	
Fries, Frank D.	"	Santa Fé, N. M.	
Francis, Mack	"	Waynesville, N. C.	
Fettes, George	"	Antonito, Col.	
Gisler, Joseph	"	Santa Fé, N. M.	
Gibbs, James P.	"	"	
Gibbie, William R.	"	Las Vegas, N. M.	
Grigsby, Braxton	"	New York, N. Y.	
Grigg, John G.	"	San Antonio, Tex.	
Gammel, Roy U.	"	Jersey Co., Ill.	
Harding, John D.	"	Socorro, N. M.	
Hood, John B.	"	New York, N. Y.	
Harkness, Daniel D.	"	Las Vegas, N. M.	
Hutchison, William M.	"	Santa Fé, N. M.	
Hall, John P.	"	Williamson Co., Tex.	Wounded in line of duty and sent to hospital July 1, 1898.
Hogle, William H.	"	Santa Fé, N. M.	
Hudson, Arthur J.	"	"	
Hulskotter, John	"	"	
Hutchason, Joseph M.	"	Jimtown, Tenn.	
Howell, William S. E.	"	Cerrillos, N. M.	
Hadden, David A.	"	San Antonio, Tex.	
Hixon, Thomas L.	"	Las Vegas, N. M.	
Heard, Judson	"	Pecos City, Tex.	
Hamlin, Warden W.	"	Chicago, Ill.	
Jones, Thomas B.	"	Santa Fé, N. M.	
Johnston, Charles E.	"	San Antonio, Tex.	
Jacobus, Charles W.	"	Santa Fé, N. M.	
Knapp, Edgar A.	"	Elizabeth, N. J.	
Kingsley, Charles E.	"	Las Vegas, N. M.	

TROOP E—*Continued.*

NAME.	RANK.	PLACE OF RESIDENCE.	REMARKS.
Kissam, William A.	Trooper	New York, N. Y.	
Lowe, Frank	"	Santa Fé, N. M.	
Ludy, Dan	"	Las Vegas, N. M.	
Livingston, Thomas C.	"	Hamilton Co., Tex.	
Lowitzki, Hyman S.	"	Santa Fé, N. M.	
Lewis, James	"	"	
Merchant, James E.	"	Cerrillos, N. M.	
Moran, William J.	"	"	
McKinnon, Samuel	"	Madrid, N. M.	
McKinley, Charles E.	"	Cerrillos, N. M.	Wounded in line of duty July 1, 1898. Head.
McKay, Charles F.	"	Santa Fé, N. M.	
McCabe, Frederick H.	"	"	
McDowell, John C.	"	"	
Morrison, Amaziah B.	"	Las Vegas, N. M.	
Mahan, Lloyd L.	"	Cerrillos, N. M.	
Martin, Henry D.	"	"	
Menger, Otto F.	"	Clayton, N. M.	Wounded in line of duty July 1, 1898, and sent to hospital. Left thigh.
Munger, William C.	"	Santa Fé, N. M.	
Nettleblade, Adolph F.	"	Cerrillos, N. M.	
Roberts, Thomas	"	Golden, N. M.	
Ryan, John E.	"	Santa Fé, N. M.	Wounded July 1, 1898, in line of duty.
Ramsey, Homer M.	"	Pearsoll, Tex.	
Seaders, Ben F.	"	Las Vegas, N. M.	
Skinner, Arthur V.	"	Santa Fé, N. M.	
Schnepple, William C.	"	"	
Scanlon, Edward	"	Cerrillos, N. M.	

Name	Rank	Residence	Remarks
Slevin, Edward	Trooper	Tampa, Fla.	
Taylor, William R.	"	New York, N. Y.	
Wagner, William W.	"	Bland, N. M.	
Wright, George	"	Madrid, N. M.	
Wynkoop, Charles W.	"	Santa Fé, N. M.	
Warren, George W.	"	"	
Discharged.			
William E. Dame	1st Sergeant	Cerrillos, N. M.	Discharged per ord. reg. com., Aug. 10, '98.
Frederick C. Wesley	Sergeant	Santa Fé, N. M.	Wounded July 1st, 2d, or 3d, near Santiago. Forearm; slight. Discharged Aug. 26, '98.
Transferred by Verbal Order Regim't'l Com., May 12, 1898.			
William R. Reber	Sergeant		
Stuart R. Price	Corporal		
Bernard, William C.	Trooper		
Brown, Hiram T.	"		
Bump, Arthur L.	"		
Cloud, William	"		
Davis, Henry Clay	"		
Duran, Jose L.	"		
Easton, Stephen	"		
Fennell, William A.	"		
Fleming, Clarence A.	"		
Holden, Prince A.	"		
Land, Oscar N.	"		
Martin, John	"		
Roberts, John P.	"		
Stephens, Orregon	"		
Torbett, John G.	"		

TROOP E—*Continued.*

NAME.	RANK.	PLACE OF RESIDENCE.	REMARKS.
William, Thomas C	Trooper.		
Zigler, Daniel J	"		
Died.			
Cochran, Irad, Jr	"		Died May 26, 1898, San Antonio, Tex. Spinal meningitis.
Miller, John S	"		Died July 16, 1898, of yellow fever, at Siboney, Cuba.
Judson, Alfred M	"		Died Aug. 17, 1898, of typhoid fever, at Montauk Point, L. I.
O'Neill, John	"		Died Aug. 3, 1898, of dysentery, at Edgmont Key, Fla.
Killed.			
Green, Henry C	"		Killed in action July 1, 1898, near Santiago.
Robison, John F	"		Killed in action July 2, 1898, near Santiago.
Alterations Sept. 7, '98.			
Sherrard Coleman	1st Lieutenant.	Santa Fé, N. M.	Originally as 2d Lt. Troop E, May 6, 1898. Promoted to Reg. Q. M. Sept. 7, 1898.
John A. McIlhenny	2d Lieutenant.		Commissioned Sept. 7, 1898. Assigned to Troop E Sept. 7, 1898.

TROOP F.

Name	Rank	Residence	Remarks
Maximiliano Luna	Captain	Santa Fé, N. M.	
Horace W. Weakley	1st Lieutenant	"	
William E. Dame	2d Lieutenant	"	
Horace E. Sherman	1st Sergeant	"	
Garfield Hughes	Sergeant	"	
Thomas D. Fennessy	"	"	
William L. Mattocks	"	"	
James Doyle	"	"	Wounded in action June 24. G. S. wrist.
George W. Armijo	"	"	
Eugene Bohlinger	"	"	
Herbert A. King	"	"	
Edward Donally	Corporal	"	
John Cullen	"	"	
Edward Hale	"	"	
Arthur P. Spencer	"	"	
John Boehnke	"	"	Wounded in action July 1, 1898. Perry Powers. Left arm.
Albert Powers	"	"	
Wentworth S. Conduit	"	"	Wounded in action June 24, 1898. G. S. right wrist.
Albers, Heyl L.	Private	"	Wounded in action June 24, '98. G. S. wrist.
Albertson, Edward J	"	"	
Alexander, James	"	"	
Abbott, Charles G	"	"	
Adams, Edgar S	"	San Antonio, Tex.	
Alexander, James F	"	Santa Fé, N. M.	
Black, James S	"	"	

TROOP F—Continued.

NAME.	RANK.	PLACE OF RESIDENCE.	REMARKS.
Bailey, Robert Z.	Private	Santa Fé, N. M.	Wounded in action June 24, 1898. G. S. both legs.
Boschen, John	"	San Antonio, Tex.	
Bell, William A.	"	Tampa, Fla.	
Brennan, Jeremiah	"	Santa Fé, N. M.	
Burris, Walter C.	"	"	
Byrne, John	"	Muskogee, I. T.	
Bell, John H.	"	Santa Fé, N. M.	
Clark, Ray V.	"	"	Contusion scalp, slight, near Santiago de Cuba, July 1, 2, or 3, 1898.
Cochran, William O.	"	"	
Clark, Frank J.	"	"	
Colbert, Benj. H.	"	San Antonio, Tex.	
Christian, Edward D.	"	Tampa, Fla.	
Clelland, Calvin G.	"	Santa Fé, N. M.	
Conley, Edward C.	"	"	
Cochran, Willard M.	"	"	
Cherry, Charles C.	"	"	
Dougherty, Louis	"	"	
De Bohun, John C.	"	"	
Farley, William	"	"	Wounded by fragment of shell in wrist July 1, 1898. Left wrist.
Freeman, Will	"	"	Gunshot wound in foot July 1, 1898.
Gibbs, Henry M.	"	"	
Galligher, William D.	"	"	
Goldberg, Samuel	"	"	Wounded in action July 1, 1898. Hip.
Glessner, Otis	"	"	

194

Name	Rank	Station	Remarks
Green, John D	Private	Santa Fé, N. M.	Gunshot wound, June 24, 1898.
Gee, Charles R	Farrier	"	
Hill, Jefferson	Wagoner	"	
Hardie, Albert C	Private	"	
Hopping, Charles O	"	"	
Hamner, George	"	"	
Kennedy, Stephen A	"	"	
Leffert, Charles E	"	"	
Lisk, Guy M	"	"	
Leach, John M	"	"	
Le Stourgeon, E. Guy	"	San Antonio, Tex.	
Lavelle, Nolan Z	"	"	
Martin, Thomas	"	Santa Fé, N. M.	
McCurdy, J. Kirk	Trumpeter	San Antonio, Tex.	
Mills, John B	Private	Santa Fé, N. M.	
McGregor, Herbert P	"		Wounded in action July 1, '98. Left shoulder.
McCarthy, F. Allan	"	San Antonio, Tex.	
Nickell, William E	"	Santa Fé, N. M.	
Nesbit, Otto W	"	"	
Newitt, George W	"	"	
Neal, John M	"	"	
Perry, Arthur L	Bugler	"	Wounded July 1, 2, or 3, 1898, Santiago de Cuba. Shoulder.
Parmele, Chas. A	Private	"	
Quier, Frank T	"	"	
Raymond, Milliard L	"	"	
Reed, Harry B	"	"	Wounded in action June 24, 1898. Arm.
Reed, Clifford L	"	"	
Renner, Charles L	"	"	
Reynolds, Edwin L	"	"	
Russell, Arthur L	"	"	

TROOP F—Continued.

NAME.	RANK.	PLACE OF RESIDENCE.	REMARKS.
Rebentisch, Adolph	Private	San Antonio, Tex.	Gunshot wound in shoulder June 24, 1898. Left shoulder.
Reyer, Adolph T.	"	Santa Fé, N. M.	
Rogers, Albert	"	"	
Rice, Lee C.	"	"	
Staub, Louis E.	"	"	
Shields, William G.	"	"	
Stockbridge, Arthur J.	"	"	
Sharland, George H.	"	"	
Skipwith, John G.	"	"	
Sennett, James B.	"	"	
Taugen, Edward	"	"	
Trump, Norman O.	"	"	
Vinnedge, George E.	"	"	
Wardwell, Louis C.	"	"	
Warren, Paul	"	"	
Watrous, Charles R.	"	"	
Weber, Beauregard	"	"	
Weller, Samuel M.	"	San Antonio, Tex.	Gunshot wounds in shoulder, arm, and leg July 1, 1898. Left leg.
Winter, John G.	"	"	
Winter, Otto R.	"	"	
Wertheim, Adolph S.	"	"	
Walsh, John	"	Santa Fé, N. M.	
Wells, Thomas J.	"	"	
Wilson, Harry W.	"	Tampa, Fla.	

Name	Rank	Residence	Remarks
Discharged.			
Doughlas, James	Private	Santa Fé, N. M.	Discharged account surgeon's certificate of disability.
Transferred.			
Maxwell Keys	2d Lieutenant	"	Promoted to Adjutant Aug. 1, 1898.
Bawcom, Joseph L.	Private	"	Transferred from F to I Troop May 12, '98.
Flynn, Joseph F.	"	"	"
Goodrich, Hedrick Ben	"	"	"
Hickey, Walter	"	"	"
Hogan, Michael	"	"	"
King, Harry Bruce	"	"	"
Kerney, George M.	"	"	"
Larsen, Louis	"	"	"
McCoy, John	"	"	"
Nehmer, Charles A.	"	"	"
Rogers, Leo G.	"	"	"
Rafalowitz, Hymon	"	"	"
Spencer-Edwards, John	"	"	"
Schearnhorst, Carl J. jr.	"	"	"
Temple, Frank	"	"	"
Died.			
Booth, Frank B.	Private	Madison, Wis.	Wounded, Las Guasimas, June 24. Died. Key West, Aug. 30. G. S. right shoulder.
Erwin, William T.	"	San Antonio, Tex.	Killed in action June 24, 1898. Las Guasimas. G. S. head.
Endsley, Gey D.	"	Somerfield, Pa.	Died in Cuba July 18, 1898, of fever.
Deserted.			
Thompson, Charles	"	Mercer Co., W. Va.	Deserted at Tampa, Fla., July 27, 1898.
Discharged.			
John A. McIlhanny	Corporal	San Antonio, Tex.	Discharged to accept commission.

TROOP G.

NAME.	RANK.	PLACE OF RESIDENCE.	REMARKS.
Wm. H. H. Llewellyn	Captain	Las Cruces, N. M.	
John Wesley Green	1st Lieutenant	Gallup, N. M.	
David J. Leahy	2d Lieutenant	Raton, N. M.	On sick leave from July 1 to Sept. 3 from wound received in San Juan battle.
Attached.			
John C. Greenway	1st Lieutenant	Hot Springs, Ark.	In Troop I; on detached service with Troop G since June 5.
Columbus H. McCaa	1st Sergeant	Gallup, N. M.	
Jacob S. Mohler	Q. M. Sergeant	"	
Raymond Morse	Sergeant	"	
Rolla A. Fullenweider	"	Raton, N. M.	
Matt T. McGehee	"	"	
James Brown	"	Gallup, N. M.	
Nicholis A. Vyne	"	Emporia, Kan.	
Raleigh L. Miller	"	Pueblo, Colo.	
Henry Kirch	Corporal	Gallup, N. M.	
James D. Ritchie	"		
Luther L. Stewart	"	Raton, N. M.	Wounded in battle June 24. G. S. left forearm. Wounded July 1. Severe; right thigh.
John McSparron	"	Gallup, N. M.	
Frank Briggs	"	Raton, N. M.	
Edward C. Armstrong	"	Albuquerque, N. M.	
William S. Reid	"	Raton, N. M.	
Hiram E. Williams	"	"	
George V. Haefner	Farrier	Gallup, N. M.	
Frank A. Hill	Saddler	Raton, N. M.	

Name	Rank	Residence	Remarks
Thomas O'Neal	Wagoner	Springer, N. M.	
Willis E. Sowers	Trumpeter	Raton, N. M.	
Edward G. Piper	"	Silver City, N. M.	
Ash, Alvin C	Trooper	Raton, N. M.	Absent, on account of wound received, from July 1 to Sept. 7. Slight; wrist.
Arnold, Edward B	"	Prescott, Ariz.	
Akin, James E	"	Dolores, Colo.	
Anderson, Arthur T	"	Albuquerque, N. M.	
Andrews, William C	"	Sulphur Springs, Tex.	
Beck, Joseph H	"	San Antonio, Tex.	Ruptured on right side about May 20. Disability occurred in line of duty.
Bishop, Louis B	"	Dolores, Colo.	
Brumley, Wm. H., Jr	"	Gallup, N. M.	
Brown, Robert	"	San Antonio, Tex.	
Brown, Edwin M	"	St. Louis, Mo.	
Brazelton, William H	"	Gallup, N. M.	
Beisel, John J	"	Raton, N. M.	
Camp, Cloid	"	"	
Camp, Marion	"	"	
Covenaugh, Thomas F	"		Abs't since June 24 acct. wound rec'd in battle. Perry F. Cavanaugh. G. S. right arm.
Cody, William F	"	St. Louis, Mo.	
Chopetal, Frank W	"	Buffalo, N. Y.	
Coyle, Michael H	"	Raton, N. M.	Absent on sick leave since June 24 on account of wound in arm gotten in battle.
Clark, Winslow	"	Milton, Mass	Absent on sick leave since July 1. G. S. wound through lungs. Severe; right lung.
Cotton, Frank W	"	Jennings, La.	
Conover, Alfred J	"	Chicasee, I. T.	
Detwiler, Sherman	"	Muscatine, Ia.	

TROOP G—*Continued.*

NAME.	RANK.	PLACE OF RESIDENCE.	REMARKS.
Dunn, Alfred B	Trooper	Calvert, Tex.	
Edmunds, John H	"	Alleghany, Pa.	
Faupel, Henry F	"	Martington, Ill.	
Fomoff, Fred	"	Albuquerque, N. M.	
Fitch, Roger S	"	Buffalo, N. Y.	
Gibson, William C	"	Gallup, N. M.	
Gevers, Louis	"	Austin, Tex.	Absent from July 1 till Aug. 2 account G. S. wound in hips, received in battle.
Goodwin, John	"	Gallup, N. M.	
Healey, Frank F	"	Brooklyn, N. Y.	
Henderson, John	"	Gallup, N. M.	Absent from July 1 to Sept. 2 acct. wound in arm received in battle. Wrist.
Henshaw, Laten R	"	El Paso, Tex.	
Johnson, Albert John	"	Raton, N. M.	
Kline, John S	"	San Marcial, N. M.	
Keeley, Bert T	"	Lamy, N. M.	
King, Henry A	"	Massitee, Mich.	
Littleton, Elias M	"	Springer, N. M.	
Lincoln, Malcolm D	"	Lucknow, I. T.	
Larson, Anton	"	Silverton, Colo.	
Lyle, James C	"	Georgetown, Colo.	
Miller, Frank P	"	Los Angeles, Cal.	
Meyers, Fred P	"	Gallup, N. M.	Reduced 1st Srgt. to Tpr. Wounded July 1; unaccounted for since. Severe; head.
Moran, Daniel	"	"	
Mann, Eugene M	"	Omaha, Neb.	

Name	Rank	Location	Remarks
McCarty, George H	Trooper	Los Angeles, Cal.	
McKinney, Frank G	"	Harrison, Ark.	
McKinney, Oliver	"	Cañon City, Colo.	
McMullen, Samuel J	"	St. Louis, Mo.	
Noish, John	"	Raton, N. M.	
Phipps, Thomas W	"	Bland, N. M.	
Petty, Arch	"	Gallup, N. M.	
Pennington, Elijah	"	San Antonio, Tex.	
Preston, Robert A	"	Stiles, Tex.	
Quigg, George H	"	Gallup, N. M.	
Quinn, Walter D	"	San Marcial, N. M.	
Ratcliff, William	"	Gallup, N. M.	
Richards, Richard	"	Albuquerque, N. M.	
Rayburn, Harry C	"	Camden, Ia.	
Reid, Robert W	"	Raton, N. M.	Absent on sick leave from June 24 to Sept. 8 acct. wound in side. G. S. right hip.
Ragland, Robert C	"	Guthrie, O. T.	
Roland, George	"	Deming, N. M.	G. S. right side.
Stillson, Earl	"	Topeka, Kan.	
Simmons, Charles M	"	Raton, N. M.	
Slaughter, Benjamin	"	San Antonio, Tex.	
Shannon, Charles W	"	Raton, N. M.	
Thomas, Neal	"	Aztec, N. M.	
Travis, Grant	"	" "	
Van Horn, Eustus E	"	Halstead, Kan.	
Welch, Toney	"	Durango, Colo.	
Whittington, Richard	"	Gallup, N. M.	Leg broken Aug. 18. Injury occurred in line of duty.
Whited, Lyman E	"	Raton, N. M.	
Wood, William D	"	Bland, N. M.	
Wright, Clarence	"	Springer, N. M.	

TROOP G—Continued.

NAME.	RANK.	PLACE OF RESIDENCE.	REMARKS.
Discharged.			
Swan, George D	Trooper	Gallup, N. M.	
Thompson, Frank M	"	Aztec, N. M.	
Deserted.			
McCulloch, Samuel T	"	Springer, N. M.	
Deaths.			
Green, J. Knox	"	Rancho, Tex	Died at Montauk Point, N. Y., Aug. 15, sickness which originated in line of duty.
Lutz, Eugene A	"	Raton, N. M	Died in Yellow Fever Hospital, in Cuba, Aug. 15, 1898.
Killed in Action.			
Haefner, Henry J	"	Gallup, N. M	Wounded in battle June 24, 1898; died in Field Hospital same day.
Russell, Marcus D	"	Troy, N. Y	Killed in action June 24, 1898.
Transferred.			
Bailie, Henry C	"	Gallup, N. M	Attached from dynamite gun detail to troop; transferred from Troop I to G Aug. 31.
Arendt, Henry J	Sergeant	Raton, N. M	Transferred to Troop I May 12.
Love, William J	Trooper	"	"
Morgan, Schuyler C	"	Hazard, Ky	"
Morgan, Ulysses G	"	"	"
Odell, William D	"	Parkersburg, W. Va	"
Donnelly, Ruth'd B. H.	"	Jefferson, O. T	"
Evans, Evan	"	Gallup, N. M	"

Groves, Oscar W	Trooper	Raton, N. M.	Transferred to Troop I May 12.
Jones, William H	"	"	" " " " " "
Kanis, Frank	"	Jamestown, N. D.	Transferred to Troop K May 11.
Pierce, Ed	"	Chicago, Ill.	Transferred to Troop I May 12.
Saville, Michael	"	"	" " " " " "
Sinnelt, Lee	"	Mayesville, W. Va.	" " " " " "
Tait, John H	"	Raton, N. M.	" " " " " "
Peabody, Harry	"	"	" " " " " "
McGowan, Alex	"	Gallup, N. M.	" " " " " "
Brown, John	"	"	" " " " " "
Crockett, Joseph B	"	Raton, N. M.	Transferred to Troop K May 11.
Corbe, M. C	Trumpeter		

TROOP H.

George Curry	Captain	Tularosa, N. M.	
William H. Kelly	1st Lieutenant	East Las Vegas, N. M.	
Charles L. Ballard	2d Lieutenant	Roswell, N. M.	
Green A. Settle	1st Sergeant	Jackson Co., Ky.	
Nevin P. Gutilins	Sergeant	Tularosa, N. M.	
William A. Mitchell	"	El Paso, Tex.	
Oscar de Montell	"	Roswell, N. M.	
Thomas Darnell	"	Denver, Colo.	
Willis J. Physive	"	Columbia, S. C.	
Michael C. Rose	"	Silver City, N. M.	
Nova A. Johnson	"	Roswell, N. M.	
Morton M. Morgan	Corporal	Silver City, N. M.	

TROOP H—Continued.

Name.	Rank.	Place of Residence.	Remarks.
Arthur E. Williams	Corporal	Las Cruces, N. M.	
Frank Murray	"	Roswell, N. M.	
Morgan O. B. Llewellyn	"	Las Cruces, N. M.	
James C. Hamilton	"	Roswell, N. M.	
George F. Jones	"	El Paso, Tex.	
Charles P. Cochran	"	Eddy, N. M.	
John M. Kelly	"	El Paso, Tex.	
Robert E. Ligon	Trumpeter	Beaumont, Tex.	
Gaston R. Dehumy	"	Santa Fé, N. M.	
Uriah Sheard	Blacksmith	El Paso, Tex.	
Robert L. Martin	Farrier	Santa Fé, N. M.	
John Shaw	Saddler	Scott Co., Ia.	
Taylor B. Lewis	Wagoner	Las Cruces, N. M.	
Allison, Jovilo	Private	Bentonville, Ark.	
Amonette, Albert B.	"	Roswell, N. M.	
Bendy, Cecil C	"	El Paso, Tex.	
Black, Columbus L.	"	Las Cruces, N. M.	
Byan, John B	"	"	
Bogardus, Frank	"	"	
Brown, Percy	"	Spring Hill, Tenn.	
Baker, Philip S.	"	Clinton, Ia.	
Bullard, John W.	"	Guadaloupe Co., Tex.	
Connell, Thomas J	"	Bennett, Tex.	
Corbett, Thomas F	"	Roswell, N. M.	
Cornish, Thomas J	"	Freestone, Tex.	
Crawford, Clinton K.	"	Cincinnati, Ohio.	
Cone, John S	"	Tularosa, N. M.	

204

Duran, Abel B	Private	Silver City, N. M.
Duran, Jose L	"	Santa Fé, N. M.
Dorsey, Lewis	"	Silver City, N. M.
Doty, George B	"	Santa Fé, N. M.
Dunkle, Fred. W	"	East Las Vegas, N. M.
Douglas, Arthur L	"	Eddy, N. M.
Eaton, Frank A	"	Silver City, N. M.
Fletcher, Augustus C	"	"
Frye, Oley B	"	Flagstaff, Ariz.
Gasser, Louis	"	El Paso, Tex.
George, Ira W	"	Quincy, Ill.
Grigsby, James B	"	Deming, N. M.
Hamilton, James M	"	"
Herring, Leary O	"	Silver City, N. M.
Hunt, Le Roy R	"	Cincinnati, Ohio.
Houston, Robert C	"	Hillsboro, N. M.
James, Frank W	"	Marion Co., Ga.
Johnson, Charles	"	Lund, Sweden.
Johnson, Harry F	"	Beaumont, Tex.
Johnson, Lewis I	"	"
Kehoe, Michael J	"	Ottawa, Canada.
Kelm, Amandus	"	Silver City, N. M.
Kinnebrugh, Ollie A	"	El Paso, Tex.
Kendall, Harry J	"	Coldsborg, Ky.
Lawson, Frank H	"	Las Cruces, N. M.
Lewis, Adelbert	"	Beaver Co., Utah.
Lannon, John	"	Hillsboro, N. M.
Mooney, Thomas A	"	Silver City, N. M.
Moneckton, William J	"	San Antonio, Tex.
McAdams, Joel H	"	Mt. Pelia, Tenn.
McAdams, Richard P	"	"

205

TROOP H—*Continued.*

NAME.	RANK.	PLACE OF RESIDENCE.	REMARKS.
McCarthy, Frederick J.	Private	Mentzville, Mo.	
Murray, George F.	"	Deming, N. M.	
Nobles, William H.	"	Silver City, N. M.	
Neff, Netderton	"	Cincinnati, Ohio.	
Owens, Clay T.	"	El Paso, Tex.	
Ott, Charles H.	"	Silver City, N. M.	
Pace, John	"	Bentonville, Ark.	
Pepkins, Price	"		
Powell, Lory H.	"	Roswell, N. M.	
Pronger, Norman W.	"	Silver City, N. M.	
Pollock, John F.	"	Tularosa, N. M.	
Piersol, James M.	"	Osborne, Mo.	
Roberson, James R.	"	Belle Co., Tex.	
Rutherford, Bruce H.	"	Reno Co., Ill.	
Regan, John J.	"	Beaumont, Tex.	
Sharp, Emerson E.	"	Wanamaker, Tenn.	
Stewart, Newton	"	El Paso, Tex.	
Scroggins, Oscar	"	Logan Co., Ill.	
St. Clair, Edward C.	"	New Orleans, La.	
Saucier, Harry S.	"	"	
Schutt, Henry	"	Warren, Pa.	
Sawyer, Benjamin	"	Hillsboro, Ill.	
Thompson, Alex. M.	"	Deming, N. M.	
Tragner, William S.	"	Wilcox, Ariz.	
Thomas, Theodore C.	"	Leavenworth, Kan.	
Waggoner, Daniel G.	"	Roswell, N. M.	
Waggoner, Curtis C.	"	"	

Name	Rank	Location	Notes
Wilson, Charles E.	Private	Boulder, Colo.	
Wilkinson, Samuel O.	"	Cincinnati, Ohio.	
Woodson, Pickins E.	"	Honey Grove, Tex.	
Wheeler, Frank G.	"	Chautauqua Co., N. Y.	
Wickham, Patrick A.	"	Socorro, N. M.	

Discharged.

Name	Rank	Location	Notes
William L. Rynerson	Sergeant	Las Cruces, N. M.	Discharged from service by S. O. No. 145, headqrs. U. S. Army, Washington, D. C.

Transferred.

Name	Rank	Location	Notes
John B. Wiley	Sergeant		Transferred to I Troop May 12, 1898.
Joseph F. Kausky	"	Santa Fé, N. M.	"
John V. Morrison	"	Dona Ana, N. M.	"
Lee. Robert E.	Private	Jack Co., Tex.	"
Bennett, Orton A.	"	El Paso, Tex.	"
Brito, Jose	"	"	"
Brito, Frank C.	"		"
Cate, James S.	"	Grapevine, Tex.	"
Casad, C. Darwin	"	Las Cruces, N. M.	"
Dolan, Thomas P.	"	Ticonderoga, N. Y.	"
Farrell, Fred. P.	"	El Paso, Tex.	"
Freuger, Numa C.	"	Las Cruces, N. M.	"
Hermeyer, Ernest H.	"	Hamilton Co., Tex.	"
Jopling, Cal.	"		"
Nehmer, William	"	Staten, Germany.	"
Roediger, August	"	Charlotte, N. C.	"
Schafer, George	"	Penos Altos, N. M.	"
Storms, Morris J.	"	Roswell, N. M.	"
Sullivan, William J.	"	Manchester, Va.	"
Fritz, William H.	"	Windsor, Conn.	"
Eberman, Henry J.	"	Bremen, Germany	Transferred from K Troop to H Troop May 16, 1898; re-transferred to K June 8, '98.

TROOP II—Continued.

NAME.	RANK.	PLACE OF RESIDENCE.	REMARKS.
Bucklin, E. W.	Private	Chautauqua Co., N. Y.	Transferred to L Troop June 8, 1898.
Wright, Grant.	"	Cold Spring, N. Y.	"
Died.			
Gosling, Frederick W.	"	Bedfordshire, England	Died in hospital at Camp Wikoff, N. Y., Aug. 19, 1898.
Casey, Edwin Eugene.	"	Las Cruces, N. M.	Died in hospital, Camp Wikoff, N. Y., Sept. 1, 1898.
Deserted.			
Ewell, Edward A.	"	Adrian, Ill.	Deserted June 28, 1898, at Tampa, Fla.
Miller, Samuel.	"	Roswell, N. M	"

TROOP I.

NAME.	RANK.	PLACE OF RESIDENCE.	REMARKS.
Schuyler A. McGinnis	Captain	Newkirk, O. T.	
Frederick W. Wientge.	1st Lieutenant.	Santa Fé, N. M.	
Samuel Greenwald	2d Lieutenant.	Prescott, Ariz.	
John B. Wylie.	1st Sergeant.	Ft. Bayard, N. M.	
Schuyler C. Morgan.	Qr. Mr. Sergt.	Durango, Col.	
John V. Morrison	Sergeant.	Springerville, Ariz.	
William R. Reber.	"		
Basil N. Ricketts	"	Lambs' Club, N. Y.	Wounded near Santiago de Cuba, July 1, 2, or 3, 1898. Thigh ; slight.
Percival Gassett	"	Dedham, Mass.	

Name	Rank	Location
James S. Cate	Sergeant	Grapevine, Tex.
Wm. H. Waffensmith	"	Raton, N. M.
August Roediger	Corporal	Charlotte, N. C.
Numa C. Freuger	"	Las Cruces, N. M.
William J. Sullivan	"	Silver City, N. M.
William J. Nehmer	"	"
Abraham L. Bainter	"	Colorado Springs, Col.
Hiram T. Brown	"	Albuquerque, N. M.
Errickson N. Nichols	"	52 E. 78th st., New York, N.Y.
George M. Kerney	"	Globe, Ariz.
Robert E. Lea	Trumpeter	Donna Ana, N. M.
Clarence H. Underwood	"	Colorado Springs, Col.
Charles A. Nehmer	Blacksmith	Chicago, Ill.
Hayes Donnelly	Farrier	Jefferson, O. T.
Leo G. Rogers	Saddler	Bogard, Mo.
Everett E. Holt	Wagoner	Coffeeville, Kan.
Alexis, George D	Private	New Orleans, La.
Arendt, Henry J	"	Hoboken, N. J.
Armstrong, Charles M	"	
Adkins, Joseph R	"	
Bates, William H	"	
Barrowe, Hallett A	"	
Bawcom, Joseph L	"	Bisbee, Ariz.
Bennett, Horton A	"	Tularosa, N. M.
Brito, Frank C	"	Pinos Altos, N. M.
Brito, Jose	"	Los Angeles, Cal.
Brush, Charles A	"	Handford, Cal.
Bassage, Albert C	"	Corning, N. Y.
Cassel, Charles D	"	Mesilla, N. M.
Cloud, William	"	
Crockett, Joseph B	"	Topeka, Kan.

TROOP I—Continued.

Name.	Rank.	Place of Residence.	Remarks.
Coe, George M.	Private	Albuquerque, N. M.	
Clark, Frank M.	"	Hiawatha, Kan.	
Davis, Henry C.	"	Santa Fé, N. M.	
Dolan, Thomas P.	"	Pinos Altos, N. M.	
Denny, Robert W.	"	Raton, N. M.	
Duke, Henry K.	"	Lipscomb, Tex.	
Evans, Evan	"	Gallup, N. M.	
Fennell, William A.	"	Reunion, Md.	
Flynn, Joseph F.	"	Albuquerque, N. M.	
Geiger, Percy A.	"	Durango, Col.	
Gooch, John R.	"	Santa Fé, N. M.	
Groves, Oscar W.	"	Raton, N. M.	
Goodrich, Ben Hedric.	"		
Giller, Alfred C.	"	Topeka, Kan.	
Hermeyer, Ernest H.	"	Roswell, N. M.	
Hickey, Walter	"	Nashua, N. H.	
Hogan, Michael	"		
Jones, William H.	"	Raton, N. M.	Left with injured hand in Washington, D. C., Aug. 12, 1898.
Jopling, Cal.	"	La Luz, N. M.	
King, Harry B.	"	Raton, N. M.	
Larsen, Louis	"		
Love, William J.	"	Jersey City, N. J.	
McCoy, John	"	Monrovia, Cal.	
McGowan, Alex.	"	Gallup, N. M.	
Martin, John	"	Decanter, Ill.	
Miller, Edwin H.	"	Junction City, Kan.	

Miller, David R.	Private	Needles, Cal.
Miller, Jacob H.	"	Durango, Col.
Morgan, U. S. Grant	"	Raton, N. M.
Morris, Ben. F. T.	"	" "
Moore, Roscoe B.	"	2 W. 35th st., New York, N. Y.
North, Franklin H.	"	Parkersburg, W. Va.
O'Dell, William W.	"	Raton, N. M.
Peabody, Harry	"	Chicago, Ill.
Pierce, Edward	"	Plattsburg, Mo.
Price, Stewart R.	"	Philadelphia, Pa.
Rafalowitz, Hyman	"	Clayton, N. M.
Roberts, John P.	"	Y. M. C. A., St. Louis, Mo.
Reisig, Max	"	New Orleans, La.
Ranlett, Charles	"	Ottawa, Kan.
Reidy, John	"	
Shornhorst, Carl J., Jr.	"	Pinos Altos, N. M.
Schafer, Geo.	"	Marysville, W. Va.
Sennett, Lee	"	Centerpoint, Tex.
Storms, Morris J.	"	Clay County, Tex.
Spencer-Edwards, John	"	
Tait, John H.	"	Lafayette, Ind.
Temple, Frank	"	Yale, Kan.
Torbett, John T	"	Windsor, Conn.
Tritz, William H.	"	Faribault, Minn.
Townsend, Charles M	"	Raton, N. M.
Twyman, John L.	"	
Thompson, George	"	
Williams, Thomas C	"	
Wiley, Harry B	"	Santa Fé, N. M.
Wisenberg, Roy O.	"	Raton, N. M.
Zeigler, Daniel J	"	Como, Mont.

211

TROOP I—*Continued.*

NAME.	RANK.	PLACE OF RESIDENCE.	REMARKS.
Discharged.			
Brown, Harry R......	Private......	....	Disch'd Tampa, Fla., Aug. 5, per S. O. 153 A. G. O. June 30; final st'm'ts to A.G.O. Aug. 3
Young, Howard G.....	"	....	Discharged to date from Aug. 23, 1898.
Transferred.			
Alfred O. Girard.....	1st Sergeant...	....	Transferred July 18 to 2d Army Corps per telegraphic instructions A. G. O.
Elliot C. Cowdin......	Corporal......	....	Transferred to Troop L, 1st U. S. V. C., June 7, 1898, per order reg. commander.
Hamilton Fish, Jr.....	Sergeant......	....	Transferred to Troop L, 1st U. S. V. C., June 7, 1898, per order reg. commander.
Wilson, Charles A.....	Private......	....	Transferred to hospital corps, 1st U. S. V. C., June 7, 1898, per order reg. com'd'r.
Bailey, Harry C......	"	....	Transferred back to Troop G Sept. 1, 1898, per verbal order reg. commander.
John C. Greenway.....	2d Lieutenant..	....	Promoted 1st Lieut. to Troop A, 1st U. S. V. C.
Died.			
William Tiffany......	" "	....	Died Aug. 26, 1898.
Deserted.			
Saville, Michael......	Private......	....	Deserted from Camp Wikoff, L. I., Aug. 20, 1898.
Brown, John	"	....	Deserted en route from Camp Wood, San Antonio, Tex., to Camp Tampa, Fla., June 3.
Farrell, Fred P.......	"	....	Deserted en route from Camp Wood, San Antonio, Tex., to Camp Tampa, Fla., June 3.

TROOP K.

Name	Rank	Address	Remarks
Woodbury Kane	Captain	319 5th av., New York City	
Joseph A. Carr	1st Lieutenant	2127 R st., Washingt'n, D.C.	
Horace K. Devereaux	2d Lieutenant	Colorado Springs, Col.	Wounded at San Juan July 1, 1898. Forearm and arm.
Frederik K. Lie	1st Sergeant	Organ P. O., N. M.	
Thaddeus Higgins	Sergeant	210 W. 104th st., N. Y. City	
Reginolds Ronalds	"	Knickerb'k'r Club, N.Y.City	
Samuel G. Devore	"	Wheeling, W. Va.	Wounded at El Poso July 1. Left forearm; shrapnel.
Philip K. Sweet	"	226 W. 121st st., N. Y. City	
William J. Breen	"	510 E. 144th st., N. Y. City	
Craig W. Wadsworth	"	Geneseo, N. Y.	
Henry W. Buel	"	319 5th av., N. Y. City	
James B. Tailor	Corporal	Ardsley-on-Hudson, N. Y.	
Joseph S. Stevens	"	Narragans't av., N'port, R.I.	
Maxwell Norman	"	Newport, R. I.	
Edwin Coakley	"	Prescott, Ariz.	
George Kerr, Jr.	"	East Downington, Pa.	
Henry S. Van Schaick	"	100 Broadway, N. Y. City	
Frederick Herrig	"	Pleasant Valley, Mont.	
Oscar Land	Trumpeter	720 S. 8th st., Denver, Col.	
George W. Knoblauch	"	205 W. 57th st., N. Y. City	
Benjamin A. Long	Saddler		Wounded at El Poso July 1. Left thigh; shrapnel.
Thomas G. Bradley	Farrier	Potomac, Montg'm'y Co. Md.	
George T. Crucius	Blacksmith	Amanda st., Mont'g'm'y, Ala	
Lee Burdwell	Wagoner	Langtry, Tex.	

TROOP K—*Continued.*

Name.	Rank.	Place of Residence.	Remarks.
Armstrong, James T.	Private	Selma, Ala.	Wounded July 1.
Adams, John H.	"	Colorado Springs, Col.	
Bell, Sherman	"	Las Vegas, N. M.	
Bernard, William C.	"	Chester, Vt.	
Batchelder, Wallace N.	"		
Bump, Arthur L.	"	New London, O.	Slightly wounded July 1.
Cameron, Charles H.	"	McDonald, Pa.	
Campbell, Douglass	"		
Cash, Walter S.	"	Colorado Springs, Col.	Wounded July 1. Slight; arm.
Cooke, Henry B.	"		
Carroll, John F.	"	Hillsboro, Tex.	
Cartmell, Nathaniel M.	"	Lexington, Va.	
Clagett, Jesse C.	"	Motero Sta., Fred'k Co., Md.	
Corle, Max C.	"	El Paso, Tex.	
Coville, Allen M.	"	Topeka, Kan.	
Crowninshield, F. B.	"	Marblehead, Mass.	
Channing, Roscoe H.	"	24 Park Place, N. Y. City.	
Daniels, Benjamin F.	"	Colorado Springs, Col.	
Davis, John	"	Tarpon Springs, Fla.	
Easton, Stephen	"	Santa Fé, N. M.	
Eberman, Edwin	"		
Emerson, Edwin	"	"Collier's Weekly," N. Y. C.	
Flemming, Clarence A.	"		
Fletcher, Henry	"	Green Point, Pa.	
Falk, Theodore	"	Oklahoma City, O. T.	
Freeman, Elisha L.	"	Burden, Kan.	
Holden, Prince A.	"	Saddler, Grayson Co., Tex.	

Name	Rank	Address	Notes
Hulme, Robert A.	Private	El Reno, O. T.	
James, William F.	"	San Antonio, Tex.	
Jordan, Andrew M.	"	Rossa, Tex.	
Kania, Frank	"	Jamestown, N. D.	
Langdon, Jesse D.	"	Fargo, N. D.	
Marshall, Creighton	"	1807 G st. N.W., W'h'n, D.C.	
Maverick, Lewis	"	San Antonio, Tex.	
McGinty, William	"	Stillwater, O. T.	
McKoy, William J.	"	Oshkosh, Wis.	
Mitchell, Mason	"	Lambs' Club, N. Y. City	Wounded at El Poso. Slight; left arm; shrapnel.
Mitchell, William H.	"	Salem, Mass.	
Montgomery, L. N.	"	Hempstead, Tex.	
Nicholson, Charles P.	"	1617 John st., Baltimore, Md	
Norris, Edmund S.	"	Guthrie, O. T	
Posey, Alfred	"		
Pollak, Albin J.	"		
Quaid, William	"	Newbery, N. Y.	
Robinson, Kenneth D.	"	55 Liberty st., N. Y. City	Wounded on July 1. Severe; right side.
Reed, Colton	"	San Antonio, Tex.	
Smith, Frederick	"	Guthrie, O. T.	
Smith, George L.	"	Frankfort, Mich.	
Smith, Joseph S.	"	1829 Brown st., Phila., Pa.	
Smith, Clarke T	"	2008 Wallace st., Phila., Pa.	
Stockton, Richard	"	218 W. Jersey st., Eliz'h, N.J.	
Stephens, Oregon	"	Purdy, I. T.	
Thorp, Henry	"	Southampton, L. I.	
Test, Clarence L.	"	Austin, Tex.	
Toy, J. Frederick	"	602 S. 43d st., Phila., Pa.	
Tudor, William	"	87 Brimer st., Boston, Mass.	
Venable, Warner M.	"	Stevenville, Tex.	

TROOP K—*Continued*.

Name.	Rank.	Place of Residence.	Remarks.
Wiberg, Axel E.	Private	Windsor Ho., Newkirk, O. T.	
Weitzel, John F.	"	Guthrie, O. T.	
Wilson, Frank M.	"	Taylor, Tex.	
Woodward, John A.	"	Cold Springs, N. Y.	
Wright, Grant.	"	688 W. 37th, Los Ang'es, Cal.	
Young, James E.	"		
Discharged.			
Maloon, Winthrop L.	"		Discharged per S. O. No. 141, A. G. O., dated June 6.
McMasters, Fred'k D.	"		Discharged per S. O. No. 178, A. G. O., dated July 30, Washington, D. C.
Robert M. Ferguson.	Sergeant	55 Liberty st., N. Y. City	Discharged Aug. 10, 1898.
William Tiffany.	"	New York City.	"
Warden, John L.	Private	27 W. 43d st., N. Y. City.	Discharged by way of favor per order from Asst. Sec'y. War, Aug. 15, Wash'n. D. C.
Cosby, Arthur F.	"		W'd July 1. D'ch'd, A. G. O., Aug. 17. Slight; r't hand. Eng'd Las Guasimas, San Juan.
Babcock, Campbell E.	"	The Plaza, Chicago, Ill.	Discharged Sept. 5.
Lee, Joseph J.	"	Knoxville, Md.	Discharged per S. O. No. 205, A. G. O., Washington, D. C., Aug. 31.
Transferred.			
Duran, Joseph L.	"	Santa Fé, N. M.	Transferred to Troop H, this Regt., July 15.
Brandon, Perry H.	"	Douglass, Kan.	Overheated July 1. Trans. to D July 29. Eng'ed battles Las Guasimas, San Juan.
David M. Goodrich	1st Lieutenant.	Akron, O.	Transferred from Troop D Aug. 11. Transferred to Troop D Sept. 5.

Died.

Name	Rank	Address	Remarks
Henry Haywood	Sergeant	Police Dept., N. Y. City	Wounded July 1. Died in Div. Hosp., Cuba, July 2 from bullet wound. Abdomen.
Ives, Gerald M.	Private	388 W. 71st st., N. Y. City	Died at his home, 388 W. 71st st., N. Y. City (date not known), from typhoid fever.

Deserted.

Name	Rank	Address	Remarks
Staley, Frank	"		Deserted from troop at San Antonio, Tex., May 14.
Curzon, ——	"		Deserted from detachment at Tampa, Fla., June 13.

Promoted.

Name	Rank	Address	Remarks
Micah J. Jenkins	Major	Youngs Island, S. C.	Promoted Major Aug. 11, 1898.

TROOP L.

Name	Rank	Address	Remarks
Richard C. Day	Captain	Vinita, I. T.	Shot through left shoulder and arm in line of duty at San Juan. Severe.
John R. Thomas	1st Lieutenant	Muscogee, I. T.	Gunshot wound in right lower leg at Las Guasimas June 24.
Frank P. Hayes	2d Lieutenant	San Antonio, Tex.	
Elhanan W. Bucklin	1st Sergeant	Jamestown, N. Y.	
Jerome W. Henderlider	Sergeant	Saranac, Mich.	
William M. Simms	"	Vinita, I. T.	Wounded at San Juan July 1, 1898, in line of duty. Leg.
Joe A. Kline	"	"	Wounded at San Juan July 1 in line of duty. (Jerry Kline.) Leg.

TROOP L—*Continued.*

NAME.	RANK.	PLACE OF RESIDENCE.	REMARKS.
William W. Carpenter.	Sergeant	Vinita, I. T.	Wounded at San Juan July 1 in line of duty. Left thigh.
James McKay	"	Guthrie, Okla.	Hurt in back by fragment of shell at El Paso July 1. Contusion back; slight.
Dillwyn M. Bell	"	"	
James E. McGuire	"	Chelsea, I. T.	Wounded at El Paso July 2, 1898, in line of duty. Right foot; slight.
George H. Seaver	Corporal	Muscogee, I. T.	
John W. Davis	"	Vinita, I. T.	Wounded at San Juan July 1, 1898. Right leg and arm.
Sam. G. Davis	"	Sardis, Ark.	Wounded at San Juan July 1, 1898.
Bud Parnell	"	Muscogee, I. T.	
Joseph J. Roger	"	Tillon, Ark.	Wounded at San Juan July 1, 1898. Abdomen and arm.
George B. Dunnigan	"	Vinita, I. T.	
Maynard R. Williams	"	Fairland, I. T.	
Elliot C. Cowden	"	New York City.	
Mike Kinney	Blacksmith	Imlay, Mich.	
John R. Kean	Farrier	Maxwell, Ont.	Wounded at Las Guasimas June 24. G. S. left shoulder and lungs.
Nicholas H. Cochran	Wagoner	Vinita, I. T.	
Guy M. Babcock	Saddler	Cherryville, Kan.	
Thomas F. Meagher	Trumpeter	Muscogee, I. T.	Wounded at Las Guasimas June 24. G. S. left forearm.
Frank R. McDonald	"	Oolagah, I. T.	Wounded at San Juan July 1, 1898. (J. R. McDonald.) Head.
Adair, John M.	Private	Claremore, I. T.	

Name	Rank	Residence	Remarks
Benson, Victor H.	Private	Clonan, Ia.	
Carey, Oren E.	"	Howells, Neb.	
Chilcoot, Fred.	"		
Cook, James.	"	Cherokee City, Ark.	Appears on list of wounded near Santiago de Cuba, July 1, 2, or 3, 1898.
Cruse, James.	"	St. Joe, Ark.	
Culver, Ed.	"	Muscogee, I. T.	Wounded at Las Guasimas June 24. G. S. breast.
Davis, James C.	"	Waggoner, I. T.	
Damet, John P.	"	Alexander, S. D.	Wounded at Las Guasimas June 24. G. S. left shoulder.
Dennis, David C.	"	Nelson, Mo.	
Dobson, William H.	"	Muscogee, I. T.	
Ennis, Richard L.	"	Cornell, Ill.	
Evans, James R.	"	Baldwin, Ark.	
Gilmore, Maurice E.	"	Muscogee, I. T.	
Haley, Robert M.	"	Waggoner, I. T.	
Hawkins, Charles D.	"	Vinita, I. T.	
Heagert, Rudolph.	"	" "	
Holderman, Bert T.	"	Arcopa, Kan.	
Hughes, Frank.	"	Vinita, I. T.	
Hughes, William E.	"	" "	
Isbell, Thomas J.	"	" "	Wounded at Las Guasimas June 24. G. S. neck, hip, and thumb.
Jones, Levi.	"	Hemasville, Mo.	
Johns, William S.	"	Muscogee, I. T.	
Kinkade, Elijah S.	"	Clinton, La.	
Knox, Robert G.	"	La Porte, Ind.	
Lawrence, Richard.	"	Chetopa, Kan.	
Lane, Ed. K.	"	Sapulpa, I. T.	
Lane, Sanford J.	"		

TROOP L—*Continued.*

Name.	Rank.	Place of Residence.	Remarks.
Lentz, Edward	Private	Bowling Green, O.	
Lewis, Frank A	"	Newark, N. J.	
Little, Rollie L	"	West Fork, Ark.	
McDonald, Asa W	"	Bearing Cross, Ark.	
McCamish, Andrew L	"	Bethel, Kan.	
Miller, John S	"	Garrison, Neb.	
Miller, Boot	"	Chelsea, I. T.	
Moore, John J	"	Vinita, I. T.	
Oskison, Richard L	"	"	Wounded at San Juan July 1. Left leg.
Owens, Ed. L	"	"	Wounded near Santiago de Cuba July 1, 2, or 3, 1898. Right thigh; severe.
Parker, Ora E	"	Dickens, Ia	
Pulley, William O	"	Marion, Ill.	
Philpot, Leigh T	"	Bryson, Ky.	
Poe, Nathaniel M	"	Adair, I. T.	Wounded at Las Guasimas June 24. G. S. foot.
Price, Ben. W	"	Eufaula, I. T.	
Rich, Allen K	"	Ft. Gibson, I. T.	
Robertson, George W	"	Muscogee, I. T.	
Robinson, Frank P	"	Borbors, Kan.	
Russell, Dan	"	Goodland, I. T.	
Scobey, Arthur E	"	Wills Point, Tex.	Wounded at San Juan Hill July 1, 1898. Right hand.
Sharp, Walter L	"	Chicago, Ill.	
Skelton, James W	"	Trinity Mills, Tex.	
Smith, Bert	"	Vinita, I. T.	
Smith, Sylvester S	"	"	

Name	Rank	Place	Remarks
Stepens, Luke B	Private	Rio Vista, I. T.	
Stidham, Theodore E	"	Eufaula, I. T.	
Swearinger, George	"	Maysville, Mo.	
Taylor, Warren F	"	Hillsboro, Tex.	
Thompson, Sylvester V	"		Wounded at San Juan July 1, 1898. Left leg and arm.
Wetmore, Robert C	"	Montclair, N. J.	
Whitney, Schuyler C	"	Pryor Creek, I. T.	Wounded at Las Guasimas June 24. G. S. neck.
Wilkins, George W	"	Vinita, I. T.	
Wilson, James E	"	Madrid, Mo.	
Winn, Arthur N	"	Muscogee, I. T.	
Discharged.			
Hutchinson, Charles N	"		
Price, Walter W	"		
Frank P. Hayes	1st Sergeant	San Antonio, Tex.	Discharged June 24, 1898, to enable him to accept commission as 2d Lieutenant.
Transferred.			
Roberts, William J	Private		Transferred to Troop M June 7, 1898.
John Byrne	Sergeant	Vinita, I. T.	Transferred to Troop F July 10, 1898.
Died.			
Allyn K. Capron	Captain	Ft. Sill	Killed at battle of Las Guasimas June 24, 1898. G. S. lungs.
Hamilton Fish	Sergeant	New York City	Killed at battle of Las Guasimas June 24, 1898. G. S. heart.
Dawson, Tilden W	Private	Vinita, I. T.	Killed at battle of Las Guasimas June 24, 1898. G. S. head.
Santo, William T	"	Chouteau, I. T.	Killed at battle of San Juan July 1, 1898. (William Sonata.)

TROOP L—Continued.

NAME.	RANK.	PLACE OF RESIDENCE.	REMARKS.
Hendricks, Milo A.	Private	Muscogee, I. T.	Mort'y wounded at battle of San Juan July 1. Died in hosp. July 6, 1898.
Enyart, Silas R.	"	Sapulpa, I. T.	Mortally wounded at San Juan July 1. Died in hosp. July 6, 1898. (Engart.)

TROOP M.

NAME.	RANK.	PLACE OF RESIDENCE.
Robert H. Bruce	Captain	Mineola, Tex.
Ode C. Nichols	1st Lieutenant	Durant, I. T.
Albert S. Johnson	2d Lieutenant	Oklahoma City, Okla.
Harry E. Berner	1st Sergeant	Durant, I. T.
Joseph L. Smith	Q. M. Sergeant	Caddo, I. T.
William E. Lloyd	Sergeant	Durant, I. T.
Fred E. Nichols	"	Purcell, I. T.
Morency A. Hawkins	"	Tioga, Tex.
Wilbert L. Poole	"	Durant, I. T.
Otis B. Weaver	"	Mt. Vernon, Tex.
Henry C. Foley	"	Muscogee, I. T.
Samuel Downing	Corporal	Atoka, I. T.
Charles S. Lynch	"	Caddo, I. T.
John N. Jackson	"	"
Frank U. Talman	"	South McAlester, I. T.
Hiram S. Creech	"	Durant, I. T.

Name	Rank	Location
Charles J. Fandree	Corporal	Caddo, I. T.
Theodore E. Schulz	"	Tampa, Fla.
William G. Jones	"	Ardmore, I. T.
Frank Marion	Trumpeter	Muscogee, I. T.
Charles J. Hokey	"	Krebs, I. T.
John McMullen	Wagoner	Ardmore, I. T.
John Hall	Farrier	Durant, I. T.
Cragg Parsons	Blacksmith	Ardmore, I. T.
Luther M. Kiethly	Saddler	Hartshorn, I. T.
Samuel Young	Chief Cook	Caddo, I. T.
Allaun, Jacob	Private	Sapulpa, I. T.
Berd, Samuel J. W.	"	Muscogee, I. T.
Boydstun, John F.	"	Caddo, I. T.
Barlow, John W.	"	Ardmore, I. T.
Barrington, John P.	"	Ardmore, I. T.
Baird, Thompson M.	"	Thurber, Tex.
Brierty, Thomas	"	Tampa, Fla.
Butler, Peter L.	"	Kiowa, I. T.
Beal, Andy R.	"	Durant, I. T.
Bruce, Peter R.	"	Waggoner, I. T.
Brown, Leon	"	Ardmore, I. T.
Barney, Leland	"	"
Burks, Jesse S.	"	"
Chase, George	"	Durant, I. T.
Calhoun, Wesley	"	"
Carter, Arthur E.	"	Ardmore, I. T.
Carden, Horace W.	"	"
Cox, Walter	"	Durant, I. T.
Cooper, Bud G	"	Muscogee, I. T.
Dorell, Charles	"	Vinita, I. T.
Dupuy, Joseph	"	Muscogee, I. T.

TROOP M—Continued.

Name.	Rank.	Place of Residence.	Remarks.
Flying, Crawford D...	Private	Muscogee, I. T.	
Fairman, Charles E...	"	Ardmore, I. T.	
Griffith, Ezra E...	"	Sapulpa, I. T.	
Garland, George W...	"	Ardmore, I. T.	
Hall, James T...	"	Waggoner, I. T.	
Hawes, Fred W...	"	Denison, Tex.	
Houchin, Willis C...	"	Durant, I. T.	
Hamilton, Troy...	"	Hartshorn, I. T.	
Howell, William...	"	Muscogee, I. T.	
Harris, Chester...	"	"	
Hoffman, George B...	"	Summerville, N. J.	
Johnson, Bankston...	"	Caddo, I. T.	
Johnson, Charles L...	"	Ardmore, I. T.	
Johnston, Gordon...	"	Birmingham, Ala.	
Jones, Charles L...	"	McAlester, I. T.	
Keithly, Ora E...	"	Hartshorn, I. T.	
King, John...	"	McAlester, I. T.	
Kearns, Edward L...	"	Tampa, Fla.	
Mitchell, William...	"	Waggoner, I. T.	
Madden, Charles E...	"	Broken, I. T.	
Murphy, Will S...	"	Caddo, I. T.	
McPherren, Charles E	"	"	
Maytubby, Bud...	"	Muscogee, I. T.	
McDaniel, Thomas E..	"	Caddo, I. T.	
McPherson, Charles E.	"	Elizabeth, N. J.	
Morrell, Robert W...	"	Oolegah, I. T.	
Owens, John M...	"		

Pipkins, Virgil A	Private	Broken, I. T.	
Rouse, John L	"	Durant, I. T.	
Rose, Lewis W	"	Los Angeles, Cal.	
Russel, Walter L	"	Caddo, I. T.	
Rynerson, Benjamin A	"	Durant, I. T.	
Reynolds, Benjamin F	"	Ardmore, I. T.	
Ross, William E	"	"	
Roberts, William J	"	Vinita, I. T.	
Sloan, Samuel P	"	South McAlester, I. T.	
Sykes, Marion	"	Muscogee, I. T.	
Stewart, Henry J	"	Caddo, I. T.	
Thomas, Jesse C	"	"	
Tyler, Edwin	"	Ardmore, I. T.	
Vickers, John W	"	South McAlester, I. T.	
Williams, Benjamin H	"	"	
Williams, George W	"	Ardmore, I. T.	
Wolfe, John W	"	"	
Webster, David	"	Durant, I. T.	
Wagner, John D	"	Caddo, I. T.	
Woog, Benjamin B	"	Washington, D. C.	
de Zychlinski, Wm. T	"	Bismarck, N. D.	
Transferred.			
Sanford, G. Lane	"	Sapulpa, I. T.	Transferred to L Troop, 1st U. S. V. C., June 8, 1898.
Died of Disease.			
Yancey, Kyle	"	McAlester, I. T.	Died of typhoid fever at Tampa, July 5, '98.

HOSPITAL CORPS.

Name.	Rank.	Place of Residence.	Remarks.
Henry La Motte	Major	Williamsburg, Mass.	Contusion scalp near Santiago de Cuba July 1, 2, or 3, 1898.
James A. Massie	1st Lieutenant	Santa Fé, N. M.	
James R. Church	1st Lieutenant	Washington, D. C.	
James B. Brady	Steward	Santa Fé, N. M.	
Herbert J. Rankin	"	Las Vegas, N. M.	
Charles A. Wilson	"	Colorado Springs, Col.	
Rawdin, John R.	Private		

The Rough Riders at Santiago
By Theodore Roosevelt

On June 30 we received orders to hold ourselves in readiness to march against Santiago, and all the men were greatly overjoyed, for the inaction was trying. The one narrow road, a mere muddy track along which the army was encamped, was choked with the marching columns. As always happened when we had to change camp, everything that the men could not carry, including, of course, the officers' baggage, was left behind.

About noon the Rough Riders struck camp and drew up in column beside the road in the rear of the First Cavalry. Then we sat down and waited for hours before the order came to march, while regiment after regiment passed by, varied by bands of tatterdemalion Cuban insurgents, and by mule-trains with ammunition. Every man carried three days' provisions. We had succeeded in borrowing mules sufficient to carry along the dynamite gun and the automatic Colts. At last, toward mid-afternoon, the First and Tenth Cavalry, ahead of us, marched, and we followed. The First was under the command of Lieutenant-Colonel Veile, the Tenth under Lieutenant Colonel Baldwin.

Every few minutes there would be a stoppage in front, and at the halt I would make the men sit or lie down beside the track, loosening their packs. The heat was intense as we passed through the still, close jungle, which formed a wall on either hand. Occasionally we came to gaps or open spaces, where some regiment was camped, and now and then one of these regiments, which apparently had been left out of its proper place, would file into the road, breaking up our line of march. As a result, we finally found ourselves following merely the tail of the regiment ahead of us, an infantry regiment being thrust into the interval. Once or twice, we had to wade streams.

Darkness came on, but we still continued to march. It was about eight o'clock when we turned to the left and climbed El Poso hill, on whose summit there was a ruined ranch and sugar factory, now, of course, deserted. Here I found General Wood, who was arranging for the camping of the brigade. Our own arrangements for the night were simple. I extended each troop across the road into the jungle, and then the men threw down their belongings where they stood and slept on their arms. Fortunately, there was no rain. Wood and I curled up under our raincoats on the saddle-blankets, while his two *aides*. Captain A. L. Mills and Lieutenant W. E. Shipp, slept near us. We were up before dawn and getting breakfast. Mills and Shipp had nothing to eat, and they breakfasted with Wood and myself, as we had been able to get some handfuls of beans, and some coffee and sugar, as well as the ordinary bacon and hardtack.

We did not talk much, for though we were in ignorance as to precisely what the day would bring forth, we knew that we should see fighting. We had slept soundly enough, although, of course, both Wood and I during the night had made a round of the sentries, he of the brigade, and I of the regiment; and I suppose that, excepting among hardened veterans, there is always a certain feeling of uneasy excitement the night before the battle.

Mills and Shipp were both tall, fine-looking men, of tried courage, and thoroughly trained in every detail of their profession; I remember being struck by the quiet, soldierly way they were going about their work early that morning. Before noon one was killed and the other dangerously wounded.

General Wheeler was sick, but with his usual indomitable pluck and entire indifference to his own personal comfort, he kept to the front. He was unable to retain command of the cavalry division, which accordingly devolved upon General Samuel Sumner, who commanded it until mid-afternoon, when the bulk of the fighting was over. General Sumner's own brigade fell to Colonel Henry Carroll. General Sumner led the advance with the cavalry, and the battle was fought by him and by General Kent, who commanded the infantry division, and whose foremost brigade was led by General Hawkins.

As the sun rose the men fell in, and at the same time a battery of field-guns was brought up on the hill-crest just beyond, between us and toward Santiago. It was a fine sight to see the great horses straining under the lash as they whirled the guns up the hill and into position.

Our brigade was drawn up on the hither side of a kind of half basin, a big band of Cubans being off to the left. As yet we had received no orders, except that we were told that the main fighting was to be done by Lawton's infantry division, which was to take El Caney, several miles to our right, while we were simply to make a diversion. This diversion was to be made mainly with the artillery, and the battery which had taken position immediately in front of us was to begin when Lawton began.

It was about six o'clock that the first report of the cannon from El Caney came booming to us across the miles of still jungle. It was a very lovely morning, the sky of cloudless blue, while the level, shimmering rays from the just-risen sun brought into fine relief the splendid palms which here and there towered above the lower growth. The lofty and beautiful mountains hemmed in the Santiago plain, making it an amphitheatre for the battle.

Immediately our guns opened, and at the report great clouds of white smoke hung on the ridge crest. For a minute or two there was no response. Wood and I were sitting together, and Wood remarked to me that he wished our brigade could be moved somewhere else, for we were directly in line of any return fire aimed by the Spaniards at the battery. Hardly had he spoken when there was a peculiar whistling, singing sound in the air, and immediately afterward the noise of something exploding over our heads. It was shrapnel from the Spanish batteries. We sprung to our feet and leaped on our horses.

Immediately afterward a second shot came which burst directly above us; and then a third. From the second shell one of the shrapnel bullets dropped on my wrist, hardly breaking the skin, but raising a bump about as big as a hickory-nut. The same shell wounded four of my regiment, one of them being Mason Mitchell, and two or three of the regulars were also hit, one losing his leg by a great fragment of shell. Another shell exploded right in the middle of the Cubans, killing and wounding a good many, while the remainder scattered like guinea-hens. Wood's led horse was also shot through the lungs. I at once hustled my regiment over the crest of the hill into the thick underbrush, where I had no little difficulty in getting them together again into column.

Meanwhile the firing continued for fifteen or twenty minutes, until it gradually died away. As the Spaniards used smokeless powder, their artillery had an enormous advantage over ours, and, moreover, we did not have the best type of modern guns, our fire being slow.

As soon as the firing ceased, Wood formed his brigade, with my regiment in front, and gave me orders to follow behind the First Brigade, which was just moving off the ground. In column of fours, we marched down the trail toward the ford of the San Juan River. We passed two or three regiments of infantry, and were several times halted before we came to the ford. The First Brigade, which was under Colonel Carroll—Lieutenant-Colonel Hamilton commanding the Ninth Regiment, Major Wessels the Third, and Captain Kerr the Sixth—had already crossed and was marching to the right, parallel to, but a little distance from, the river. The Spaniards in the trenches and block-houses on top of the hills in front were already firing at the brigade in desultory fashion. The extreme advance of the Ninth Cavalry was under Lieutenants McNamee and Hartwick. They were joined by General Hawkins, with his staff, who was looking over the ground and deciding on the route he should take his infantry brigade.

Our orders had been of the vaguest kind, being simply to march to the right and connect with Lawton—with whom, of course, there was no chance of our connecting. No reconnaissance had been made, and the exact position and strength of the Spaniards was not known. A captive balloon was up in the air at this moment, but it was worse than useless. A previous proper reconnaissance and proper look-out from the hills would have given us exact information. As it was, Generals Kent, Sumner, and Hawkins had to be their own reconnaissance, and they fought their troops so well that we won anyhow.

I was now ordered to cross the ford, march half a mile or so to the right, and then halt and await further orders; and I promptly hurried my men across, for the fire was getting hot, and the captive balloon, to the horror of everybody, was coming down to the ford. Of course, it was a special target for the enemy's fire. I got my men across before it reached the ford. There it partly collapsed and remained, causing severe loss of life, as it indicated the exact position where the Tenth and the First Cavalry, and the infantry, were crossing.

As I led my column slowly along, under the intense heat, through the high grass of the open jungle, the First Brigade was to our left, and the firing between it and the Spaniards on the hills grew steadily hotter and hotter. After a while I came to a sunken lane, and as by this time the First Brigade had stopped and was engaged in a stand-up fight, I halted my men and sent back word for orders. As we faced toward the Spanish hills my regiment was on the right with next to it and a little in advance the First Cavalry, and behind them the Tenth. In our front the Ninth held the right, the Sixth the centre, and the Third the left; but in the jungle the lines were already overlapping in places. Kent's infantry were coming up, farther to the left.

Captain Mills was with me. The sunken lane, which had a wire fence on either side, led straight up toward, and between, the two hills in our front, the hill on the left, which contained heavy blockhouses, being farther away from us than the hill on our right, which we afterward grew to call Kettle Hill, and which was surmounted merely by some large ranch buildings or haciendas, with sunken brick-lined walls and cellars.

I got the men as well sheltered as I could. Many of them lay close under the bank of the lane, others slipped into the San Juan River and crouched under its hither bank, while the rest lay down behind the patches of bushy jungle in the tall grass. The heat was intense, and many of the men were already showing signs of exhaustion. The sides of the hills in front were bare; but the country up to them was, for the most part, covered with such dense jungle that in charging through it no accuracy of formation could possibly be preserved.

The fight was now on in good earnest, and the Spaniards on the hills were engaged in heavy volley firing. The Mauser bullets drove in sheets through the trees and the tall jungle grass, making a peculiar whirring or rustling sound; some of the bullets seemed to pop in the air, so that we thought they were explosive; and, indeed, many of those which were coated with brass did explode, in the sense that the brass coat was ripped off, making a thin plate of hard metal with a jagged edge, which inflicted a ghastly wound. These bullets were shot from a .45-calibre rifle carrying smokeless powder, which was much used by the guerillas and irregular Spanish troops.

The Mauser bullets themselves made a small clean hole, with the result that the wound healed in a most astonishing manner. One or two of our men who were shot in the head had the skull blown open, but elsewhere the wounds from the minute steel-coated bullet, with its very high velocity, were certainly nothing like as serious as those made by the old large-calibre, low-power rifle. If a man was shot through the heart, spine, or brain he was, of course, killed instantly; but very few of the wounded died—even under the appalling conditions which prevailed, owing to the lack of attendance and supplies in the field-hospitals with the army.

While we were lying in reserve we were suffering nearly as much as afterward when we charged. I think that the bulk of the Spanish fire was practically unaimed, or at least not aimed at any particular man, and only occasionally at a particular body of men; but they swept the whole field of battle up to the edge of the river, and man after man in

Rough Riders Fording the San Juan River while Moving to the Front.

our ranks fell dead or wounded, although I had the troopers scattered out far apart, taking advantage of every scrap of cover.

Devereux was dangerously shot while he lay with his men on the edge of the river. A young West Point cadet, Ernest Haskell, who had taken his holiday with us as an acting second lieutenant, was shot through the stomach. He had shown great coolness and gallantry, which he displayed to an even more marked degree after being wounded, shaking my hand and saying, "All right. Colonel, I'm going to get well. Don't bother about me, and don't let any man come away with me." When I shook hands with him, I thought he would surely die; yet he recovered.

The most serious loss that I and the regiment could have suffered befell just before we charged. Bucky O'Neill was strolling up and down in front of his men, smoking his cigarette, for he was inveterately addicted to the habit. He had a theory that an officer ought never to take cover—a theory which was, of course, wrong, though in a volunteer organisation the officers should certainly expose themselves very fully, simply for the effect on the men; our regimental toast on the transport running, "*The officers; may the war last until each is killed, wounded, or promoted.*"

As O'Neill moved to and fro, his men begged him to lie down, and one of the sergeants said, "Captain, a bullet is sure to hit you." O'Neill took his cigarette out of his mouth, and blowing out a cloud of smoke laughed and said, "Sergeant, the Spanish bullet isn't made that will kill me." A little later he discussed for a moment with one of the regular officers the direction from which the Spanish fire was coming. As he turned on his heel a bullet struck him in the mouth and came out at the back of his head; so that even before he fell his wild and gallant soul had gone out into the darkness.

My orderly was a brave young Harvard boy, Sanders, from the quaint old Massachusetts town of Salem. The work of an orderly on foot, under the blazing sun, through the hot and matted jungle, was very severe, and finally the heat overcame him. He dropped; nor did he ever recover fully, and later he died from fever. In his place I summoned a trooper whose name I did not know. Shortly afterward, while sitting beside the bank, I directed him to go back and ask whatever general he came across if I could not advance, as my men were being much cut up. He stood up to salute and then pitched forward across my knees, a bullet having gone through his throat, cutting the carotid.

When O'Neill was shot, his troop, who were devoted to him, were for the moment at a loss whom to follow. One of their number, Henry Bardshar, a huge Arizona miner, immediately attached himself to me as my orderly, and from that moment he was closer to me, not only in the fight, but throughout the rest of the campaign, than any other man, not even excepting the colour-sergeant, Wright.

Captain Mills was with me; gallant Shipp had already been killed. Mills was an invaluable aide, absolutely cool, absolutely unmoved or flurried in any way.

I sent messenger after messenger to try to find General Sumner or General Wood and get permission to advance, and was just about making up my mind that in the absence of orders I had better "march toward the guns," when Lieutenant-Colonel Dorst came riding up through the storm of bullets with the welcome command "to move forward and support the regulars in the assault on the hills in front." General Sumner had obtained authority to advance from Lieutenant Miley, who was representing General Shafter at the front, and was in the thick of the fire.

The general at once ordered the First Brigade to advance on the hills, and the Second to support it. He himself was riding his horse along the lines, superintending the fight. Later I overheard a couple of my men talking together about him. What they said illustrates the value of a display of courage among the officers in hardening their soldiers; for their theme was how, as they were lying down under a fire which they could not return, and were in consequence feeling rather nervous, General Sumner suddenly appeared on horseback, sauntering by quite unmoved; and, said one of the men, "That made us feel all right. If the general could stand it, we could."

The instant I received the order I sprang on my horse and then my "crowded hour" began. The guerillas had been shooting at us from the edges of the jungle and from their perches in the leafy trees, and as they used smokeless powder, it was almost impossible to see them, though a few of my men had from time to time responded. We had also suffered from the hill on our right front, which was held chiefly by guerillas, although there were also some Spanish regulars with them, for we found their dead. I formed my men in column of troops, each troop extended in open skirmishing order, the right resting on the wire fences which bordered the sunken lane. Captain Jenkins led the first squadron, his eyes literally dancing with joyous excitement.

I started in the rear of the regiment, the position in which the colonel should theoretically stay. Captain Mills and Captain McCor-

General Sumner, who Commanded the Cavalry Division During the San Juan Fight.

mick were both with me as *aides*; but I speedily had to send them off on special duty in getting the different bodies of men forward. I had intended to go into action on foot as at Las Guasimas, but the heat was so oppressive that I found I should be quite unable to run up and down the line and superintend matters unless I was mounted; and, moreover, when on horseback, I could see the men better and they could see me better.

A curious incident happened as I was getting the men started forward. Always when men have been lying down under cover for some time, and are required to advance, there is a little hesitation, each looking to see whether the others are going forward. As I rode down the line, calling to the troopers to go forward, and rasping brief directions to the captains and lieutenants, I came upon a man lying behind a little bush, and I ordered him to jump up. I do not think he understood that we were making a forward move, and he looked up at me for a moment with hesitation, and I again bade him rise, jeering him and saying: "Are you afraid to stand up when I am on horseback?"

As I spoke, he suddenly fell forward on his face, a bullet having struck him and gone through him lengthwise. I suppose the bullet had been aimed at me; at any rate, I, who was on horseback in the open, was unhurt, and the man lying flat on the ground in the cover beside me was killed. There were several pairs of brothers with us; of the two Nortons one was killed; of the two McCurdys one was wounded.

I soon found that I could get that line, behind which I personally was, faster forward than the one immediately in front of it, with the result that the two rearmost lines of the regiment began to crowd together; so, I rode through them both, the better to move on the one in front. This happened with every line in succession, until I found myself at the head of the regiment.

Both lieutenants of B Troop from Arizona had been exerting themselves greatly, and both were overcome by the heat; but Sergeants Campbell and Davidson took it forward in splendid shape. Some of the men from this troop and from the other Arizona troop (Bucky O'Neill's) joined me as a kind of fighting tail.

The Ninth Regiment was immediately in front of me, and the First on my left, and these went up Kettle Hill with my regiment. The Third, Sixth, and Tenth went partly up Kettle Hill (following the Rough Riders and the Ninth and First), and partly between that and the block-house hill, which the infantry were assailing. General Sumner in person gave the Tenth the order to charge the hills; and it went forward at a rapid gait. The three regiments went forward more or less intermingled, advancing steadily and keeping up a heavy fire.

Up Kettle Hill Sergeant George Berry, of the Tenth, bore not only his own regimental colours but those of the Third, the colour-sergeant of the Third having been shot down; he kept shouting, "Dress on the colours, boys, dress on the colours!" as he followed Captain Ayres, who was running in advance of his men, shouting and waving his hat. The Tenth Cavalry lost a greater proportion of its officers than any other regiment in the battle—eleven out of twenty-two. By the time I had come to the head of the regiment we ran into the left wing of the Ninth Regulars, and some of the First Regulars, who were lying down; that is, the troopers were lying down, while the officers were walking to and fro. The officers of the white and coloured regiments alike took the greatest pride in seeing that the men more than did their duty; and the mortality among them was great.

I spoke to the captain in command of the rear platoons, saying that I had been ordered to support the regulars in the attack upon the hills, and that in my judgment we could not take these hills by firing at them, and that we must rush them. He answered that his orders were to keep his men lying where they were, and that he could not charge without orders. I asked where the colonel was, and as he was not in sight, said, "Then I am the ranking officer here and I give the order to charge"—for I did not want to keep the men longer in the open suffering under a fire which they could not effectively return. Naturally the captain hesitated to obey this order when no word had been received from his own colonel.

So, I said, "Then let my men through, sir," and rode on through the lines, followed by the grinning Rough Riders, whose attention had been completely taken off the Spanish bullets, partly by my dialogue with the regulars, and partly by the language I had been using to themselves as I got the lines forward, for I had been joking with some and swearing at others, as the exigencies of the case seemed to demand. When we started to go through, however, it proved too much for the regulars, and they jumped up and came along, their officers and troops mingling with mine, all being delighted at the chance.

When I got to where the head of the left wing of the Ninth was lying, through the courtesy of Lieutenant Hartwick, two of whose coloured troopers threw down the fence, I was enabled to get back into the lane, at the same time waving my hat, and giving the order to charge the hill on our right front. Out of my sight, over on the right,

Captains McBlain and Taylor, of the Ninth, made up their minds independently to charge at just about this time; and at almost the same moment Colonels Carroll and Hamilton, who were off, I believe, to my left, where we could see neither them nor their men, gave the order to advance. But of all this I knew nothing at the time.

The whole line, tired of waiting, and eager to close with the enemy, was straining to go forward; and it seems that different parts slipped the leash at almost the same moment. The First Cavalry came up the hill just behind, and partly mixed with my regiment and the Ninth. As already said, portions of the Third, Sixth, and Tenth followed, while the rest of the members of these three regiments kept more in touch with the infantry on our left.

By this time, we were all in the spirit of the thing and greatly excited by the charge, the men cheering and running forward between shots, while the delighted faces of the foremost officers, like Captain C. J. Stevens, of the Ninth, as they ran at the head of their troops, will always stay in my mind. As soon as I was in the line, I galloped forward a few yards until I saw that the men were well started, and then galloped back to help Goodrich, who was in command of his troop, get his men across the road so as to attack the hill from that side.

Captain Mills had already thrown three of the other troops of the regiment across this road for the same purpose. Wheeling around, I then again galloped toward the hill, passing the shouting, cheering, firing men, and went up the lane, splashing through a small stream; when I got abreast of the ranch buildings on the top of Kettle Hill, I turned and went up the slope. Being on horseback I was, of course, able to get ahead of the men on foot, excepting my orderly, Henry Bardshar, who had run ahead very fast in order to get better shots at the Spaniards, who were now running out of the ranch buildings.

Sergeant Campbell and a number of the Arizona men, and Dudley Dean, among others, were very close behind. Stevens, with his platoon of the Ninth, was abreast of us; so were McNamee and Hartwick. Some forty yards from the top I ran into a wire fence and jumped, off turning him loose. He had been scraped by a couple of bullets, one of which nicked my elbow, and I never expected to see him again. As I ran up to the hill, Bardshar stopped to shoot, and two Spaniards fell as he emptied his magazine. These were the only Spaniards I actually saw fall to aimed shots by any one of my men, with the exception of two guerillas in trees.

Almost immediately afterward the hill was covered by the troops,

Little Texas—Colonel Roosevelt's War Horse.

both Rough Riders and the coloured troopers of the Ninth, and some men of the First. There was the usual confusion, and afterward there was much discussion as to exactly who had been on the hill first. The first guidons planted there were those of the three New Mexican troops, G, E, and F, of my regiment, under their captains, Llewellen, Luna, and Muller, but on the extreme right of the hill, at the opposite end from where we struck it, Captains Taylor and McBlain and their men of the Ninth were first up. Each of the five captains was firm in the belief that his troop was first up. As for the individual men, each of whom honestly thought he was first on the summit, their name was legion. One Spaniard was captured in the buildings, another was shot as he tried to hide himself, and a few others were killed as they ran.

Among the many deeds of conspicuous gallantry here performed, two, both to the credit of the First Cavalry, may be mentioned as examples of the others, not as exceptions. Sergeant Charles Karsten, while close beside Captain Tutherly, the squadron commander, was hit by a shrapnel bullet. He continued on the line, firing until his arm grew numb; and he then refused to go to the rear, and devoted himself to taking care of the wounded, utterly unmoved by the heavy fire. Trooper Hugo Brittain, when wounded, brought the regimental standard forward, waving it to and fro, to cheer the men.

No sooner were we on the crest than the Spaniards from the line of hills in our front, where they were strongly entrenched, opened a very heavy fire upon us with their rifles. They also opened upon us with one or two pieces of artillery, using time fuses which burned very accurately, the shells exploding right over our heads.

On the top of the hill was a huge iron kettle, or something of the kind, probably used for sugar refining. Several of our men took shelter behind this. We had a splendid view of the charge on the San Juan block-house to our left, where the infantry of Kent, led by Hawkins, were climbing the hill. Obviously, the proper thing to do was to help them, and I got the men together and started them volley-firing against the Spaniards in the San Juan block-house and in the trenches around it. We could only see their heads; of course, this was all we ever could see when we were firing at them in their trenches. Stevens was directing not only his own coloured troopers, but a number of Rough Riders; for in a *mêlée* good soldiers are always prompt to recognise a good officer, and are eager to follow him.

We kept up a brisk fire for some five or ten minutes; meanwhile we were much cut up ourselves. Gallant Colonel Hamilton, than whom there was never a braver man, was killed, and equally gallant Colonel Carroll wounded. When near the summit Captain Mills had been shot through the head, the bullet destroying the sight of one eye permanently and of the other temporarily. He would not go back or let any man assist him, sitting down where he was and waiting until one of the men brought him word that the hill was stormed. Colonel Veile planted the standard of the First Cavalry on the hill, and General Sumner rode up. He was fighting his division in great form, and was always himself in the thick of the fire. As the men were much excited by the firing, they seemed to pay very little heed to their own losses.

Suddenly, above the cracking of the carbines, rose a peculiar drumming sound, and some of the men cried, "The Spanish machine-guns!" Listening, I made out that it came from the flat ground to the left, and jumped to my feet, smiting my hand on my thigh, and shouting aloud with exultation, "It's the Gatlings, men, our Gatlings!" Lieutenant Parker was bringing his four Gatlings into action, and shoving them nearer and nearer the front.

Now and then the drumming ceased for a moment; then it would resound again, always closer to San Juan hill, which Parker, like ourselves, was hammering to assist the infantry attack. Our men cheered lustily. We saw much of Parker after that, and there was never a more welcome sound than his Gatlings as they opened. It was the only sound which I ever heard my men cheer in battle.

The infantry got nearer and nearer the crest of the hill. At last, we could see the Spaniards running from the rifle-pits as the Americans came on in their final rush. Then I stopped my men for fear they should injure their comrades, and called to them to charge the next line of trenches, on the hills in our front, from which we had been undergoing a good deal of punishment. Thinking that the men would all come, I jumped over the wire fence in front of us and started at the double; but, as a matter of fact, the troopers were so excited, what with shooting and being shot, and shouting and cheering, that they did not hear, or did not heed me; and after running about a hundred yards, I found I had only five men along with me.

Bullets were ripping the grass all around us, and one of the men. Clay Green, was mortally wounded; another, Winslow Clark, a Harvard man, was shot first in the leg and then through the body. He made not the slightest murmur, only asking me to put his water canteen where he could get at it, which I did; he ultimately recovered.

There was no use going on with the remaining three men, and I bade them stay where they were while I went back and brought up the rest of the brigade. This was a decidedly cool request, for there was really no possible point in letting them stay there while I went back; but at the moment it seemed perfectly natural to me, and apparently so to them, for they cheerfully nodded, and sat down in the grass, firing back at the line of trenches from which the Spaniards were shooting at them.

Meanwhile, I ran back, jumped over the wire fence, and went over the crest of the hill, filled with anger against the troopers, and especially those of my own regiment, for not having accompanied me. They, of course, were quite innocent of wrong-doing; and even while I taunted them bitterly for not having followed me, it was all I could do not to smile at the look of injury and surprise that came over their faces, while they cried out, "We didn't hear you, we didn't see you go. Colonel; lead on now, we'll sure follow you."

I wanted the other regiments to come too, so I ran down to where General Sumner was and asked him if I might make the charge; and he told me to go and that he would see that the men followed. By this time everybody had his attention attracted and when I leaped over the fence again, with Major Jenkins beside me, the men of the various regiments which were already on the hill came with a rush, and we started across the wide valley which lay between us and the Spanish

Charge at San Juan

entrenchments.

Captain Dimmick, now in command of the Ninth, was bringing it forward; Captain McBlain had a number of Rough Riders mixed in with his troop, and led them all together; Captain Taylor had been severely wounded. The long-legged men like Greenway, Goodrich, sharpshooter Proffit, and others, outstripped the rest of us, as we had a considerable distance to go. Long before we got near them the Spaniards ran, save a few here and there, who either surrendered or were shot down. When we reached the trenches, we found them filled with dead bodies in the light blue and white uniform of the Spanish Regular Army. There were very few wounded. Most of the fallen had little holes in their heads from which their brains were oozing; for they were covered from the neck down by the trenches.

It was at this place that Major Wessels, of the Third Cavalry, was shot in the back of the head. It was a severe wound, but after having it bound up, he again came to the front in command of his regiment. Among the men who were foremost was Lieutenant Milton F. Davis, of the First Cavalry. He had been joined by three men of the Seventy-first New York, who ran up, and, saluting, said, "Lieutenant, we want to go with you, our officers won't lead us."

One of the brave fellows was soon afterward shot in the face. Lieutenant Davis's first sergeant, Clarence Gould, killed a Spanish soldier with his revolver, just as the Spaniard was aiming at one of my Rough Riders. At about the same time I also shot one. I was with Henry Bardshar, running up at the double, and two Spaniards leaped from the trenches and fired at us, not ten yards away. As they turned to run, I closed in and fired twice, missing the first and killing the second. My revolver was from the sunken battleship *Maine*, and had been given me by my brother-in-law, Captain W. S. Cowles, of the navy. At the time I did not know of Gould's exploit, and supposed my feat to be unique; and although Gould had killed his Spaniard in the trenches, not very far from me, I never learned of it until weeks after. It is astonishing what a limited area of vision and experience one has in the hurly-burly of a battle.

There was very great confusion at this time, the different regiments being completely intermingled—white regulars, coloured regulars, and Rough Riders. General Sumner had kept a considerable force in reserve on Kettle Hill, under Major Jackson, of the Third Cavalry. We were still under a heavy fire and I got together a mixed lot of men and pushed on from the trenches and ranch-houses which we had just taken, driving the Spaniards through a line of palm-trees, and over the crest of a chain of hills.

When we reached these crests, we found ourselves overlooking Santiago. Some of the men, including Jenkins, Greenway, and Goodrich, pushed on almost by themselves far ahead. Lieutenant Hugh Berkely, of the First, with a sergeant and two troopers, reached the extreme front. He was, at the time, ahead of everyone; the sergeant was killed and one trooper wounded; but the lieutenant and the remaining trooper stuck to their post for the rest of the afternoon until our line was gradually extended to include them.

While I was reforming the troops on the chain of hills, one of General Sumner's aides, Captain Robert Howze—as dashing and gallant an officer as there was in the whole gallant cavalry division, by the way—came up with orders to me to halt where I was, not advancing farther, but to hold the hill at all hazards. Howze had his horse, and I had some difficulty in making him take proper shelter; he stayed with us for quite a time, unable to make up his mind to leave the extreme front, and meanwhile jumping at the chance to render any service, of risk or otherwise, which the moment developed.

I now had under me all the fragments of the six cavalry regiments which were at the extreme front, being the highest officer left there, and I was in immediate command of them for the remainder of the afternoon and that night. The Ninth was over to the right, and the Thirteenth Infantry afterward came up beside it. The rest of Kent's infantry was to our left. Of the Tenth, Lieutenants Anderson, Muller, and Fleming reported to me; Anderson was slightly wounded, but he paid no heed to this. All three, like every other officer, had troopers of various regiments under them; such mixing was inevitable in making repeated charges through thick jungle; it was essentially a troop commanders', indeed, almost a squad leaders', fight.

The Spaniards who had been holding the trenches and the line of hills, had fallen back upon their supports and we were tinder a very heavy fire both from rifles and great guns. At the point where we were, the grass-covered hill-crest was gently rounded, giving poor cover, and I made my men lie down on the hither slope.

On the extreme left Captain Beck, of the Tenth, with his own troop, and small bodies of the men of other regiments, was exercising a practically independent command, driving back the Spaniards whenever they showed any symptoms of advancing. He had received his orders to hold the line at all hazards from Lieutenant Andrews, one of General Sumner's *aides*, just as I had received mine from Captain Howze. Finally, he was relieved by some infantry, and then rejoined the rest of the Tenth, which was engaged heavily until dark, Major Wint being among the severely wounded. Lieutenant W. N. Smith was killed. Captain Bigelow had been wounded three times.

Our artillery made one or two efforts to come into action on the firing-line of the infantry, but the black powder rendered each attempt fruitless. The Spanish guns used smokeless powder, so that it was difficult to place them. In this respect they were on a par with their own infantry and with our regular infantry and disjointed cavalry; but our only two volunteer infantry regiments, the Second Massachusetts and the Seventy-First New York, and our artillery, all had black powder. This rendered the two volunteer regiments, which were armed with the antiquated Springfield, almost useless in the battle, and did practically the same thing for the artillery wherever it was formed within rifle range.

When one of the guns was discharged a thick cloud of smoke shot out and hung over the place, making an ideal target, and in a half minute every Spanish gun and rifle within range was directed at the particular spot thus indicated; the consequence was that after a more or less lengthy stand the gun was silenced or driven off. We got no appreciable help from our guns on July 1. Our men were quick to realise the defects of our artillery, but they were entirely philosophic about it, not showing the least concern at its failure.

On the contrary, whenever they heard our artillery open they would grin as they looked at one another and remark, "There go the guns again; wonder how soon they'll be shut up," and shut up they were sure to be. The light battery of Hotchkiss one-pounders, under Lieutenant J. B. Hughes, of the Tenth Cavalry, was handled with conspicuous gallantry.

On the hill-slope immediately around me I had a mixed force composed of members of most of the cavalry regiments, and a few infantrymen. There were about fifty of my Rough Riders with Lieutenants Goodrich and Carr. Among the rest were perhaps a score of coloured infantrymen, but, as it happened, at this particular point without any of their officers. No troops could have behaved better than the coloured soldiers had behaved so far; but they are, of course, peculiarly dependent upon their white officers. Occasionally they produce non-commissioned officers who can take the initiative and accept responsibility precisely like the best class of whites; but this cannot be expected normally, nor is it fair to expect it.

With the coloured troops there should always be some of their own officers; whereas, with the white regulars, as with my own Rough Riders, experience showed that the non-commissioned officers could usually carry on the fight by themselves if they were once started, no matter whether their officers were killed or not.

At this particular time it was trying for the men, as they were lying flat on their faces, very rarely responding to the bullets, shells, and shrapnel which swept over the hilltop, and which occasionally killed or wounded one of their number. Major Albert G. Forse, of the First Cavalry, a noted Indian fighter, was killed about this time. One of my best men, Sergeant Greenly, of Arizona, who was lying beside me, suddenly said: "Beg pardon, Colonel; but I've been hit in the leg."

I asked, "Badly?"

He said, "Yes, Colonel; quite badly." After one of his comrades had helped him fix up his leg with a first-aid-to-the-injured bandage, he limped off to the rear.

None of the white regulars or Rough Riders showed the slightest sign of weakening; but under the strain the coloured infantrymen (who had none of their officers) began to get a little uneasy and to drift to the rear, either helping wounded men, or saying that they wished to find their own regiments. This I could not allow, as it was depleting my line, so I jumped up, and walking a few yards to the rear, drew my revolver, halted the retreating soldiers, and called out to them that I appreciated the gallantry with which they had fought and would be sorry to hurt them, but that I should shoot the first man who, on any pretence whatever, went to the rear.

My own men had all sat up and were watching my movements with the utmost interest; so was Captain Howze. I ended my statement to the coloured soldiers by saying: "Now, I shall be very sorry to hurt you, and you don't know whether or not I will keep my word, but my men can tell you that I always do;" whereupon my cow-punchers, hunters, and miners solemnly nodded their heads and commented in chorus, exactly as if in a comic opera, "He always does; he always does!"

This was the end of the trouble, for the "smoked Yankees"—as the Spaniards called the coloured soldiers—flashed their white teeth at one another, as they broke into broad grins, and I had no more trouble with them, they seeming to accept me as one of their own officers. The coloured cavalrymen had already so accepted me; in return, the

Rough Riders, although for the most part Southwesterners, who have a strong colour prejudice, grew to accept them with hearty goodwill as comrades, and were entirely willing, in their own phrase, "to drink out of the same canteen." Where all the regular officers did so well, it is hard to draw any distinction; but in the cavalry division a peculiar meed of praise should be given to the officers of the Ninth and Tenth for their work, and under their leadership the coloured troops did as well as any soldiers could possibly do.

In the course of the afternoon the Spaniards in our front made the only offensive movement which I saw them make during the entire campaign; for what were ordinarily called "attacks" upon our lines consisted merely of heavy firing from their trenches and from their skirmishers. In this case they did actually begin to make a forward movement, their cavalry coming up as well as the marines and reserve infantry, while their skirmishers, who were always bold, redoubled their activity. It could not be called a charge, and not only was it not pushed home, but it was stopped almost as soon as it began, our men immediately running forward to the crest of the hill with shouts of delight at seeing their enemies at last came into the open. A few seconds' firing stopped their advance and drove them into the cover of the trenches.

They kept up a very heavy fire for some time longer, and our men again lay down, only replying occasionally. Suddenly we heard on our right the peculiar drumming sound which had been so welcome in the morning, when the infantry were assailing the San Juan blockhouse. The Gatlings were up again! I started over to inquire, and found that Lieutenant Parker, not content with using his guns in support of the attacking forces, had thrust them forward to the extreme front of the fighting line, where he was handling them with great effect.

From this time on, throughout the fighting, Parker's Gatlings were on the right of my regiment, and his men and mine fraternised in every way. He kept his pieces at the extreme front, using them on every occasion until the last Spanish shot was fired. Indeed, the dash and efficiency with which the Gatlings were handled by Parker was one of the most striking features of the campaign; he showed that a first-rate officer could use machine guns, on wheels, in battle and skirmish, in attacking and defending trenches, alongside of the best troops, and to their great advantage.

As night came on, the firing gradually died away. Before this happened, however, Captains Morton and Boughton, of the Third Cavalry, came over to tell me that a rumour had reached them to the effect that there had been some talk of retiring and that they wished to protest in the strongest manner. I had been watching them both, as they handled their troops with the cool confidence of the veteran regular officer, and had been congratulating myself that they were off toward the right flank, for as long as they were there, I knew I was perfectly safe in that direction. I had heard no rumour about retiring, and I cordially agreed with them that it would be far worse than a blunder to abandon our position.

To attack the Spaniards by rushing across open ground, or through wire entanglements and low, almost impassable jungle, without the help of artillery, and to force unbroken infantry, fighting behind earthworks and armed with the best repeating weapons, supported by cannon, was one thing; to repel such an attack ourselves, or to fight our foes on anything like even terms in the open, was quite another thing. No possible number of Spaniards coming at us from in front could have driven us from our position, and there was not a man on the crest who did not eagerly and devoutly hope that our opponents would make the attempt, for it would surely have been followed, not merely by a repulse, but by our immediately taking the city. There was not an officer or a man on the firing-line, so far as I saw them, who did not feel this way.

As night fell, some of my men went back to the buildings in our rear and foraged through them, for we had now been fourteen hours charging and fighting without food. They came across what was evidently the Spanish officers' mess, where their dinner was still cooking, and they brought it to the front in high glee. It was evident that the Spanish officers were living well, however the Spanish rank and file were faring. There were three big iron pots, one filled with beef-stew, one with boiled rice, and one with boiled peas; there was a big demijohn of rum (all along the trenches which the Spaniards held were empty wine and liquor bottles); there were a number of loaves of rice-bread; and there were even some small cans of preserves and a few salt fish. Of course, among so many men, the food, which was equally divided, did not give very much to each, but it freshened us all.

Soon after dark, General Wheeler, who in the afternoon had resumed command of the cavalry division, came to the front. A very few words with General Wheeler reassured us about retiring. He had been through too much heavy fighting in the Civil War to regard the present fight as very serious, and he told us not to be under any apprehension, for he had sent word that there was no need whatever of retiring, and was sure we would stay where we were until the chance came to advance. He was second in command; and to him more than to any other one man was due the prompt abandonment of the proposal to fall back—a proposal which, if adopted, would have meant shame and disaster.

Shortly afterward General Wheeler sent us orders to entrench. The men of the different regiments were now getting in place again and sifting themselves out. All of our troops who had been kept at Kettle Hill came forward and rejoined us after nightfall. During the afternoon Greenway, apparently not having enough to do in the fighting, had taken advantage of a lull to explore the buildings himself, and had found a number of Spanish entrenching tools, picks, and shovels, and these we used in digging trenches along our line. The men were very tired indeed, but they went cheerfully to work, all the officers doing their part.

Crockett, the ex-Revenue officer from Georgia, was a slight man, not physically very strong. He came to me and told me he didn't think he would be much use in digging, but that he had found a lot of Spanish coffee and would spend his time making coffee for the men, if I approved. I did approve very heartily, and Crockett officiated as cook for the next three or four hours until the trench was dug, his coffee being much appreciated by all of us.

So many acts of gallantry were performed during the day that it is quite impossible to notice them all, and it seems unjust to single out any; yet I shall mention a few, which it must always be remembered are to stand, not as exceptions, but as instances of what very many men did. It happened that I saw these myself. There were innumerable others, which either were not seen at all, or were seen only by officers who happened not to mention them; and, of course, I know chiefly those that happened in my own regiment.

Captain Llewellen was a large, heavy man, who had a grown-up son in the ranks. On the march he had frequently carried the load of some man who weakened, and he was not feeling well on the morning of the fight. Nevertheless, he kept at the head of his troop all day. In the charging and rushing, he not only became very much exhausted, but finally fell, wrenching himself terribly, and though he remained with us all night, he was so sick by morning that we had to take him behind the hill into an improvised hospital.

Lieutenant Day, after handling his troop with equal gallantry and

Troop K, Rough Riders.

efficiency, was shot, on the summit of Kettle Hill. He was hit in the arm and was forced to go to the rear, but he would not return to the States, and rejoined us at the front long before his wound was healed. Lieutenant Leahy was also wounded, not far from him. Thirteen of the men were wounded and yet kept on fighting until the end of the day, and in some cases never went to the rear at all, even to have their wounds dressed. They were Corporals Waller and Fortescue and Trooper McKinley of Troop E; Corporal Roades of Troop D; Troopers Albertson, Winter, McGregor, and Ray Clark of Troop F; Troopers Bugbee, Jackson, and Waller of Troop A; Trumpeter McDonald of Troop L; Sergeant Hughes of Troop B; and Trooper Gievers of Troop G.

One of the Wallers was a cowpuncher from New Mexico, the other the champion Yale high-jumper. The first was shot through the left arm so as to paralyze the fingers, but he continued in battle, pointing his rifle over the wounded arm as though it had been a rest. The other Waller, and Bugbee, were hit in the head, the bullets merely inflicting scalp wounds. Neither of them paid any heed to the wounds except that after nightfall each had his head done up in a bandage. Fortescue I was at times using as an extra orderly. I noticed he limped, but supposed that his foot was skinned. It proved, however, that he had been struck in the foot, though not very seriously, by a bullet, and I never knew what was the matter until the next day I saw him making wry faces as he drew off his bloody boot, which was stuck fast to the foot. Trooper Rowland again distinguished himself by his fearlessness.

For gallantry on the field of action Sergeants Dame, Ferguson, Tiffany, Greenwald, and, later on, McIlhenny, were promoted to second lieutenancies, as Sergeant Hayes had already been. Lieutenant Carr, who commanded his troop, and behaved with great gallantry throughout the day, was shot and severely wounded at nightfall. He was the son of a Confederate officer; his was the fifth generation which, from father to son, had fought in every war of the United States. Among the men whom I noticed as leading in the charges and always being nearest the enemy, were the Pawnee, Pollock, Simpson of Texas, and Dudley Dean. Jenkins was made major, Woodbury Kane, Day, and Frantz captains, and Greenway and Goodrich first lieutenants, for gallantry in action, and for the efficiency with which the first had handled his squadron, and the other five their troops—for each of them, owing to some accident to his superior, found himself in command of his troop.

Dr. Church had worked quite as hard as any man at the front in caring for the wounded; as had Chaplain Brown. Lieutenant Keyes, who acted as adjutant, did so well that he was given the position permanently. Lieutenant Coleman similarly won the position of quartermaster.

We finished digging the trench soon after midnight, and then the worn-out men laid down in rows on their rifles and dropped heavily to sleep. About one in ten of them had blankets taken from the Spaniards. Henry Bardshar, my orderly, had procured one for me. He, Goodrich, and I slept together. If the men without blankets had not been so tired that they fell asleep anyhow, they would have been very cold, for, of course, we were all drenched with sweat, and above the waist had on nothing but our flannel shirts, while the night was cool, with a heavy dew.

Before anyone had time to wake from the cold, however, we were all awakened by the Spaniards, whose skirmishers suddenly opened fire on us. Of course, we could not tell whether or not this was the forerunner of a heavy attack, for our Cossack posts were responding briskly. It was about three o'clock in the morning, at which time men's courage is said to be at the lowest ebb; but the cavalry division was certainly free from any weakness in that direction. At the alarm everybody jumped to his feet and the stiff, shivering, haggard men, their eyes only half-opened, all clutched their rifles and ran forward to the trench on the crest of the hill.

The sputtering shots died away and we went to sleep again. But in another hour dawn broke and the Spaniards opened fire in good earnest. There was a little tree only a few feet away, under which I made my headquarters, and while I was lying there, with Goodrich and Keyes, a shrapnel burst among us, not hurting us in the least, but with the sweep of its bullets killing or wounding five men in our rear, one of whom was a singularly gallant young Harvard fellow, Stanley Hollister. An equally gallant young fellow from Yale, Theodore Miller, had already been mortally wounded. Hollister also died.

The Second Brigade lost more heavily than the First; but neither its brigade commander nor any of its regimental commanders were touched, while the commander of the First Brigade and two of its three regimental commanders had been killed or wounded.

In this fight our regiment had numbered 490 men, as, in addition to the killed and wounded of the first fight, some had had to go to the hospital for sickness and some had been left behind with the baggage, or were detailed on other duty. Eighty-nine were killed and wounded: the heaviest loss suffered by any regiment in the cavalry division. The Spaniards made a stiff fight, standing firm until we charged home. They fought much more stubbornly than at Las Guasimas. We ought to have expected this, for they have always done well in holding entrenchments. On this day they showed themselves to be brave foes, worthy of honour for their gallantry. In the attack on the San Juan hills our forces numbered about 6,600. There were about 4,500 Spaniards against us.

★★★★★★★★★★★★★★★★★

According to the official reports, 5,104 officers and men of Kent's infantry, and 2,649 of the cavalry had been landed. My regiment is put down as 542 strong, instead of the real figure, 490, the difference being due to men who were in hospital and on guard at the seashore, etc. In other words, the total represents the total landed; the details, etc., are included. General Wheeler, in his report of July 7, puts these details as about fifteen per cent of the whole of the force which was on the transports; about eighty-five per cent got forward and was in the fight.

The total Spanish force in Santiago under General Linares was 6,000: 4,000 regulars, 1,000 volunteers, and 1,000 marines and sailors from the ships. (Diary of the British Consul, Frederick W. Ramsden, entry of July 1.) Four thousand more troops entered next day. Of the 6,000 troops, 600 or thereabouts were at El Caney, and 900 in the forts at the mouth of the harbour. Lieutenant Tejeiro states that there were 520 men at El Caney, 970 in the forts at the mouth of the harbour, and 3,000 in the lines, not counting the cavalry and civil guard which were in reserve. He certainly very much understates the Spanish force; thus, he nowhere accounts for the engineers mentioned earlier; and his figures would make the total number of Spanish artillerymen but 32.

He excludes the cavalry, the civil guard, and the marines which had been stationed at the Plaza del Toros; yet he later mentions that these marines were brought up, and their commander, Bustamente, severely wounded; he states that the cavalry advanced to cover the retreat of the infantry, and I myself saw the cavalry come forward, for the most part dismounted, when the Spaniards attempted a forward movement late in the afternoon, and we shot many of their horses; while later I saw and conversed with officers and men of the civil guard who had been wounded at the same time—this in connection with returning them their wives and children, after the latter had fled from the city. Although the engineers are excluded, Lieutenant Tejeiro mentions that their colonel, as well as the colonel of the artillery, was wounded.

Four thousand five hundred is surely an understatement of the forces which resisted the attack of the forces under Wheeler. Lieutenant Tejeiro is very careless in his figures. Thus, in one place he states that the position of San Juan was held by two companies comprising 250 soldiers. Later he says it was held by three companies, whose strength he puts at 300—thus making them average 100 instead of 125 men apiece. He then mentions another echelon of two companies, so situated as to cross their fire with the others. Doubtless the block house and trenches at Fort San Juan proper were only held by three or four hundred men; they were taken by the Sixth and Sixteenth Infantry under Hawkins's immediate command; and they formed but one point in the line of hills, trenches, ranch-houses, and blockhouses which the Spaniards held, and from which we drove them. When the city capitulated later, over 8,000 unwounded troops and over 16,000 rifles and carbines were surrendered; by that time the marines and sailors had of course gone, and the volunteers had disbanded.

In all these figures I have taken merely the statements from the Spanish side. I am inclined to think the actual numbers were much greater than those here given. Lieutenant Wiley, in his book, "In Cuba with Shafter," which is practically an official statement, states that nearly 11,000 Spanish troops were surrendered; and this is the number given by the Spaniards themselves in the remarkable letter the captured soldiers addressed to General Shafter, which Wiley quotes in full. Lieutenant Tejeiro, explains that the volunteers had disbanded before the end came, and the marines and sailors had of course gone, while nearly a thousand men had been killed or captured or had died of wounds and disease, so that there must have been at least 14,000 all told. Subtracting the reinforcements who arrived on the 2d, this would mean about 10,000 Spaniards present on the 1st; in which case Kent and Wheeler were opposed by at least equal numbers.

In dealing with the Spanish losses. Lieutenant Tejeiro contradicts himself. He puts their total loss on this day at 593, including 94 killed, 121 missing, and 2 prisoners—217 in all. Yet he states that of the 520 men at Caney but 80 got back, the remaining 440 being killed, captured, or missing. When we captured the city, we found in the hospitals over 2,000 seriously wounded and sick Spaniards; on making inquiries, I found that over a third were wounded. From these facts I feel that it is safe to put down the total Spanish loss in battle as at least 1,200, of whom over a thousand were killed and wounded.

Lieutenant Tejeiro, while rightly claiming credit for the courage shown by the Spaniards, also praises the courage and resolution of the Americans, saying that they fought, "con un arrojo y una decision verdaderamente admirables." He dwells repeatedly upon the determination with which our troops kept charging though themselves unprotected by cover. As for the Spanish troops, all *who fought them that day will most freely admit the courage they showed. At El Caney, where they were nearly hemmed in, they made a most desperate defence; at San Juan the way to retreat was open, and so, though they were seven times as numerous, they fought with less desperation, but still very gallantly.*

★★★★★★★★★★★★★★★★

Our total loss in killed and wounded was 1,071. Of the cavalry division there were, all told, some 2,300 officers and men, of whom 375 were killed and wounded. In the division over a fourth of the officers were killed or wounded, their loss being relatively half as great again as that of the enlisted men—which was as it should be.

I think we suffered more heavily than the Spaniards did in killed and wounded (though we also captured some scores of prisoners). It would have been very extraordinary if the reverse was the case, for we did the charging; and to carry earthworks on foot with dismounted cavalry, when these earthworks are held by unbroken infantry armed with the best modern rifles, is a serious task.

ALSO FROM LEONAUR
AVAILABLE IN SOFTCOVER OR HARDCOVER WITH DUST JACKET

AN APACHE CAMPAIGN IN THE SIERRA MADRE by John G. Bourke—An Account of the Expedition in Pursuit of the Chiricahua Apaches in Arizona, 1883.

BILLY DIXON & ADOBE WALLS by Billy Dixon and Edward Campbell Little—Scout, Plainsman & Buffalo Hunter, *Life and Adventures of "Billy" Dixon* by Billy Dixon and *The Battle of Adobe Walls* by Edward Campbell Little (*Pearson's Magazine*).

WITH THE CALIFORNIA COLUMN by George H. Petis—Against Confederates and Hostile Indians During the American Civil War on the South Western Frontier, *The California Column, Frontier Service During the Rebellion* and *Kit Carson's Fight With the Comanche and Kiowa Indians*.

THRILLING DAYS IN ARMY LIFE by George Alexander Forsyth—Experiences of the Beecher's Island Battle 1868, the Apache Campaign of 1882, and the American Civil War.

INDIAN FIGHTS AND FIGHTERS by Cyrus Townsend Brady—Indian Fights and Fighters of the American Western Frontier of the 19th Century.

THE NEZ PERCÉ CAMPAIGN, 1877 by G. O. Shields & Edmond Stephen Meany—Two Accounts of Chief Joseph and the Defeat of the Nez Percé, *The Battle of Big Hole* by G. O. Shields and *Chief Joseph, the Nez Percé* by Edmond Stephen Meany.

CAPTAIN JEFF OF THE TEXAS RANGERS by W. J. Maltby—Fighting Comanche & Kiowa Indians on the South Western Frontier 1863-1874.

SHERIDAN'S TROOPERS ON THE BORDERS by De Benneville Randolph Keim—The Winter Campaign of the U. S. Army Against the Indian Tribes of the Southern Plains, 1868-9.

GERONIMO by Geronimo—The Life of the Famous Apache Warrior in His Own Words.

WILD LIFE IN THE FAR WEST by James Hobbs—The Adventures of a Hunter, Trapper, Guide, Prospector and Soldier.

THE OLD SANTA FE TRAIL by Henry Inman—The Story of a Great Highway.

LIFE IN THE FAR WEST by George F. Ruxton—The Experiences of a British Officer in America and Mexico During the 1840's.

ADVENTURES IN MEXICO AND THE ROCKY MOUNTAINS by George F. Ruxton—Experiences of Mexico and the South West During the 1840's.

AVAILABLE ONLINE AT **www.leonaur.com**
AND FROM ALL GOOD BOOK STORES

ALSO FROM LEONAUR

AVAILABLE IN SOFTCOVER OR HARDCOVER WITH DUST JACKET

AFGHANISTAN: THE BELEAGUERED BRIGADE by G. R. Gleig—An Account of Sale's Brigade During the First Afghan War.

IN THE RANKS OF THE C. I. V by Erskine Childers—With the City Imperial Volunteer Battery (Honourable Artillery Company) in the Second Boer War.

THE BENGAL NATIVE ARMY by F. G. Cardew—An Invaluable Reference Resource.

THE 7TH (QUEEN'S OWN) HUSSARS: Volume 4—1688-1914 by C. R. B. Barrett—Uniforms, Equipment, Weapons, Traditions, the Services of Notable Officers and Men & the Appendices to All Volumes—Volume 4: 1688-1914.

THE SWORD OF THE CROWN by Eric W. Sheppard—A History of the British Army to 1914.

THE 7TH (QUEEN'S OWN) HUSSARS: Volume 3—1818-1914 by C. R. B. Barrett—On Campaign During the Canadian Rebellion, the Indian Mutiny, the Sudan, Matabeleland, Mashonaland and the Boer War Volume 3: 1818-1914.

THE KHARTOUM CAMPAIGN by Bennet Burleigh—A Special Correspondent's View of the Reconquest of the Sudan by British and Egyptian Forces under Kitchener—1898.

EL PUCHERO by Richard McSherry—The Letters of a Surgeon of Volunteers During Scott's Campaign of the American-Mexican War 1847-1848.

RIFLEMAN SAHIB by E. Maude—The Recollections of an Officer of the Bombay Rifles During the Southern Mahratta Campaign, Second Sikh War, Persian Campaign and Indian Mutiny.

THE KING'S HUSSAR by Edwin Mole—The Recollections of a 14th (King's) Hussar During the Victorian Era.

JOHN COMPANY'S CAVALRYMAN by William Johnson—The Experiences of a British Soldier in the Crimea, the Persian Campaign and the Indian Mutiny.

COLENSO & DURNFORD'S ZULU WAR by Frances E. Colenso & Edward Durnford—The first and possibly the most important history of the Zulu War.

U. S. DRAGOON by Samuel E. Chamberlain—Experiences in the Mexican War 1846-48 and on the South Western Frontier.

AVAILABLE ONLINE AT www.leonaur.com
AND FROM ALL GOOD BOOK STORES

ALSO FROM LEONAUR
AVAILABLE IN SOFTCOVER OR HARDCOVER WITH DUST JACKET

THE 9TH—THE KING'S (LIVERPOOL REGIMENT) IN THE GREAT WAR 1914 - 1918 by Enos H. G. Roberts—Mersey to mud—war and Liverpool men.

THE GAMBARDIER by Mark Severn—The experiences of a battery of Heavy artillery on the Western Front during the First World War.

FROM MESSINES TO THIRD YPRES by Thomas Floyd—A personal account of the First World War on the Western front by a 2/5th Lancashire Fusilier.

THE IRISH GUARDS IN THE GREAT WAR - VOLUME 1 by Rudyard Kipling—Edited and Compiled from Their Diaries and Papers—The First Battalion.

THE IRISH GUARDS IN THE GREAT WAR - VOLUME 1 by Rudyard Kipling—Edited and Compiled from Their Diaries and Papers—The Second Battalion.

ARMOURED CARS IN EDEN by K. Roosevelt—An American President's son serving in Rolls Royce armoured cars with the British in Mesopotamia & with the American Artillery in France during the First World War.

CHASSEUR OF 1914 by Marcel Dupont—Experiences of the twilight of the French Light Cavalry by a young officer during the early battles of the great war in Europe.

TROOP HORSE & TRENCH by R.A. Lloyd—The experiences of a British Lifeguardsman of the household cavalry fighting on the western front during the First World War 1914-18.

THE EAST AFRICAN MOUNTED RIFLES by C.J. Wilson—Experiences of the campaign in the East African bush during the First World War.

THE LONG PATROL by George Berrie—A Novel of Light Horsemen from Gallipoli to the Palestine campaign of the First World War.

THE FIGHTING CAMELIERS by Frank Reid—The exploits of the Imperial Camel Corps in the desert and Palestine campaigns of the First World War.

STEEL CHARIOTS IN THE DESERT by S. C. Rolls—The first world war experiences of a Rolls Royce armoured car driver with the Duke of Westminster in Libya and in Arabia with T.E. Lawrence.

WITH THE IMPERIAL CAMEL CORPS IN THE GREAT WAR by Geoffrey Inchbald—The story of a serving officer with the British 2nd battalion against the Senussi and during the Palestine campaign.

AVAILABLE ONLINE AT **www.leonaur.com**
AND FROM ALL GOOD BOOK STORES

www.ingramcontent.com/pod-product-compliance
Lightning Source LLC
Chambersburg PA
CBHW031625160426
43196CB00006B/281